MW00607876

FLAVORS OF FRIULI

FLAVORS OF FRIULI

A Culinary Journey through Northeastern Italy

୬୦୯ଅ

Elisabeth Antoine Crawford

EQUILIBRIO
San Francisco, CA

Copyright © 2009 by Elisabeth Antoine

All rights reserved. No part of this publication may be reproduced, stored in a retrieval system, or transmitted, in any form or by any means, electronic, mechanical, photocopying, recording, or otherwise, without the prior written permission of the publisher.

ISBN 978-0-9703716-1-4
Library of Congress Control Number 2009929086

Published by Equilibrio
San Francisco, California
www.Flavors-of-Friuli.com

10 9 8 7 6 5 4 3 2 1
Printed in China

All photography by the author, excepting the following credits:
    Image of Gianni Cosetti (page 78) courtesy of Gabriella Cosetti
    Image of pitina (page 187) by Filippo Bier
    Image of the Grotta Gigante (page 262) courtesy of the Società Alpina delle Giulie
    Images of the Carnevale Muggesano (pages 314-15) courtesy of the Associazione delle Compagnie
        del Carnevale Muggesano
    Cover portrait by Michael Antoine
Map illustration (page 349) by David Caggiano

PREVIOUS PAGE: *Trieste's Palazzo del Governo.*

Acknowledgements

Many heartfelt thanks to the following individuals:

My good friends Steno and Liviana Dondè for introducing me to Friulian cuisine and for treating me to some of my most memorable meals in Friuli.

The Stoppar family at Pasticceria Penso for making me feel at home in Trieste and allowing me to join them in the kitchen for so many weeks. I truly felt like I was part of their family.

Gianna Modotti who invited me to her cooking school in Udine and provided valuable insight into the history and cuisine of the region.

Brothers Mario, Maurizio, and Enzo Mancini at Osteria Al Vecchio Stallo who welcomed me into their restaurant night after night during my lengthy visits to Udine.

Bepi Salon at Ristorante Salon in Piano d'Arta for answering all of my questions with both patience and passion. Also to Matteo for being such an amiable host.

Joško and Loredana Sirk at La Subida in Cormòns for serving such fantastic meals at my favorite restaurant in all of Friuli.

Franca Schneider at Locanda Alla Pace in Sauris di Sotto for her gracious hospitality.

Giuseppe "Rocky" DeSantis at Osteria Al Tulat in Forni di Sopra for allowing me to spend hours browsing through his cookbook collection.

Rosanna Clochiatti at Ristorante Alle Vecchie Carceri in San Daniele for sending me such extensive information about her beloved Friuli, as well as her husband's recipe for cjalsòns.

Tiziana Romanin at Albergo Al Sole in Forni Avoltri for treating me to a fabulous meal on the house—and introducing me to the mayor.

And most importantly, my family for their unconditional love and support.

To Michael and David

CONTENTS

Southern Friuli: Adriatic Coast...219

PREFACE

Mandi! This heartfelt Friulian greeting—meaning both hello and goodbye—symbolizes to me the warmth and openness of the Friulian people, perhaps even a sense of kinship that extends across nationalities. It is the greeting I heard so often from complete strangers as I was, for instance, boarding a bus or perhaps crossing the street. It represents an invitation into the Friulian community, to come in out of the cold and sit by the *fogolâr*. I certainly have felt welcomed in Friuli, more so than in many other regions. This genuine hospitality combined with the spirit of living off the land forms the essence of Friuli, a character that appears in all aspects of Friulian life, including the region's cuisine.

My obsession with Italy began long before I discovered Friuli. As far back as I can remember, images of Italian life infused my soul with longing. Even as a child, I felt a deep, unexplained attraction to this country in which I had never set foot. When I made my first trip post-college, it was as if I had discovered my true purpose—even though I did not yet know precisely what it was.

Drawn like a magnet, I pursued every possible opportunity to travel in Italy, but it was my initial visit to Friuli that changed my course in life. In preparation for the publication of my first book, *Balance on the Ball: Exercises Inspired by the Teachings of Joseph Pilates*, I had arranged to visit the factory where the Ledragomma exercise balls are produced. The owner, Steno Dondè, took me to lunch in San Daniele, where we discussed business over glasses of Merlot and feasted on a gigantic platter of prosciutto. Having learned of my interest in Italian cooking, he later treated me to dinner at Osteria Al Vecchio Stallo, one of Udine's oldest restaurants. He ordered for me some of the local specialties—*cjalsòns*, *frico* with polenta, and *brovada*. While the pickled turnips were not love-at-first-bite, I was enamored with the gooey cheesiness of the *frico* and the complex sweet and savory flavors of the *cjalsòns*. Needless to say, I was immediately hooked.

During the next few years, I often found myself returning to Friuli, enticed by memories of pillow-light gnocchi, creamy *baccalà*, and of course, the *cjalsòns*. I sampled more *cjalsòns* than any other dish, close to twenty different varieties. Some were uninspired, but most were divine. Armed with pages of notes, I scoured restaurant menus for local dishes and practically ate my way through the region. I savored *goulasch* at the top of Monte Santo di Lussari near Tarvisio; I gorged on a *piatto misto* of at least six types of pork in Trieste's oldest buffet; and I devoured countless pastries in bakeries from Aquileia to Zuglio.

Along the way, I collected cookbooks, interviewed chefs, and talked to the local people. Whenever I tasted an outstanding dish in a restaurant, I asked the chef for the recipe. Most were happy to oblige or at least give me a verbal run-down of ingredients. In each case, I referred to the chef's recipe in conjunction with published cookbook recipes to create my own rendition of a particular dish. My job was to then translate the Italian recipes, convert their metric measurements, and test and retest until eventually getting it right. My goal was to make each recipe simple to prepare and, in the case of some of the more complex dishes and desserts, to at least give the home cook confidence to prepare them. Since my culinary experience is entirely self-taught, I believe that if I can master an apple strudel or *torta Dobos*, then my readers will achieve the same success.

In addition to the hurdle of metric conversions, I have had to cope with the frustration of vague measurements that are so typical of foreign recipes—a handful of this, a spoonful of that—or even no measurements at all. I relied a great deal on my notes and memories to create an authentic interpretation. After struggling with this challenge, I have come to realize that in Italy cooking is not an exact science but an art. It takes a true understanding of ingredients to orchestrate the final result.

Surprisingly to me, determining those ingredients turned out to be as difficult a task as calculating the quantities. While most previously published recipes were fairly similar, many questions still arose as to the most traditional method of preparation. For example, is it typical for Italians to add tomatoes to their *goulasch*? Does Trieste-style *baccalà* include potatoes, tomatoes, or both? Is there any intrinsic difference between *gubana*, *presnitz*, and *putizza*? Should I use puff pastry or strudel dough in my *strucolo de pomi*? Are the Austro-Hungarian cakes *Sacher*, *Dobos*, and *Rigojanci* any different in Trieste than in central Europe? (To answer that last question, I traveled to both Vienna and Budapest to find out.) I ended up sampling more than my fair share of certain dishes, asking opinions from everyone I met, and ultimately making a judgment call based on what I found to be either most pervasive or most representative of Friuli's traditional cuisine.

While working on this project, the question I have heard most often is, why Friuli? Friends who appreciate my passion for Italy have found it strange that I have been drawn to one of the country's most *un*-Italian regions. My answer is that possibly this is what intrigues me the most—the fact that it is so distinctive. For the same reason, I am drawn to fusion cuisine at home in San Francisco. Dishes that run the gamut from mildly unusual to outlandishly bizarre are simply more interesting to me. Maybe I bore easily—or perhaps I secretly yearn to disguise my dessert as a first course—but I have always been attracted to exotic foods, especially if I can conceivably prepare them at home.

As I look back on the years of researching and writing this book, I am struck not only by my memories of food but of the people as well. Their generosity has been simply overwhelming. For example, the Stoppar family of Pasticceria Penso helped me find an apartment across the street one autumn, so that I could spend three solid weeks in their bakery kitchen. On another trip, cooking instructor Gianna Modotti welcomed me into her home and gave me a complimentary spot in one of her cooking classes. In Forni Avoltri, the mayor—whom I just happened to chance on in a restaurant—invited me to be a special guest at a cookbook-signing event that evening.

All along the way, so many chefs and restaurateurs were willing to share with me their recipes and their passion for food: Bepi Salon, Joško Sirk, "Rocky" DeSantis, Mario Mancini, and Franca Schneider, to name just a few. Even ordinary folk revealed unforgettable kindness, such as the townspeople of Venzone who helped me catch the last bus of the day when the trains were, unbeknownst to me, on strike. And I will never forget the Italian family I met having lunch at Malga Pozôf; after offering me a ride down Monte Zoncolan, they stopped at the side of the road to forage for porcini mushrooms and to share with me an impromptu snack of homemade custard with fresh raspberries.

After getting to know these individuals and building what I hope will be lasting friendships, I have developed a deeper appreciation of the Friulian culture and its influence on the region's cuisine. In this book, I hope to pass this appreciation on to you.

Buon Appetito!

INTRODUCTION

Tucked away between mountains and sea in Italy's extreme northeast corner, Friuli-Venezia Giulia is a veritable melting pot of cultures. Today, the only clear boundary lines are political: those that separate Italy from the neighboring countries of Austria and Slovenia, those that mark the border between Friuli-Venezia Giulia and Italy's Veneto region, and those that delineate Friuli's four provinces, Trieste, Udine, Gorizia, and Pordenone. From a cultural point of view, these borders remain somewhat blurred, as there is considerable overlap in ethnicity, traditions, and cuisine. There are, however, three distinct geographical areas within Friuli-Venezia Giulia whose individual characteristics have played a significant role in the region's culinary history.

Northern Mountains

Until the mid-1900s, much of Friuli's mountainous north had been isolated from the rest of the region. The harsh climate and rugged terrain prevented the free-flowing trade of goods that flourished elsewhere. Friulians had to become self-sufficient, making use of wild mushrooms, herbs, fruits, and berries that could be gathered in their forests and fields.

Central Hills and Plains

Like their neighbors to the north, the people of central Friuli subsisted on a simple diet of hearty grains and vegetables. The fertile plains of this region have encouraged the development of a booming wine industry, while its rolling hills were found to have the perfect climate for salt-curing Friuli's famous prosciutto.

Southern Coastline

The southern portion of Friuli lies along the Adriatic Sea. Naturally, seafood takes center stage here. While the cooking along the western coast shows a considerable Venetian influence, Austrian and Slavic dishes are most pervasive around the capital city of Trieste.

The rocky Dolomite range towers above Forni di Sopra (TOP); *vineyards and farmland blanket the plains near Cormòns* (CENTER); *the Barcolana boat race sails past Castello di Miramare on Trieste's coastline* (BOTTOM); *the Torre dell'Orologio, or "clock tower," of Udine's Porticato di San Giovanni was modeled after the one in Venice's Piazza San Marco* (OPPOSITE).

To fully appreciate the cuisine of Friuli-Venezia Giulia, it is necessary to understand a little of the region's history.

Invasion of the Celts

Around 500 BC, Celtic warriors advanced across central Europe and invaded much of northern Italy. They are recognized for introducing to the region their original method of salt-curing ham. Another group of Celtic settlers, called the Carni, also arrived during this period. A more peaceful tribe, they inhabited the mountains that eventually came to be known as Carnia.

The Roman Empire

The Romans arrived in 186 BC, seizing the village that would later become Aquileia, one of the most important cities of the Roman Empire. Another significant settlement was founded by Julius Caesar in 50 BC. Called Forum Iulii, or "Julius's market," it was to become, centuries later, the town of Cividale. (The name Forum Iulii evolved into the region's name Friuli, while Venezia Giulia was derived from the term "Julian Venice.")

The Romans were responsible for building an infrastructure of roads; the principal thoroughfare, Via Giulia Augusta, connected the Alps to the sea and was vital in establishing a spice trade between the European continent and the East. Though geographically isolated from the rest of the region, the coastal city Tergeste—now Trieste—was also strategically valuable to the Romans.

The Patriarch of Aquileia

The region saw the arrival of Christianity in the early 4th century AD, and Aquileia was established as the seat of the patriarch, the ecclesiastical ruler of the region. After numerous barbaric invasions—particularly the attacks by Attila the Hun and the Lombards during the 5th and 6th centuries, respectively—the patriarch relocated to the port of Grado, while much of the population fled west along the coast, settling on some uninhabited islands in the lagoon. This new community based itself on the enlightened political values of ancient Rome and would eventually evolve into the almighty Republic of Venice.

Roman ruins in the town of Zuglio (ABOVE); *the Basilica Patriarcale of Aquileia* (RIGHT); *remains of an ancient Roman basilica at Castello di San Giusto in Trieste* (OPPOSITE).

The Lombard Invasion

When the Lombards invaded Friuli in 568, they established their first Italian duchy in Cividale. With a strategic location along the Natisone River and a legacy of Roman culture, Cividale once again became a center of prosperity. The town's position later attracted a rival patriarch of Aquileia to move there; Cividale remained a patriarchal seat until the 11th century.

The Holy Roman Empire

After a few centuries of Lombard rule, the region saw the beginnings of the Holy Roman Empire. In 776, King Charlemagne's Franks invaded Friuli. By making generous donations to the church, Charlemagne contributed to Christianity's rise in power during the Middle Ages. When the pope crowned Otto I of Saxony the Holy Roman Emperor in 962, long-lasting ties were established between the Italian peninsula and the Germanic world. During this period, the emergence of the feudal system created a rigid division between rich and poor populations, and times of war and famine fell upon medieval Europe.

A Revitalization of Commerce

In 1019, Patriarch Poppone sacked Grado and transferred the patriarchate back to Aquileia. This jump-started a general rebirth of the region. During the 12th century, friendly relations between the pope and emperor allowed for a revitalization of commerce with transalpine countries. As trade expanded, towns began to flourish, and feudalism withdrew to the countryside. Townspeople were free to choose their own professions, and each town developed a particular identity. Udine blossomed into the region's largest city when the patriarch moved there in the 13th century; it remained a thriving community until 1420, when the Venetian lion of Saint Mark took Friuli under its protective wing.

The Venetians and the Hapsburgs

As two competing powers—the Venetian Republic and the Austro-Hungarian Empire—were emerging, the region saw another period of unrest, and cities were forced to align with one of the two sides. In 1382, when Venetian forces threatened to occupy the entire coastline, Trieste turned to Hapsburg Austria for protection. Nevertheless, Venice went on a vast conquering spree, taking control of Udine, Pordenone, and Gorizia, as well as considerable territory beyond. In the early 16th century, Venetian power waned, and Gorizia was eventually handed over to Austria.

Cividale's Chiesa di San Francesco on the banks of the Natisone River (ABOVE)*; the Loggia del Lionello in Udine's Piazza della Libertà* (LEFT).

Napoleon's Invasion

Powers shifted again in 1797 when Napoleon Bonaparte and his troops conquered Venice. The subsequent Treaty of Campoformido ceded Venetian Friuli—along with much of northern Italy—to Austria. The entire region remained under Austrian rule until the mid-19th century.

Palmanova was built by the Venetians in the 16th century to protect against a Turkish invasion. The surrounding fortress, shaped like a nine-pointed star, was reinforced by Napoleon following his occupation of Friuli. Three arched gates provide the only access to the town (ABOVE).

The Unification of Italy

For decades, in a movement called the Risorgimento, cities throughout the Italian peninsula had been struggling to break free from the various powers that dominated and to unite to form a single nation. After many battles, the Kingdom of Italy was proclaimed in 1861. Five years later, after the Austro-Prussian War, western Friuli was ceded to Italy. The smaller region of Venezia Giulia, however, remained under Austrian control.

World War I

Around the turn of the 20th century, there was a strong Irredentist movement in Trieste that sought to unite Venezia Giulia with Italy. In fact, unification was one of Italy's main objectives during World War I. Italian patriots got their wish—following the war, the Venezia Giulia region was awarded to Italy along with sections of the Istrian peninsula.

World War II

Prior to World War II, Italy had been ruled for two decades by the Fascist dictator Mussolini. After siding with Hitler and eventually surrendering to the Allies, Italy ceded parts of Venezia Giulia and Istria to Yugoslavia. A new border between Italy and Yugoslavia was drawn during the Paris Peace Treaty of 1947, dividing the Italian city of Gorizia right down the middle. After the war, Trieste was declared a free territory and spent years in limbo under an Anglo-American military government; in 1954, the city was once again united with Italy.

The two regions, Friuli and Venezia Giulia, were joined into one autonomous region in 1964. Friuli takes up the vast majority of land area and comprises the provinces of Udine and Pordenone, while the smaller provinces of Trieste and Gorizia make up Venezia Giulia. For the sake of brevity in this book, the entire region may occasionally be referred to as Friuli.

It is evident that the continuous shifting of power has caused substantial political tension and countless wars, but these fuzzy borders have also been instrumental in shaping a unique fusion of cuisines. As various parts of Friuli have passed through Celtic, Roman, Lombard, Venetian, Austro-Hungarian, and Slavic rule, those very cultures have put their stamp on recipes handed down through the ages. Since Roman times, the region has served as a gateway for spices and other wares from afar, providing kitchens with unusual ingredients not indigenous to the land. During the free port era of Hapsburg Trieste, foreign merchants left behind fragments of their culture, while immigrants integrated the flavors of their native countries into their new home. Although present-day Friuli-Venezia Giulia has emerged as an essentially Italian body, its spirit demonstrates a clear intermingling of Germanic, Latin, and Slavic traditions.

Trieste's Palazzo del Municipio sports a banner honoring the forty-year anniversary of an autonomous Friuli-Venezia Giulia (ABOVE); the winged lion of Saint Mark guards the entrance to the Castello di Gorizia (OPPOSITE).

NORTHERN FRIULI:
Carnia Mountains

The mountains of northern Friuli may be divided geographically into three areas: the Carnian Alps in the west, the Giulian Alps to the east, and the foothills often referred to as Alto Friuli. For centuries, this land was ruled by the Hapsburg Empire, and as you travel deeper into this region, you will discover abundant clues to Friuli's Austro-Hungarian heritage. Onion-domed church steeples, gabled chalets, and Alpine farmhouses dot the landscape, while aromas of smoked pork and *goulasch* waft onto village streets at mealtime.

Venture into the mountains where the rolling, grassy meadows invite you to sing and the hills are as alive as a Von Trapp family picnic. The air is refreshing and brisk; the fragrance of wildflowers and pine lingers in the gentle breeze. The only sounds to caress your ears are the wind in the trees and the chirping of an occasional bird. For visitors, Carnia is an escape from the hassles of urban life—a retreat into the solitude of nature.

Carnia takes its name from the region's first inhabitants, a Celtic tribe called the Carni. Thought to be less barbaric in nature than their warrior cousins, these Celts wandered across the

The majestic Dolomite range seen from the wildflower-strewn hills of Forni di Sopra (ABOVE); *Chiesa di Sant'Osvaldo towers above a traditional Alpine home in Sauris di Sotto* (OPPOSITE).

Alps in search of a quiet place to raise cattle. Modern-day residents have inherited their ancestors' peaceful ways, as well as their spiritual connection to nature. Celebrations such as the Festa del Solstizio d'Estate and various legends involving witches and wood goblins are linked to pagan customs of the ancient Celts.

For the most part, the Carnian people keep to themselves and their deep-rooted traditions. Many locals still speak Furlan, a nearly obsolete Romance language with German and Slavic influences. Despite their limited contact with the outside world—or perhaps encouraged by it—Carnians tend to be exceedingly hospitable to foreigners.

Throughout history, the Carnian people were poor and often plagued by famine. This was especially true during the long, brutal winters when snow would barricade the few existing roads, leaving families to fend for themselves. When the weather prevented work outdoors, women and children would huddle around the *fogolâr*, or "fireplace," subsisting on meager food rations, while the men turned to weaving, carpentry, or woodcrafts. Often the men would leave town in early autumn to spend the winter working as woodsmen, stonecutters, or merchants in foreign lands, returning home to work in the fields at the first sign of spring. At times, communities encouraged permanent emigration so as to keep the population at a level consistent with agricultural production. Today, emigration continues as the younger generations leave to join the urban workforce in cities like Udine and Pordenone.

Alto Friuli

Nestled at the base of the Carnian and Giulian Alps are the towns Venzone and Gemona del Friuli. Gemona is, unfortunately, best known as the epicenter of the devastating earthquakes of 1976. Following a lengthy restoration, the town has lost some of its quaintness, although great effort was made to retain architectural and historical integrity. Also severely damaged in the earthquake, nearby Venzone has kept more of its original charm. Situated in the heart of pumpkin country, this medieval town hosts the popular Festa della Zucca every autumn.

A log pile becomes a decorative alcove for flowers (ABOVE); *goats graze in the hills above Sauris di Sopra* (RIGHT); *traditional Carnian shoes called* scarpèts (OPPOSITE, TOP); *ancient Carnian memorabilia at the Mondo delle Malghe festival in Ovaro* (OPPOSITE, BOTTOM).

Giulian Alps

From Venzone, the *autostrada* winds north to the Austrian border and the Tarvisiano, or Giulian Alps. Here, mountain peaks may remain capped with snow late into spring and summer. Ski resorts in Tarvisio and neighboring towns such as Sella Nevea and Camporosso draw crowds throughout the winter season, while hikers flock to these mountains during warmer months. The Fusine lakes and the sanctuary at Monte Santo di Lussari are popular excursions.

Carnian Alps

To the west lies Tolmezzo, the gateway to the Carnian Alps. The most industrial town in Carnia, Tolmezzo is famous for its long history of textile production, as well as for fostering the most renowned chef in all of Friuli, Gianni Cosetti.

In ancient times, the Romans built one of their major roads, Via Giulia Augusta, from Aquileia through Tolmezzo and across the Alps. On this road just north of Tolmezzo lies Zuglio, an ancient Roman village, the ruins of which can still be seen today right in the center of town. Zuglio's advantageous location alongside the Tagliamento River no doubt drew the Romans to the site and allowed their civilization to thrive for centuries.

Through these rugged mountains run many tributaries of the Tagliamento River. In places the gravelly riverbed is dry with only a trickle of water, but when the snow melts in springtime, the clear water rushes past dozens of low-lying villages on its way to the Adriatic Sea. The Carnian town of Forni Avoltri bottles this pure spring water to sell throughout the region, while vacationers travel to Arta Terme for its famous thermal baths and spa treatments.

The river has cut seven valleys, along which lie many of Carnia's twenty-eight villages and 121 hamlets. Other towns have situated themselves atop the mountains' towering peaks. Several, such as Ravascletto and Forni di Sopra, are now popular ski resorts. The latter

has an especially scenic location at the western edge of Carnia, with spectacular views of the rugged Dolomite range. Nearby Sauris di Sopra, at 4600 feet, boasts the highest altitude of any Carnian town.

The difficulty of reaching Carnia is perhaps the prime reason the area sees few visitors. Roads are long and treacherous, with narrow hairpin turns winding up mountainsides and dark tunnels boring through them. It is precisely this isolation that has forced many Carnian communities to become self-sufficient. Even today, as supermarkets are few and far between, many families continue their ancient tradition of raising livestock and farming the land. Though the soil here is remarkably fertile, the rocky terrain and harsh climate have made large-scale agriculture difficult. As a result, Carnians have learned to gather what food they can find in the fields and forests.

Wild mushrooms, herbs, berries, and apples not only appear seasonally in local dishes but are honored by various towns with annual festivals. Every spring, wild herbs are celebrated in Forni di Sopra, as are the wild asparagus, mushrooms, and radicchio in Arta Terme. In the summer, Forni Avoltri pays tribute to its wild berries, while Tolmezzo hosts an apple festival in September.

In ancient times, the region was known for cultivating a vast quantity of apples—some native to the hilly fields of Carnia and others brought from lands far away. One orchard in Enemonzo is striving to reintroduce many of these ancient species to the contemporary palate. In addition to 150 varieties of apples, they are growing fifty types of pears and twenty kinds of plums. Apple cider, sometimes called the "wine of the poor" and typically drunk at religious ceremonies such as weddings and baptisms, is made by fermenting leftover fruits that have been bruised or are otherwise undesirable.

As in the rest of Friuli-Venezia Giulia, the foods of poverty—polenta, beans, and potatoes—are dietary staples. Pork remains the principal meat, although game meats such as venison and pheasant are quite common as well. Fresh fish, particularly trout, are plentiful in Carnia's rivers and lakes.

*A rustic lunch (*ABOVE*); dried corn for making polenta adorns a gateway in Piano d'Arta (*RIGHT*); wildflowers abound in the hilly fields around Sauris di Sopra (*OPPOSITE*).*

Before refrigeration was invented, meats had to be eaten immediately to avoid spoilage. As in much of the world, salt- and smoke-curing were employed in order to maintain a food's shelf life. The small village of Sauris di Sotto is home to one of Carnia's most recognized products, *prosciutto di Sauris*. Here, the Petris family smokes their ham using a combination of herbs, juniper, and beech wood.

At one time, the economy of Carnia depended almost exclusively on the breeding of cattle. Even the poorest family owned at least one cow. Today, cows are still raised primarily for dairy purposes, the milk used to make fresh butter, yogurt, and cheese. Since olive trees typically do not thrive in Friuli—only in the warmer Mediterranean climate along the coast—butter takes the place of oil here, giving Carnian cuisine its trademark richness.

Montasio cheese is one of Friuli's top food exports and is produced in three varieties: fresh, semi-aged, and aged. *Ricotta affumicata*, on the other hand, is more difficult to acquire outside the region. Smoking fresh ricotta above a *fogolâr* gives this cheese its unique flavor, making it a perfect garnish for pasta and gnocchi. Even rarer still is the seasonal *formaggio di malga*. This cheese is produced only in the summertime, when cows are brought from the valleys' *latterie*, or "dairy farms," to vacation at *malghe*, tiny mountain huts where the cows can graze to their hearts' content in tranquil Alpine pastures.

While the majority of Carnia's food has always been grown or gathered on its land, there has been one significant food source from the outside world—the *cramârs*. These traveling peddlers brought home an assortment of goods from the markets of central Europe, including exotic spices and herbs. Spices such as cinnamon and nutmeg have added a unique touch to many local dishes, *cjalsòns* in particular. Perhaps Carnia's most distinctive dish, *cjalsòns* are a type of stuffed pasta with a complex filling of sweet and savory ingredients. Every cook in Carnia has his or her

Menu offerings at a pizzeria in Sauris di Sopra include cjarsòns *and* frico *(ABOVE); a hand-crafted straw man on display at the Mondo delle Malghe festival in Ovaro (LEFT);* prosciutto *hangs to cure at Prosciuttificio Wolf Sauris (OPPOSITE).*

own time-honored recipe that may include potato, cheese, herbs, fruit, nuts, or chocolate.

Austria's former supremacy is evident in the numerous varieties of gnocchi that appear on menus and tables throughout Friuli. In Carnia, dumplings are prepared with local ingredients such as ricotta cheese, pumpkin, herbs, and *prosciutto di Sauris*.

Delicious jams, fruit syrups, and honey are produced throughout Carnia. While honey made from *tarassaco* (dandelion) is perhaps the most characteristic, also look for rhododendron, blueberry, mint, rosemary, chestnut, sunflower, heather, and clover honey. For those who can't decide, the intense, amber-colored *millefiori* honey is made with a variety of flowers.

Desserts in Carnia are simple and rustic, the polar opposite of Trieste's lavish Viennese tortes and even less intricate than the homey *gubana* of Cividale. Cakes, tarts, breads, and strudels are made with locally grown apples, pears, berries, pumpkin, or nuts. Unlike most of Carnia's traditional sweets, the *esse di Raveo* has a fairly modern history. This S-shaped cookie was first baked in 1920 in the town of Raveo and is now sold in bakeries throughout the Val Degano.

Although the Alpine environment is not particularly conducive to winemaking, Carnia does produce a variety of spirits, namely in the hamlet of Cabia near Arta Terme. For several centuries, the Casato dei Capitani distillery has been making Sliwovitz (plum brandy) and similar liqueurs distilled from pears and cherries, as well as grappas flavored with herbs and berries.

*Honey (*ABOVE*) and liqueur flavored with blackberries and raspberries (*RIGHT*) for sale in Carnia's outdoor markets; wintertime on Monte Santo di Lussari (*OPPOSITE*).*

Clockwise from top left: *Ravascletto's grassy ski slopes in summertime; rooftops of Sauris di Sotto with Lago di Sauris in the distant valley; Prato Carnico nestled in the green hills of the Val Pesarina; the hilltop church of San Pietro towers above Zuglio; the town of Timau near the Austrian border.*

Opposite: *the Bût River flows through Arta Terme.*

Seven Valleys of Carnia & Their Principal Villages

Val Tagliamento ✦ Tolmezzo, Villa Santina, Ampezzo, Forni di Sopra
Val Lumiei ✦ Sauris
Val Degano ✦ Forni Avoltri, Ovaro, Raveo
Valcalda ✦ Ravascletto, Sutrio
Valle del Bût ✦ Arta Terme, Zuglio, Paluzza
Val Pesarina ✦ Prato Carnico
Valle del Chiarsò ✦ Paularo

Two Valleys of Tarvisiano

Valcanale ✦ Pontebba to Tarvisio
Canal del Ferro ✦ Pontebba to Gemona

Northern Friuli: ANTIPASTI

Insalata di Pere e Montasio   *Pear and Montasio Salad*

Carnian chef Gianni Cosetti recommended garnishing this salad with walnuts or sesame seeds, although there is much creative variation to be found depending on available ingredients. For example, when I ordered this salad at Antica Trattoria Cooperativa in Tolmezzo, it came with a sprinkling of ground coriander. If Montasio fresco is not available, you may substitute fresh Asiago.

4 ounces arugula or mixed baby greens

1 tablespoon olive oil

2 ripe pears, peeled, cored, and sliced

1 cup shredded Montasio fresco

1/4 cup coarsely chopped walnuts

ဢ In a large bowl, toss the arugula with the olive oil. Season to taste with salt. Divide the arugula among serving plates. Top with the pear slices, Montasio cheese, and chopped walnuts.

Serves 4.

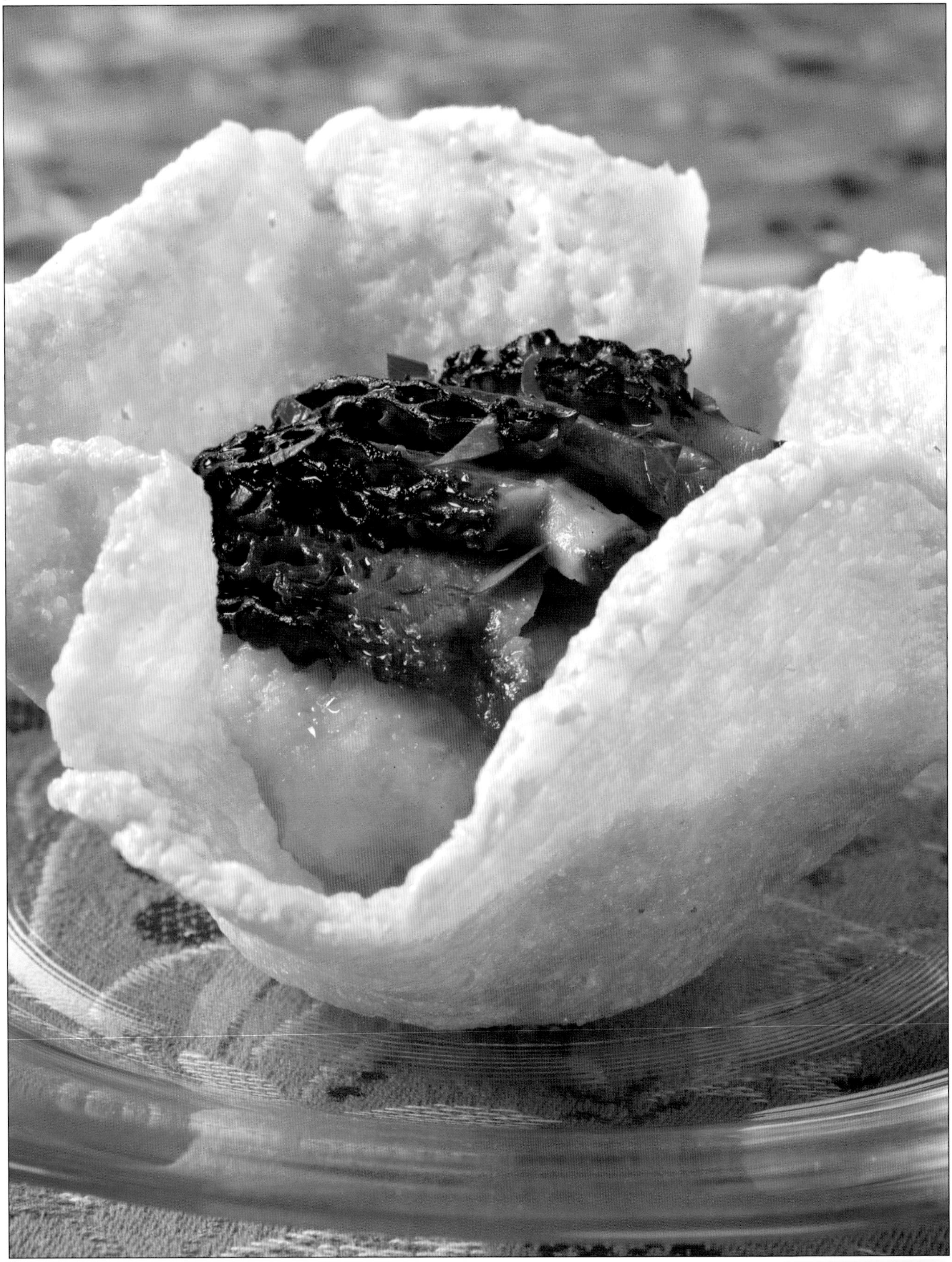

Frico Croccante

Montasio Cheese Crisps

The first recipe for frico dates back to the 15th century and is attributed to Martino da Como, chef for the patriarch of Aquileia. The original frico was a sweet dish of fried cheese sprinkled with sugar and cinnamon, but for the peasants of Carnia, frico was merely a way of utilizing leftovers. The women of the house would toss old rinds of Montasio into a cauldron on the fogolâr; by the time the men returned for their daily meal, the cheese would have melted into a crisp pancake.

Today, you will find two main varieties: frico croccante and frico con patate (page 93). While frico made with potatoes is usually served as a main course, frico croccante, or "crispy frico," is served as an appetizer in the form of a basket to hold such treats as polenta, mushrooms, or wild herbs and greens (including the widespread radicchio di montagna). A third, albeit less common, variety is frico friabile, a deep-fried mass of cheese that puffs into what looks like a porous sea sponge. If Montasio stagionato is not available, you may substitute any aged cheese such as Parmigiano-Reggiano.

4 cups grated Montasio stagionato, divided

  Preheat a large nonstick skillet over medium heat. Sprinkle 1 cup Montasio cheese into the skillet, making a 6-inch circle. Cook until the edges begin to turn golden brown, about 5 minutes. (Watch carefully as the cooking time will vary depending on the precise temperature of the skillet.) Gently remove the frico from the pan and drape over an upside-down glass or bowl. (Allowing the frico to cool in the skillet for a couple seconds off the heat will help the spatula release the cheese from the pan.) The frico will harden in less than a minute, at which point it can be removed from its mold. Repeat with the remaining cheese.

Serves 4.

VARIATION:

  Frico croccante may also be served as small wafers, perhaps garnishing an appetizer portion of polenta or simply eaten as a snack with a glass of wine. To make a smaller frico, sprinkle 1 tablespoon cheese into a preheated skillet, making a 2-inch circle. Cook until golden brown, about 2 minutes on each side. Repeat with the remaining cheese.

The Fogolâr

Derived from the same Latin root as the Italian word *focolare*, meaning "fireplace," the *fogolâr* is a centuries-old tradition at the heart of Carnian culture. What began as a primitive pile of firewood developed over time into the functional structure that remains in use today. A raised hearth typically positioned in the center of a home's main living space, the *fogolâr* is lined with tile or slabs of stone and features a grill for roasting meat, an elaborately constructed andiron with several revolving spits, coal-filled side furnaces used to cook food away from the live flame, and a flared hood for carrying away smoke and odors. Firewood may be stored in a small opening near the ground, while copper pots, kettles, and utensils hang from hooks above the stove.

Soups, stews, and the ubiquitous polenta are cooked in a large cauldron made of cast-iron or copper and suspended from a heavy chain directly over the flame. The polenta is stirred using a long wooden paddle, with the cauldron resting on a wrought-iron trivet to hold it steady. Bread may be cooked under the ashes in the side ovens, the dough wrapped in cabbage leaves to protect it from the dirty soot.

In the early days, when roofs were made of straw, a normal chimney would have been a dangerous fire hazard. So instead, a small opening was cut above the door in order for smoke to escape. Even so, smoke would fill the house, depositing black soot on the walls and rafters, the smell permeating hair, clothes, and food. Families became accustomed to this smokiness and utilized it to shape the characteristic flavors of Friulian cooking. Cheese and pork were the most common foods left to smoke over the *fogolâr*, hence the origin of *ricotta affumicata* and *prosciutto di Sauris*.

Another tradition was to hang a single herring to smoke on the first day of Lent. On each day during this religious period, the family would take turns touching the herring to their polenta, giving the meal just the slightest hint of smoky flavor. Often this ritual turned into a game of sorts, where the smoked fish was tossed from father to oldest son and so forth, perhaps serving to distract the family from the meagerness of their meal.

In times such as this, the *fogolâr* functioned not only as a kitchen stove but also as a gathering place for family and friends. The hearth was once the home's main source of heat, and on cold winter evenings, families would huddle around the fire to stay warm, often singing or telling stories.

Even today, the *fogolâr* still represents warmth. Many traditional restaurants and hotels feature this old-fashioned hearth as an inviting symbol of hos-

pitality. Modern homes are fitted with both a gas stove in the kitchen and a *fogolâr* in the living area. Although it is no longer used primarily for cooking, the *fogolâr* remains a gathering place, the heart of the Friulian home and an element central to the region's identity.

An iron cauldron is suspended over the hearth of a typical fogolâr (ABOVE)*; the* fogolâr *at the restaurant Polenta e Frico in Forni di Sopra* (LEFT)*; the* fogolâr *at Hotel Ristorante Bellavista in Ravascletto* (OPPOSITE).

Malghe of Carnia

Every summer, throughout the rural hills of Carnia, cows are herded from dairy farms in the valleys to mountain huts called *malghe*. In mid-June, the parade of cattle up into the mountains is a celebrated event, as is the descent each September. All summer long, cows can graze in tranquil Alpine pastures, providing their milk twice a day for the standard products: *formaggio di malga*, *formaggio salato*, ricotta (both fresh and smoked), and butter.

Formaggio di malga is the artisanal counterpart to the generic *latteria* cheese from the valleys, the difference being simply the cows' diet of grass and the subtle variations in flavor this provides. Like Montasio and all *latteria* cheese, there are varying stages of maturation, from young and milky to golden and crumbly. *Formaggio salato* literally means "salted cheese" and includes many varieties, all soaked in a saltwater bath prior to aging.

In addition to the rooms designated for cheese production, every *malga* undoubtedly has a smoking room. Here, in a tiny, soot-filled cabin, balls of ricotta rest for several days above a *fogolâr* until the cheese's exterior turns a smoky, brownish orange.

Unfortunately, *malghe* are almost always difficult to reach. Some are accessible by narrow gravel roads winding up the mountainside, while others require a strenuous hike through steep forest trails. Malga Pramosio and Malga Pozôf (also known as Casera Marmoreana) are two that are easily reached by car. Set amid green meadows with stunning panoramic vistas, these particular *malghe* also serve traditional meals of gnocchi, *frico*, *goulasch*, sausages, and of course, samples of *formaggio di malga*.

Sauris, Prato Carnico, and Ovaro are among the towns that celebrate Carnia's *malghe* with the Mondo delle Malghe festival every summer. The "World of the Malghe" features many varieties of *formaggio di malga*, as well as other traditional foods and crafts produced by local artisans.

Cows roam freely in the meadows around Malga Pozôf, located on Monte Zoncolan above Ravascletto (ABOVE); Casera Festons in the hills above Sauris di Sopra (LEFT); Malga Pramosio, located high above Timau near the Austrian border (OPPOSITE, TOP AND BOTTOM LEFT); cows resting outside the stables at Malga Pozôf (OPPOSITE, BOTTOM RIGHT).

Formaggio di Malga

The term formaggio di malga *denotes any type of cheese produced at a malga. Like* latteria *cheese—any cheese made at a commercial latteria, or "dairy farm"—there are varying stages of maturation, from young and milky to golden and crumbly. The towns Sauris, Prato Carnico, and Ovaro all hold Mondo delle Malghe festivals dedicated to the "world of the malghe" during the summer months.*

Wheels of cheese line the walls at Malga Pozôf (RIGHT); cheese is pressed in metal molds (OPPOSITE, TOP RIGHT) and ready for visitors to sample (OPPOSITE, TOP LEFT) at Malga Pramosio; vendors offer many varieties of formaggio di malga at Ovaro's Mondo delle Malghe festival (BELOW).

Ricotta Affumicata

The name ricotta literally means "recooked." Called *scuète* in Furlan, ricotta is made using the whey from *latteria* cheese (a generic term for most semi-firm or hard cheeses made at a *latteria*, or "dairy farm"). The whey is fermented and then heated until curds form. This mixture is wrapped in cheesecloth and pressed to extract the excess liquid. At this stage, the fresh ricotta may be used in dishes such as *toç in braide* and gnocchi.

Once upon a time, Carnia's dairy farmers produced more ricotta than their families could eat. They soon discovered that curing the cheese over the hood of a *fogolâr* was an excellent method of preservation. It also gave the cheese a distinctive smoky flavor, as well as a brownish orange exterior. Smoked ricotta—called *ricotta affumicata*—is Friuli's traditional topping for gnocchi and *cjalsòns*.

Clockwise from below: *smoke-curing gives* ricotta affumicata *a brownish orange exterior as well as a smoky flavor; balls of ricotta are hung over a fogolâr to smoke at Malga Pozôf;* ricotta affumicata *for sale in Udine's premier cheese shop, La Baita dei Formaggi; ricotta is wrapped in cheesecloth and pressed to extract the liquid at Malga Pramosio.*

Ricotta affumicata *for sale in one of Carnia's local markets* (opposite, top)*; ricotta being pressed at Malga Pramosio* (opposite, bottom)*.*

Montasio

The earliest documentation of Montasio appears on a 1775 market pricing list from San Daniele del Friuli; however, the cheese has been produced in Friuli's mountain region as far back as the 13th century. Benedictine monks from the abbey in Moggio Udinese observed the cheese-making of local shepherds and refined their techniques to create a cheese worthy of export. The abbey's Canal del Ferro location, along the ancient Roman road connecting the Alps to the Adriatic, helped broaden the cheese's distribution past the valleys of Carnia into the plains of Friuli and the Veneto. Eventually, the cheese was named after Friuli's tallest massif, Monte Montasio, the mountain from which the milk originated.

Even though technology has evolved, the essence of production has remained the same. Cow's milk is obtained from two daily milkings. The evening's milk is partially skimmed before being mixed with milk from the following morning. After pasteurization, the milk is heated to around 100°F; rennet is added, and the mixture begins to solidify. Then, the coagulated milk is broken apart using a tool called a *lira*—named after the musical instrument "lyre"—and crumbled into small grains. These are heated to around 115°F in order to separate the curd from the whey. The curds are then wrapped in cheesecloth and pressed to remove any excess liquid. After resting for one day, the cheese is immersed in a salt bath for forty-eight hours and then covered with dry salt. The cheese is now ready for aging. This process takes place in a climate-controlled room—60°F and 80–85 percent humidity—where the cheese is turned every three to four days. Aging may last anywhere from two months to two years, depending on the desired product.

There are three categories of Montasio: *fresco* (aged two to four months), *mezzano* (aged five to ten months), and *stagionato* (aged more than ten months). The fresh cheese is white with a flexible, straw-colored rind. The flavor is mild and delicate with a soft, creamy texture. As the cheese ripens, the aroma becomes stronger, the flavor piquant, almost tangy. The color turns golden yellow, the

rind darkens, and the cheese becomes firmer. All three stages contain small holes, or "eyes," and the *stagionato* develops a crumbly, granular texture that is ideal for grating.

Montasio cheese is a highly standardized industry. A local consortium regulates all matters of quality control, from the basic ingredients and technique to the final product's size and taste. The cheese has also received the official DOP (Denominazione d'Origine Protetta) mark from the European Union, which guarantees and protects the product's origin. The cheese may only be legally produced within Friuli-Venezia Giulia and certain provinces of the Veneto.

Used to garnish numerous Friulian dishes, Montasio is perhaps at its best in Carnia's signature dish, *frico*. This, and other traditional recipes, may be sampled at the Sapore di Montasio festival, part of the larger fair Fiera di San Simone, held annually in Codroipo.

A wheel of aged Montasio (ABOVE); *cows that graze in Friuli's Alpine pastures are believed to produce the best milk for making Montasio cheese* (OPPOSITE).

Northern Friuli: PRIMI

Toç in Braide

Polenta with Ricotta Sauce

In the Carnia of centuries past, where winters were brutally cold and food scarce, polenta was often the centerpiece of a meal. The creamy polenta in this dish is topped with a simple ricotta sauce and crunchy cornmeal browned in butter. Carnian chef Gianni Cosetti suggested serving the dish with asparagus, shaved truffle, or sautéed mushrooms (see funghi in padella on page 113), depending on the season.

POLENTA:

3 cups water

2 cups whole milk

1 cup coarsely ground cornmeal

1 teaspoon salt

. . .

SAUCE:

8 ounces fresh ricotta

¼ cup whole milk

. . .

TOPPING:

2 tablespoons butter

*2 tablespoons coarsely ground
   cornmeal*

FOR THE POLENTA:

› Bring 3 cups water and 2 cups milk to a boil in a medium pot over high heat. Add the cornmeal and salt. When the liquid returns to a boil, reduce heat to low; cook and stir until soft, about 25 minutes.

FOR THE SAUCE:

› Combine the ricotta and milk in a double boiler; heat until just warm. (Do not bring to a boil.)

FOR THE TOPPING:

› Melt the butter in a small skillet over medium-low heat. Add the cornmeal; cook and stir until the butter has browned, about 5 minutes.

› Divide the polenta among serving bowls. Top with the ricotta sauce; drizzle with the browned butter and cornmeal.

Serves 6.

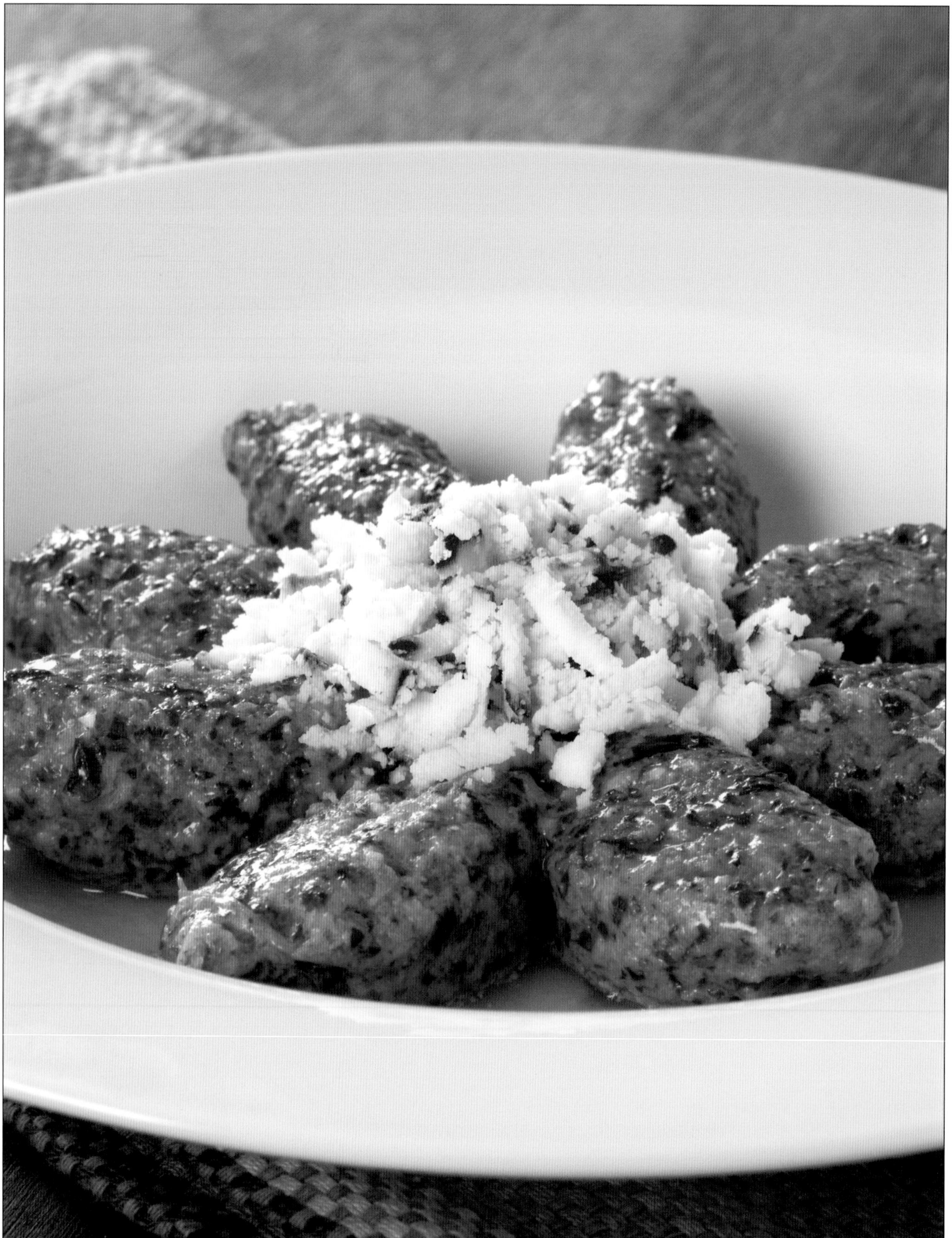

Gnocchi alle Erbe

Herb Gnocchi

Spinach gnocchi is common throughout much of Italy, and in Carnia, cooks will typically use local wild herbs and greens as well. Use two teaspoons to shape the dough into small, oblong balls as you drop the dumplings into the cooking water. With this technique, the dough requires less flour, giving the gnocchi a fluffier texture. If ricotta affumicata is not available, you may substitute ricotta salata.

8 ounces fresh spinach leaves

4 ounces arugula

2 cups (packed) fresh basil
   leaves

1/2 cup chopped fresh chives

1/2 cup chopped fresh Italian
   parsley

1 1/4 cups all-purpose flour

1/2 cup fresh ricotta

1 teaspoon salt

1/2 teaspoon ground nutmeg

1/4 teaspoon ground black
   pepper

1 egg

. . .

1/2 cup (1 stick) butter

1/2 cup grated ricotta affumicata

 Place the spinach, arugula, and basil (plus 1–2 tablespoons water if using packaged, prewashed spinach) in a large pot over medium-low heat. Cook, covered, until nearly wilted, about 8 minutes, stirring occasionally. Add the chives and parsley; cook 2–3 minutes longer. Drain the greens thoroughly, squeezing out all excess liquid. Purée the greens in a food processor; cool to room temperature.

 Transfer the puréed greens to a medium bowl. Stir in the flour, ricotta, salt, nutmeg, black pepper, and egg.

 Bring a large pot of lightly salted water to a boil over high heat. Working in batches, drop rounded teaspoonfuls of dough into the water, taking care not to overcrowd the pot. Cook until the gnocchi rise to the surface; remove them promptly with a slotted spoon.

 Melt the butter in a large skillet over medium heat; remove from heat. Add the gnocchi and toss to coat with butter. Serve topped with grated ricotta affumicata.

Serves 4.

Gnocchi di Zucca

Butternut Squash Gnocchi

These gnocchi have a delicate, cloud-like texture. For faster preparation, you may substitute 2 cups canned pumpkin for the butternut squash. As with the gnocchi alle erbe (page 55), use two teaspoons to shape the dough as you drop the dumplings into the cooking water. If ricotta affumicata is not available, you may substitute ricotta salata.

1 large butternut squash (about
   2 to 3 pounds), halved
   lengthwise
1 cup all-purpose flour
½ teaspoon salt
1 egg

· · ·

½ cup (1 stick) butter
2 tablespoons thinly sliced
   fresh sage leaves
½ cup grated ricotta affumicata

৭০ Preheat oven to 375°F. Place the squash halves on a baking sheet. Bake until tender, about 45–50 minutes. When the squash is cool enough to handle, remove and discard the seeds and membrane. Scoop out enough flesh to measure 2 cups. (Reserve any extra for another use.) Place in a medium bowl; mash well. Cool to room temperature.

৭০ Stir the flour, salt, and egg into the mashed squash.

৭০ Bring a large pot of lightly salted water to a boil over high heat. Working in batches, drop rounded teaspoonfuls of dough into the water, taking care not to overcrowd the pot. Cook until the gnocchi rise to the surface; remove them promptly with a slotted spoon.

৭০ Melt the butter in a large skillet over medium-low heat. Cook and stir until the butter has browned, about 8–10 minutes; remove from heat. Stir in the sliced sage leaves; add the gnocchi and toss to coat with butter. Serve topped with grated ricotta affumicata.

Serves 4.

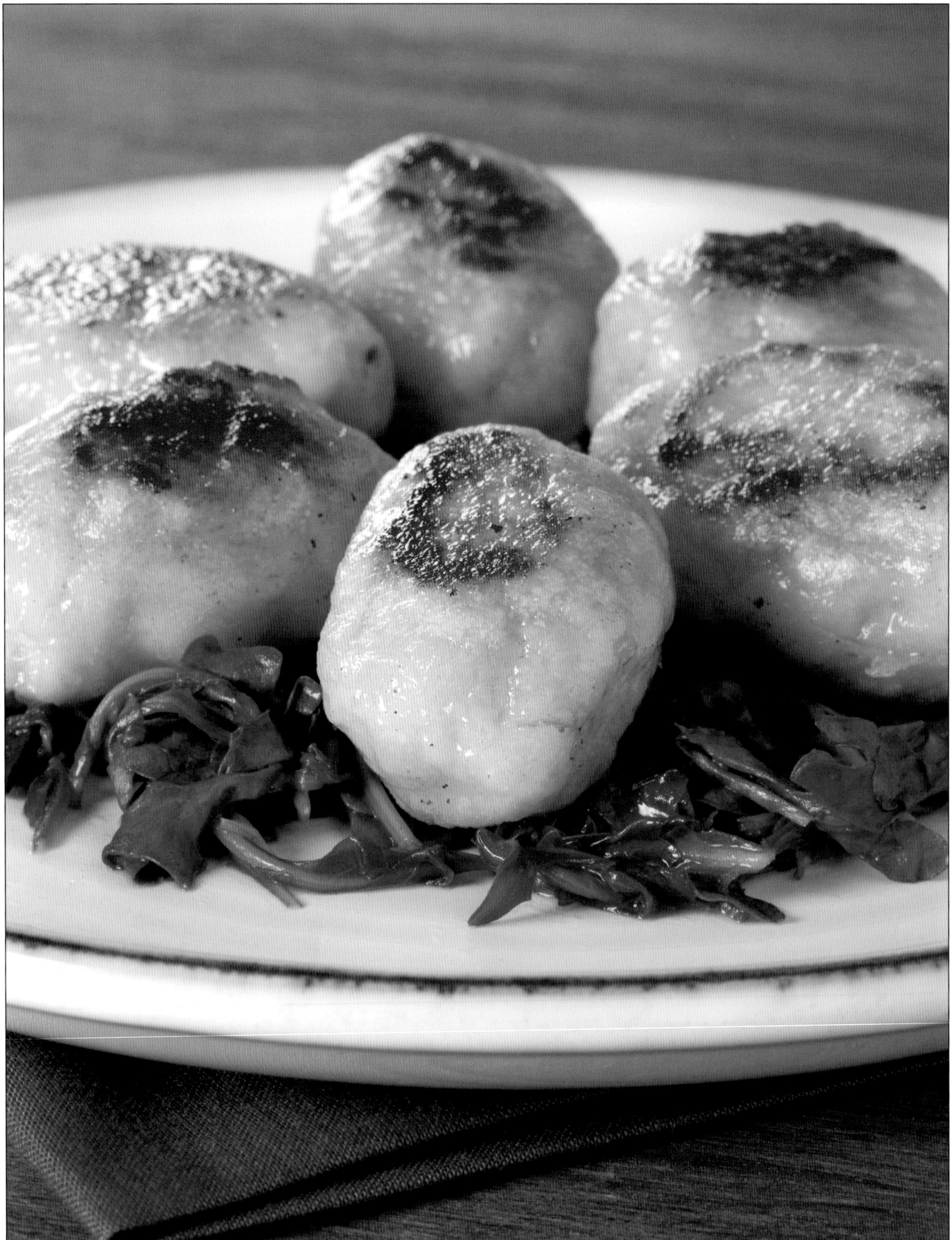

Gnocchi Croccanti di Sauris   *Crispy Stuffed Gnocchi*

Gnocchi croccanti (crispy dumplings) are a specialty at Locanda Alla Pace in Sauris. Not to be confused with the similarly termed gnocchi di Sauris—a bread-based gnocchi like the one on page 259—this dish recalls an ancient Carnian recipe for stuffed gnocchi. If Montasio stagionato is not available, you may substitute any aged cheese such as Parmigiano-Reggiano; you may also use prosciutto di San Daniele in place of the prosciutto di Sauris.

FILLING:

8 ounces prosciutto di Sauris,
    coarsely chopped

1/2 cup grated Montasio
    stagionato

1 tablespoon whole milk

2 tablespoons chopped fresh
    chives

. . .

DOUGH:

1 1/2 pounds white potatoes,
    peeled and quartered

3 cups all-purpose flour

1 tablespoon salt

1 egg

. . .

6 tablespoons butter, divided

12 ounces arugula

FOR THE FILLING:

⁞ Blend the prosciutto, Montasio cheese, and milk in a food processor until the mixture forms a smooth paste. Stir in the chives. Form the mixture into three dozen balls.

FOR THE DOUGH:

⁞ Place the potatoes in a large pot filled with water; bring to a boil over high heat. Cook until tender, about 20–25 minutes. Drain the potatoes and place in a large bowl; mash well. Cool to room temperature. Add the flour, salt, and egg; mix thoroughly to form a soft dough, adding a little extra flour if the dough appears too sticky to handle. Form the dough into three dozen balls. Press a ball of filling inside each ball of dough, wrapping the dough around the filling to seal tightly. Roll gently to form an oblong shape.

TO PREPARE:

⁞ Bring a large pot of lightly salted water to a boil over high heat. Working in batches, place the gnocchi in the water, taking care not to overcrowd the pot. Cook until the gnocchi rise to the surface; remove them promptly with a slotted spoon.

⁞ Melt 2 tablespoons butter in a large skillet over medium heat. Add half the gnocchi; cook until the bottoms are crisp and golden brown, about 3–5 minutes. Turn the gnocchi over and cook 3–5 minutes to brown the other side. Repeat with an additional 2 tablespoons butter and the remaining gnocchi.

⁞ Meanwhile, melt the remaining 2 tablespoons butter in a large pot over medium-low heat. Add the arugula; cook, covered, until wilted, about 4–5 minutes, stirring occasionally. Season to taste with salt and black pepper. Divide the arugula among serving plates. Top with the gnocchi; drizzle with any excess butter from the skillet.

Serves 6.

Orzotto ai Funghi

Barley with Mushrooms

Orzotto is to "orzo" (barley) as risotto is to "riso" (rice)—both are cooked slowly over low heat with the gradual addition of liquid to bring out the starch in the grain. In Carnia, orzotto may be prepared with any number of seasonal ingredients. Mushrooms seem to be one of the most popular, as I have tasted this dish in quite a few restaurants. If Montasio stagionato is not available, you may substitute any aged cheese such as Parmigiano-Reggiano.

1 cup pearl barley

6 tablespoons butter, divided

12 ounces assorted mushrooms
(such as porcini, morels, or
chanterelles), sliced

1 medium yellow onion,
chopped

2 ounces pancetta, chopped

½ cup dry white wine

6 cups chicken or vegetable
broth, heated

¾ cup grated Montasio
stagionato

¼ cup chopped fresh Italian
parsley

½ teaspoon ground black
pepper

   In advance, place the barley in a medium bowl and cover with water. Let soak for 1 hour; drain.

   Melt 3 tablespoons butter in a large skillet over medium heat. Add the mushrooms; cook and stir until tender, about 6–8 minutes.

   Melt the remaining 3 tablespoons butter in a large pot over medium heat. Add the onion and pancetta; cook and stir until the onion softens and the pancetta is brown and crisp, about 10 minutes. Add the barley; cook and stir for 2 minutes to allow the grains to absorb the butter. Add the white wine; cook and stir until the liquid has been absorbed, about 2–3 minutes. Reduce heat to medium-low. Add ½ cup warm chicken broth; cook and stir until the barley has absorbed most of the liquid. Continue stirring in broth, ½ cup at a time, until the barley is cooked, about 60–70 minutes. Stir in the mushrooms, Montasio cheese, parsley, and black pepper. Season to taste with salt.

Serves 6.

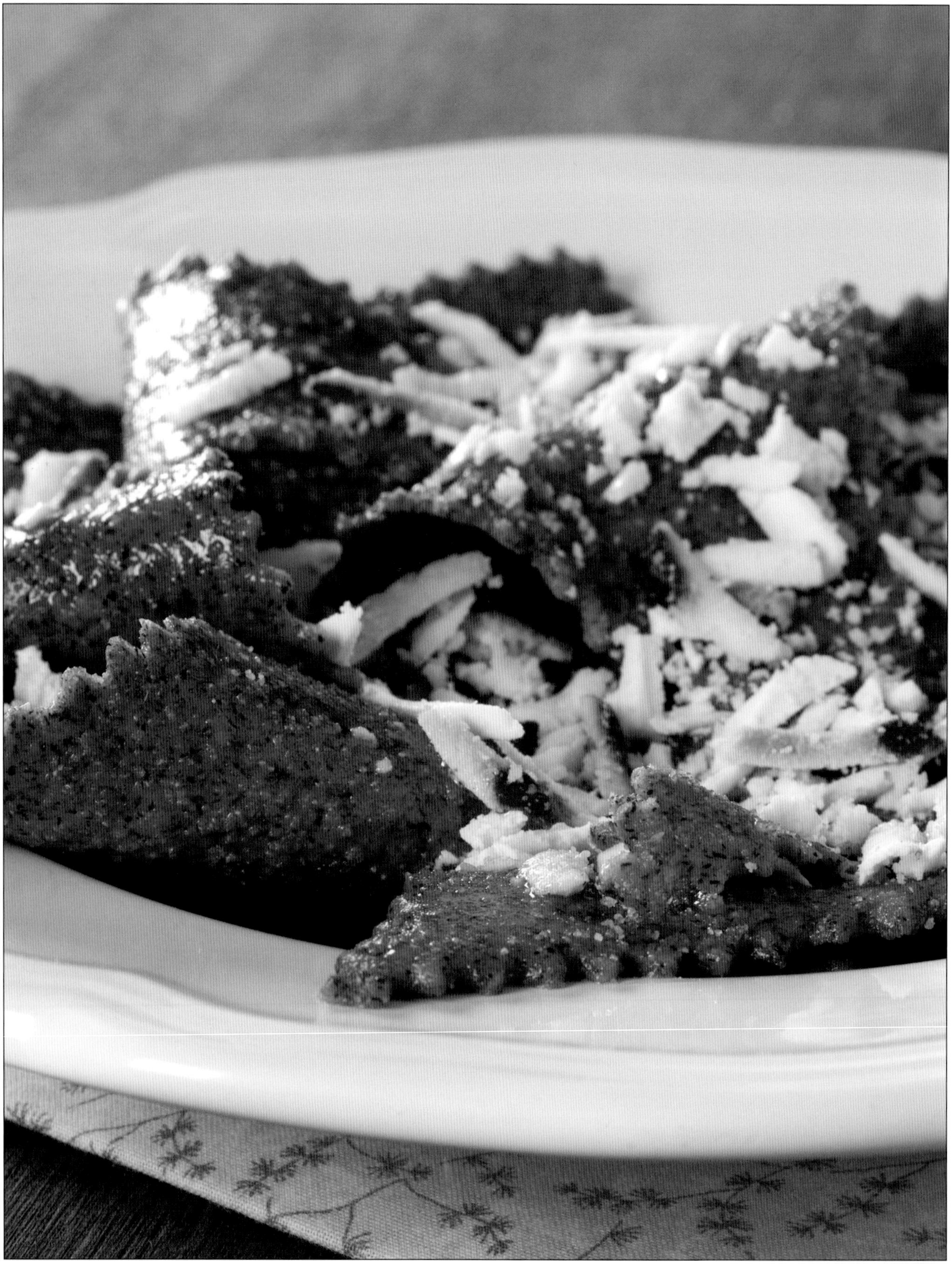

Blècs

Buckwheat Pasta

In restaurants, chefs often serve blècs—also called "bleons"—with a sauce made from seasonal ingredients. For example, during several summertime visits, I tasted the pasta in a cream sauce with mushrooms and prosciutto, in a stew-like sauce of wild game and mushrooms, and with a simple mushroom sauce and cheese. Some locals maintain, however, that the dish is most authentic tossed solely with browned butter and smoked ricotta, as shown here. Cornmeal is often added to the butter for additional texture. If ricotta affumicata is not available, you may substitute ricotta salata.

³/₄ cup all-purpose flour

³/₄ cup buckwheat flour

¹/₂ teaspoon salt

2 eggs

2 tablespoons butter, melted

1 tablespoon water, or as needed

. . .

¹/₂ cup (1 stick) butter

2 tablespoons finely ground cornmeal

¹/₂ cup grated ricotta affumicata

⁂ In a medium bowl, combine the all-purpose flour, buckwheat flour, and salt. Mix in the eggs and 2 tablespoons melted butter. Add about 1 tablespoon water, a little at a time, until the dough forms a solid mass but is not sticky. Transfer the dough to a clean surface; knead until the mixture becomes smooth and elastic, about 10 minutes. (If the dough is too dry or crumbly, lightly moisten your fingers with water during kneading until you reach the desired texture.) Cover with plastic wrap and let rest for 30 minutes.

⁂ Working in batches, feed the dough through the rollers of a pasta machine until moderately thin (setting #5 on most machines). Cut the dough into 4- by 5-inch rectangles; cut these diagonally to form triangles.

⁂ Bring a large pot of lightly salted water to a boil over high heat. Add the pasta; cook until just tender, about 3 minutes. Drain.

⁂ Melt ¹/₂ cup butter in a large skillet over medium-low heat. Add the cornmeal; cook and stir until the butter has browned, about 8–10 minutes. Remove from heat; add the cooked pasta and toss to coat with butter. Serve topped with grated ricotta affumicata.

Serves 4 to 6.

Cjalsòns

Served in nearly every restaurant throughout northern Friuli, *cjalsòns* are one of the region's best-loved specialties. The word derives from the same root as the *calzone* from Naples, and the numerous spelling variations include *cjalcions* and *cjarzòns*. Pronunciation also varies with location. The dish has been mentioned in documents as far back as medieval times, but due to the involved preparation and sometimes lengthy ingredient list, *cjalsòns* were originally prepared only for Easter celebrations.

Cjalsòns are a type of stuffed pasta with a multitude of possible fillings. In every lush valley of the Carnia mountains, each cook prepares his or her own unique recipe, merging herbs and spices and creating a distinct shape and form for the dough. While there are generally two varieties—sweet and savory—the flavors often tend to overlap. The sweet *cjalsòns* may be filled with apples, pears, crushed biscotti, dried fruit, nuts, chocolate, and spices, but often contain savory herbs such as parsley, basil, and marjoram. Likewise, the savory *cjalsòns* have undertones of sweetness, combining such unlikely ingredients as potatoes, raisins, onions, cocoa, spinach, jam, and cheese. Both sweet and savory *cjalsòns* are served in melted butter and are typically topped with *ricotta affumicata* and a sprinkle of sugar and cinnamon.

Renowned chef Gianni Cosetti, an expert on his local Carnian cuisine, became fascinated by *cjalsòns* and their countless methods of preparation. In 1973, he sponsored a competition, and the result was an astounding forty distinct recipes. Today, Friuli hosts festivals dedicated to *cjalsòns* in the towns of Pontebba and Cleulis.

If *ricotta affumicata* is not available, you may substitute *ricotta salata* in the following recipes.

This latteria *in Arta Terme sells packages of frozen* cjarsòns, *a rare example of modernization in Carnian cooking* (BELOW).

Basic Pasta Dough

Cjalsòns can be made with either a potato-based dough (similar to gnocchi) or a basic pasta dough, as shown here. Although potato dough is very common, especially in the sweet cjalsòns, I find its doughiness often overpowers the complex flavors in the filling. I much prefer using a pasta dough. Its delicate texture brings out all the delicious nuances that make cjalsòns so ethereal. This dough is used in the following four recipes: cjalsòns della Valle del Bût (page 66), cjalsòns di Treppo Carnico (page 69), cjalsòns di Pontebba (page 70), and cjalsòns di Piedim (page 73).

1 cup semolina flour

¼ cup boiling water, plus extra
  as needed

1 tablespoon olive oil

In a medium bowl, combine the flour, boiling water, and olive oil. Transfer the dough to a clean surface; knead until the flour is fully incorporated and the mixture becomes smooth and elastic, about 10 minutes. (If the dough is too dry or crumbly, lightly moisten your fingers with water during kneading until you reach the desired texture.) Cover with plastic wrap and let rest for 30 minutes.

Cjalsòns della Valle del Bût

*Pasta Filled with
Fruit and Herbs*

These sweet-savory cjalsòns—also spelled "cjarsòns"—from Ristorante Salon in Piano d'Arta are filled with fruit and herbs. In addition to the herbs listed below, the restaurant also uses leaves of lemon balm, lemon verbena, and geranium. I have tasted many versions of cjalsòns, and these are, without a doubt, my absolute favorite.

FILLING:

1 white potato (about 8
　　ounces), peeled and
　　quartered

¼ cup finely crushed biscotti

¼ cup grated apple

¼ cup grated pear

3 tablespoons grated ricotta
　　affumicata

2 tablespoons dried currants

2 tablespoons apricot jam

2 teaspoons sugar

1 teaspoon freshly grated
　　lemon peel

¼ teaspoon unsweetened cocoa
　　powder

¼ teaspoon ground cinnamon

Pinch salt

1 teaspoon butter

1 tablespoon chopped fresh
　　Italian parsley

1 tablespoon chopped fresh
　　basil

1 tablespoon chopped fresh
　　mint

1 tablespoon chopped fresh
　　marjoram

· · ·

Basic Pasta Dough (see recipe
　　on page 65)

· · ·

½ cup (1 stick) butter

½ cup grated ricotta affumicata

2 tablespoons sugar

1 teaspoon ground cinnamon

FOR THE FILLING:

&❦ Place the potato in a medium pot filled with water; bring to a boil over high heat. Cook until tender, about 20 minutes. Drain the potato and place in a medium bowl; mash well. Cool to room temperature. Stir in the crushed biscotti, apple, pear, ricotta affumicata, currants, apricot jam, sugar, lemon peel, cocoa powder, cinnamon, and salt.

&❦ Melt 1 teaspoon butter in a small skillet over medium heat. Add the parsley, basil, mint, and marjoram; cook and stir until wilted, about 1 minute. Stir into the potato mixture. Refrigerate for 1 hour, or until ready to use.

TO PREPARE:

&❦ Working in batches, feed the dough through the rollers of a pasta machine until very thin (setting #7 on most machines). Cut out 3-inch circles from the dough. Place 1 teaspoon filling on each circle. Moisten the edges with water and fold in half to make a semi-circle, sealing the edges tightly. Pinch the sealed edge into four points.

&❦ Bring a large pot of lightly salted water to a boil over high heat. Working in batches, place the cjalsòns in the water; cook until they rise to the surface, about 1–2 minutes. Drain.

&❦ Melt ½ cup butter in a large skillet over medium heat; remove from heat. Stir in the ricotta affumicata, sugar, and cinnamon; add the cjalsòns and toss to coat with butter.

Serves 4.

Cjalsòns di Treppo Carnico

Pasta Filled with Potato and Raisins

This version of cjalsòns is served at Ristorante Alle Vecchie Carceri in San Daniele, although the recipe hails from the Carnian village of Treppo Carnico near Timau.

FILLING:

1/4 cup raisins

12 ounces white potatoes, peeled and quartered

3 tablespoons plus 1 teaspoon olive oil, divided

1 medium yellow onion, chopped

2 tablespoons chopped fresh Italian parsley

2 tablespoons sugar

1 teaspoon freshly grated lemon peel

1/4 teaspoon salt

. . .

Basic Pasta Dough (see recipe on page 65)

. . .

1/2 cup (1 stick) butter

1/2 cup grated ricotta affumicata

Ground cinnamon

Sugar

. . .

Raisins (optional)

Cinnamon sticks (optional)

FOR THE FILLING:

🙹 Place the raisins in a small bowl and cover with water. Let soak for 30 minutes; drain. Place the potatoes in a medium pot filled with water; bring to a boil over high heat. Cook until tender, about 20 minutes. Drain the potatoes and place in a medium bowl; mash well. Cool to room temperature.

🙹 Heat 3 tablespoons olive oil in a large skillet over medium-low heat. Add the onion; cook and stir until golden brown and caramelized, about 30–40 minutes. Purée the onion in a food processor; stir into the mashed potatoes.

🙹 Heat 1 teaspoon olive oil in a small skillet over medium heat. Add the parsley; cook and stir until wilted and beginning to brown, about 2 minutes. Stir into the potato mixture, along with the drained raisins, sugar, lemon peel, and salt. Refrigerate for 1 hour, or until ready to use.

TO PREPARE:

🙹 Working in batches, feed the dough through the rollers of a pasta machine until very thin (setting #7 on most machines). Cut out 3-inch circles from the dough. Place 1 heaping tablespoon filling on half the circles. Moisten the edges with water; cover each with another circle of dough, sealing the edges tightly.

🙹 Bring a large pot of lightly salted water to a boil over high heat. Working in batches, place the cjalsòns in the water; cook until they rise to the surface, about 1–2 minutes. Drain.

🙹 Melt the butter in a large skillet over medium heat; remove from heat. Add the cjalsòns and toss to coat with butter. Divide the cjalsòns among serving plates; drizzle with any excess butter from the skillet. Top with grated ricotta affumicata; sprinkle with cinnamon and sugar. Garnish with extra raisins and cinnamon sticks, if desired.

Serves 4.

Cjalsòns di Pontebba   *Pasta Filled with Dried Fruit and Ricotta*

I sampled these cjalsòns at the Sagra dei Cjalsòns in Pontebba, a small village near Tarvisio. Cooking instructor Gianna Modotti, originally from Pontebba and now living in Udine, makes a similar recipe.

FILLING:

8 dried figs

8 dried plums

1/4 cup golden raisins

1 cup medium-bodied red wine
    (such as Merlot)

1 cup fresh ricotta

1/4 teaspoon ground cinnamon

. . .

Basic Pasta Dough (see recipe
    on page 65)

. . .

1/2 cup (1 stick) butter

2 tablespoons sugar

1 teaspoon ground cinnamon

FOR THE FILLING:

∞ Place the dried figs, plums, and raisins in a small saucepan; pour in the red wine. (The fruit should be mostly submerged; if it is not, slice any large figs and plums in half.) Bring to a boil over high heat. Reduce heat to low; simmer until the liquid has evaporated and the fruit is soft, about 20–25 minutes. Remove from heat; cool to room temperature.

∞ Purée the fruit in a food processor. Transfer to a medium bowl; stir in the ricotta and cinnamon. Refrigerate for 1 hour, or until ready to use.

TO PREPARE:

∞ Working in batches, feed the dough through the rollers of a pasta machine until very thin (setting #7 on most machines). Cut out 3 1/2-inch circles from the dough. Place 1 tablespoon filling on each circle. Moisten the edges with water and fold in half to make a semi-circle, sealing the edges tightly. Place filled-side down, pressing slightly so it will stand on end like a purse. Pinch the seal to form a scalloped edge (like a fluted pie crust).

∞ Bring a large pot of lightly salted water to a boil over high heat. Working in batches, place the cjalsòns in the water; cook until they rise to the surface, about 3–4 minutes. Drain.

∞ Melt the butter in a large skillet over medium heat; remove from heat. Stir in the sugar and cinnamon; add the cjalsòns and toss to coat with butter.

Serves 4.

Cjalsòns di Piedim

Pasta Filled with Chocolate and Nuts

Although cjalsòns are typically served as a first course, some restaurants will include sweet cjalsòns on their "dolci" menu. This rich, chocolatey version, from the village of Piedim near Paularo, would definitely qualify as a dessert.

FILLING:

½ cup fresh ricotta

½ cup finely crushed biscotti

⅓ cup finely chopped unsalted peanuts

¼ cup finely chopped walnuts

¼ cup diced candied lemon peel

1 ounce semisweet chocolate, grated

2 tablespoons grappa or rum

1 tablespoon plum or mixed berry jam

1 teaspoon honey

1 teaspoon unsweetened cocoa powder

1 teaspoon ground cinnamon

1 teaspoon freshly grated lemon peel

. . .

Basic Pasta Dough (see recipe on page 65)

. . .

½ cup (1 stick) butter

2 tablespoons sugar

1 teaspoon ground cinnamon

½ cup grated ricotta affumicata

FOR THE FILLING:

❧ In a medium bowl, combine the ricotta, crushed biscotti, peanuts, walnuts, candied lemon peel, chocolate, grappa, plum jam, honey, cocoa powder, cinnamon, and lemon peel. Refrigerate for 1 hour, or until ready to use.

TO PREPARE:

❧ Working in batches, feed the dough through the rollers of a pasta machine until very thin (setting #7 on most machines). Cut out 3-inch circles from the dough. Place 1 heaping teaspoon filling on each circle. Moisten the edges with water and fold in half to make a semi-circle, sealing the edges tightly.

❧ Bring a large pot of lightly salted water to a boil over high heat. Working in batches, place the cjalsòns in the water; cook until they rise to the surface, about 1–2 minutes. Drain.

❧ Melt the butter in a large skillet over medium heat; remove from heat. Stir in the sugar and cinnamon; add the cjalsòns and toss to coat with butter. Serve topped with grated ricotta affumicata.

Serves 4.

Sauris di Sopra
&
Sauris di Sotto

CLOCKWISE FROM ABOVE: *tranquil Sauris di Sopra, at 4600 feet, boasts the highest altitude of any Carnian town; Locanda Alla Pace in Sauris di Sotto specializes in local cuisine; the man-made Lago di Sauris was created in the 1940s with the construction of the Lumiei River dam; nestled in the Carnian Alps, the lower town of Sauris di Sotto is home to Prosciuttificio Wolf Sauris; a traditional Sauris home adorned with colorful flowers.*

OPPOSITE: *Chiesa di San Lorenzo perches on a hill just below Sauris di Sopra.*

Prosciuttificio Wolf Sauris

In the town of Sauris during the mid-19th century, Pietro Schneider was the village eccentric. Going by the nickname "Wolf," Schneider was the church's sexton, an unofficial dentist of sorts (he pulled teeth), and a self-proclaimed healer. Many people claimed to have been cured by his herbal remedies, although Schneider was once taken to court by local doctors over a paste he declared would heal broken bones—the case was ultimately thrown out.

In addition, Schneider was a pork butcher. Most families at that time kept at least one pig, and during slaughter season—November through March—he went from home to home preparing prosciutto and other *salumi*. In 1862, he began selling these hams, which he seasoned and smoked using a variety of local herbs and wood. Schneider's family continued this tradition for a full century; in 1962, his grandson Beppino Petris took over the business, officially naming the new company Prosciuttificio Wolf Sauris.

To keep up with orders, a new plant was built in 1983—and a later addition in 2001. Cradled in the hills above Sauris di Sotto, Wolf's barn-like factory turns out an annual eighty thousand legs of prosciutto, one hundred thousand legs of *speck* (prosciutto without the bone), and hundreds of tons of pancetta, salami, *cotechino*, *ossocollo*, and *coppa*.

The smoky flavor and aroma so characteristic of Carnia are the qualities that make Wolf's prosciutto unique in the world of hams. The legs are smoked four to five days using a combination of various woods and herbs, including beech, maple, fir, birch, oak, pine, chestnut, juniper, thyme, sage, and rosemary. Following the typical procedure, the hams are salted with sea salt and aged, but unlike *prosciutto di San Daniele*, the pig's trotter is always removed.

In a town of only four hundred citizens, Wolf employs more than sixty people. It is no wonder, then, that this company has come to embody the heart and soul of Sauris. Every July, two full weekends are dedicated to the Festa del Prosciutto, and visitors arrive from all over the region to eat, dance, and celebrate in the streets of this charming town.

Prosciutto hangs to cure (RIGHT); *the hills of Sauris di Sotto provide the perfect environs for the Wolf factory* (BELOW AND OPPOSITE, BOTTOM RIGHT); *salami* (OPPOSITE, TOP) *and prosciutto* (OPPOSITE, BOTTOM LEFT) *for sale in the factory's store.*

Gianni Cosetti

There is not a single cook in Carnia—and possibly in all of Friuli—who has not been influenced by Gianni Cosetti. Nicknamed the *orsetto*, or "bear," of Carnia, Cosetti gained his reputation as chef at the Albergo Roma in Tolmezzo. Author of the cookbook, *Vecchia e Nuova Cucina di Carnia*, Cosetti made it his mission to document the traditional cuisine of the region, ensuring that ancient recipes handed down through generations will not be forgotten.

In addition to chronicling recipes, Cosetti strove to promote a greater awareness of Carnian culture through various classes and cooking contests. One such competition in 1973 featured the stuffed pasta *cjalsòns*—the event yielded an astonishing forty versions of the dish, each recipe unique, passed down from the cook's grandmother or great-grandmother.

Cosetti died on February 20, 2001, but the legacy of the "Bear of Carnia" carries on in kitchens throughout the region. To honor the chef's memory, local officials have established the Orsetto d'Oro, or "Golden Bear," an annual contest for aspiring Friulian chefs. The contest was designed to inspire the young chefs to follow in Cosetti's footsteps and keep the cuisine of Carnia alive for generations to come.

Cosetti enjoying a glass of wine at a local enoteca (BELOW LEFT); *Cosetti was the chef at Albergo Ristorante Roma for many years—the restaurant has been reopened after a long closure following the chef's death* (BELOW RIGHT).

Cramârs

Thanks to the *cramârs*, the cuisine of Friuli has become known for blending local ingredients with exotic flavors such as cinnamon, nutmeg, cloves, saffron, chocolate, coffee, black pepper, paprika, cumin, caraway seeds, and poppy seeds. Their name having derived from the German word *krämer*, meaning "shop owner," *cramârs* were traveling peddlers who traded spices, medicinal herbs, fabrics, and other goods throughout central Europe. Many made their home in the mountains of Carnia, tending to crops and livestock during the spring and summer months, then leaving their families alone for the harsh winter. Often hiking in treacherous conditions, they traversed the Alps—from Friuli to Austria, Bavaria, and beyond—carrying goods on their backs in a wooden apothecary cabinet called a *crassigne*.

These spice merchants also acted the part of medicinal healer, weighing and mixing special concoctions of herbs and spices as remedies for various maladies. After four centuries of practice, this profession began to die out in the late 18th century, due mainly to advances in medicine that rendered the *cramârs'* folkloric customs obsolete, even suspicious. Their impact, though, has survived until present times. When the *cramârs* returned to Friuli every year at the first sign of spring, they carried home more than just unsold spices. In their travels, they picked up foreign languages and assimilated other cultures, and so brought to Carnia a certain level of sophistication not yet apparent in other Alpine regions.

Sbilfs

The mountains of Carnia are rich with pine, spruce, maple, and oak trees, the forest floor covered with a dense carpet of underbrush. A thousand forms of life populate these woods, among which dwell—in tree trunks, shady thickets, steep ravines, and abandoned barns—some fantastical creatures called *sbilfs*. An evolution of Celtic folklore, *sbilfs* represent the spirit of the forest and of nature.

Sbilfs are furtive beings, rarely noticed by humankind. Though fundamentally benevolent, they can be spiteful and are notorious for playing jokes on solitary hikers. Legend has created numerous *sbilf* characters, each with an individual personality and history. One of the most popular is Mazzaròt, an impish gnome with a mocking laugh and sneer. Although he is adept at camouflage, he often loves to wear red. Look for him in his favorite hiding spot—the wrinkled roots of old tree stumps. Superstition warns not to trample on his footsteps or you will lose your bearings and become hopelessly lost.

Bergul is another prankster, preferring hideouts that are thick and bushy. He adorns himself with leaves and twigs, rendering himself practically invisible. The rascal's favorite sport is to trip distracted passers-by with branches or entangle them in vines.

The squat, stumpy Gjan is unusually robust and endowed with a Herculean strength. Unlike many others of his kind, this *sbilf* is disposed to help humans in trouble. For centuries, he would come to the aid of woodsmen chopping timber, but nowadays—annoyed by the noise and fumes of power tools—he tends to avoid mankind for the solace of the deep woods.

An integral part of Carnian culture, the legend of the *sbilfs* imparts a love and respect for the environment. It is said that *sbilfs* will only approach humans of pure heart, that only those with a true love of nature are worthy of their company. For better luck finding a *sbilf*, Carnians say to thread three yellow primroses in your buttonhole and then venture with patience into the heart of the forest.

Every year, the town of Ravascletto marks the summer solstice with the Festa del Solstizio d'Estate. Children and adults dress in *sbilf* costumes to celebrate through stories, dance, and music. The festival lasts through June 24, coinciding with the Catholic Festa di San Giovanni. These two events merge into a continuous festival that blends religious tradition with pagan customs.

A sbilf *guards the entrance to an artist's shop in Tolmezzo* (OPPOSITE).

Ristorante Salon

In the hilltop hamlet of Piano d'Arta, on a serene lane lined with shady trees and wisteria blossoms, Hotel Ristorante Salon has long been recognized for its innovative local cuisine. When Arta Terme's thermal baths first opened in the late 19th century, the sudden influx of visitors spawned a proliferation of new restaurants and hotels in the valley. Salon was one of the originals, opened by Osvaldo Salon in 1910—first as an *osteria* and then expanding a few years later into a small *pensione*.

It was when Osvaldo passed the business down to his son Bepi, a budding mycologist, that the restaurant saw a significant transformation. In a tourist market where hotel menus typically featured "national" dishes such as *spaghetti al ragù*, *lasagne*, and *tortellini in brodo*, Bepi Salon pioneered the use of local ingredients and regional specialties. With his wife, Fides, commanding the kitchen, the pair introduced guests to such Carnian peasant fare as polenta, frittata, and *goulasch*.

Through the decades, nearly every ingredient has been raised, cultivated, or hand-picked by the Salon family, or at least procured from a local source. From the garden are fresh greens and vegetables, which are displayed on a rolling cart so that waiter Matteo can individually prepare each guest's salad tableside. Chickens, ducks, and guinea hens are raised in backyard pens, while wild game is obtained from local hunters. Trout, fresh from the valley's river and streams, are purchased weekly and kept live in tanks until ready to cook.

It is Carnia's abundance of wild edibles, though, that has contributed most to the restaurant's fame. With the sprightly nature of a *sbilf*, Bepi Salon would rise at the crack of dawn for his daily trek through Carnia's forests and meadows, returning just hours later bearing baskets of freshly picked mushrooms, herbs, and berries. Signora Fides, drawing inspiration from her mother's family recipes, would then prepare such creations as mushroom soufflé, risotto with seasonal greens, and crêpes with mushrooms and truffles. Daughter Antonella, who has recently joined Fides in the kitchen, specializes in pastries and has a particular flair for incorporating wild strawberries, blackberries, blueberries, raspberries, and currants into her desserts.

In his old age, Bepi has had to relinquish his daily hike, but Ristorante Salon continues to feature those indigenous ingredients. Every May, as part of the lengthily named Festa dell'Asparago di Bosco, del Radicchio di Montagna, e dei Funghi di Primavera, the restaurant offers a fixed-price tasting menu that highlights the region's herbs and mushrooms. At least eight courses are served and may include such dishes as herb fritters, fillet of trout marinated in wild fennel, *orzotto* with morel mushrooms and herbs, pheasant breast with marjoram and potatoes, and wild strawberry *semifreddo*.

Among the regular menu listings at Salon, there is one standout that deserves mention—the *cjarsòns*. Many experts have judged these to be the best in existence, and after sampling numerous recipes throughout Friuli, I wholeheartedly concur. (See my rendition on page 66.) Filled with a complex blend of eighteen ingredients, Salon's *cjarsòns* offer the perfect flavor combination of herbs and fruit, sweet and savory, salty and smoky. The pasta is delicate, never doughy, and the cinnamon-laced butter is enhanced by just the right amount of *ricotta affumicata*. So even if you are not drawn to Arta Terme for the thermal baths or one of the town's gastronomic festivals, the *cjarsòns* at Ristorante Salon alone merit a special trip.

Salon's bustling waiter, Matteo, ready to serve at the restaurant's bar (ABOVE); the hotel is located on a shady street in the hamlet of Piano d'Arta (OPPOSITE).

Northern Friuli:
SECONDI

Toç de Purcit

Carnian Pork Stew

This pork stew uses spices brought to Carnia by the cramârs and is often prepared for holiday meals, accompanied by polenta (page 196). If pork liver is not available, you may substitute beef or chicken liver.

2 tablespoons olive oil

1 medium yellow onion, chopped

4 ounces pancetta, chopped

1 1/2 pounds pork shoulder or butt, cut into 1-inch cubes

4 ounces pork liver, chopped

1/2 teaspoon ground black pepper

1/4 teaspoon ground cloves

1/4 teaspoon ground cinnamon

2 cups dry white wine

2 tablespoons all-purpose flour

1 1/2 cups water, divided

1/4 cup dry bread crumbs

1 teaspoon freshly grated lemon peel

  Heat the olive oil in a large, deep skillet over medium heat. Add the onion and pancetta; cook and stir until the onion softens and the pancetta is brown and crisp, about 10 minutes. Add the pork; cook and stir until just browned, about 10 minutes. Stir in the liver, black pepper, cloves, and cinnamon. Add the white wine; bring to a boil over high heat. Reduce heat to medium-low; simmer until the liquid is reduced by half, about 20 minutes.

  In a medium bowl, whisk the flour into 1/4 cup water. Stir in the bread crumbs, lemon peel, and remaining 1 1/4 cups water. Add this mixture to the skillet; bring to a boil over high heat. Reduce heat to medium-low; cook, covered, until the pork is tender, about 1 hour, stirring occasionally. Season to taste with salt.

Serves 4 to 6.

Costicine in Brodo di Polenta   *Pork Ribs in Polenta*

Pork cooked with polenta has been a common meal in Carnian homes for centuries. This recipe may also be prepared with pork chops.

2 ½ pounds pork ribs

3 tablespoons olive oil

1 cup dry white wine

2 tablespoons chopped fresh
   rosemary

2 garlic cloves, minced

3 cups water

¾ cup coarsely ground
   cornmeal

1 teaspoon salt

. . .

Freshly ground black pepper

෨ Slice the pork into individual ribs; sprinkle with salt and black pepper.

෨ Heat the olive oil in a large, deep skillet over medium-high heat. Add the ribs; cook for 20 minutes, turning to brown all sides. Add the white wine, rosemary, and garlic; reduce heat to medium-low and simmer for 5 minutes. Add 3 cups water; stir in the cornmeal and salt. Bring to a boil over high heat. Reduce heat to medium-low; cook, covered, until the polenta is soft, about 25 minutes, stirring occasionally. Sprinkle with freshly ground black pepper.

Serves 4.

Trota al Burro e Salvia   *Trout with Butter and Sage*

Trout is abundant in the Tagliamento River, especially in the many tributaries that run through Carnia's valleys. The fish is typically grilled or, as shown here, pan-fried with butter and fresh sage.

2 whole trout, heads and tails
   removed
⅓ cup all-purpose flour
4 tablespoons butter
¼ cup chopped fresh sage
   leaves
    . . .
1 lemon, cut into wedges

₧ Cut each trout in half lengthwise into two fillets; remove all bones. Sprinkle the fish fillets with salt and black pepper; dredge in flour.

₧ Melt the butter in a large skillet over medium heat; stir in the chopped sage. Place the fish fillets in the skillet, skin-side down; cook until golden brown, about 3–5 minutes on each side. Serve with lemon wedges.

Serves 4.

Frico con Patate
Montasio Cheese and Potato Pancake

Unlike the appetizer frico croccante (page 39), frico cooked with potatoes most often appears as a main course, accompanied by polenta (page 196). It may be served as a single pancake, as shown here, or as a wedge cut from a larger round, which is fairly common in restaurants. Variations include the addition of onion or pancetta—or even substituting butternut squash for the potatoes (a specialty at Venzone's Festa della Zucca). If Montasio cheese is not available, you may substitute Parmigiano-Reggiano for the Montasio stagionato and fresh Asiago for the Montasio fresco.

1 pound white potatoes, peeled
    and quartered
2 cups shredded Montasio
    fresco
1 cup grated Montasio
    stagionato
1/4 teaspoon salt
1/4 teaspoon ground black
    pepper
1 teaspoon olive oil

Place the potatoes in a large pot filled with water; bring to a boil over high heat. Cook until tender, about 20–25 minutes. Drain the potatoes and place in a medium bowl; mash well. Cool to room temperature. Stir in both Montasio cheeses, salt, and black pepper. Divide the mixture into four equal parts. Form each into a round mass and then flatten into a 4-inch disk.

Heat the olive oil in a small skillet over medium heat. One at a time, cook each frico until crisp and golden brown, about 3–4 minutes on each side. Drain any excess oil from the skillet, leaving about 1 teaspoon for cooking the next frico. (To expedite the process, use two skillets or a large griddle.)

Serves 4.

VARIATION: Frico con patate e pancetta
Over medium heat, cook and stir 4 ounces chopped pancetta until brown and crisp, about 5–6 minutes. Drain off the excess oil and stir the pancetta into the potato mixture. Omit the teaspoon olive oil used for cooking the first frico, as there will be residual oil in the skillet.

VARIATION: Frico con patate e cipolla
Over medium-low heat, cook and stir 2/3 cup finely chopped onion in 1 tablespoon olive oil until soft, about 10 minutes. Stir the onion into the potato mixture. Omit the teaspoon olive oil used for cooking the first frico, as there will be residual oil in the skillet.

VARIATION: Frico con la zucca
Substitute 2 cups mashed butternut squash for the potato. If there is little or no residual oil in the skillet after cooking the first frico, add 1 teaspoon olive oil to the skillet for each subsequent frico.

Frittata alle Erbe

Herb Frittata

Called "fertàe cu lis jàrbis" in Furlan, this thin frittata is cooked on the stovetop. The tricky part is flipping it, so make sure you use a nonstick pan and keep a large plate handy. You may add or substitute any herbs that you like, such as thyme, sage, or marjoram. In Carnia, cooks will typically use a few handfuls of wild herbs and greens picked from their backyard meadows. If Montasio stagionato is not available, you may substitute any aged cheese such as Parmigiano-Reggiano.

3 tablespoons butter, divided

1 cup coarsely chopped fresh
　spinach leaves

1/2 cup chopped fresh basil

1/4 cup chopped fresh Italian
　parsley

2 tablespoons chopped fresh
　mint

2 tablespoons chopped fresh
　chives

6 eggs

1/3 cup whole milk

1/3 cup grated Montasio
　stagionato

1/2 teaspoon salt

1/4 teaspoon ground black
　pepper

• Melt 2 tablespoons butter in a 10- or 11-inch nonstick skillet over medium heat. Add the spinach, basil, parsley, mint, and chives; cook and stir until just wilted, about 2 minutes. Remove from heat; cool to room temperature.

• In a medium bowl, whisk the eggs and milk until blended. Stir in the Montasio cheese, salt, and black pepper, along with the cooked spinach mixture.

• Using the same skillet, melt 1 tablespoon butter over medium heat; pour in the egg mixture. Cook until the bottom is golden brown, about 8–10 minutes. To flip, slide the frittata onto a large plate. Place the skillet upside-down over the frittata; holding the plate and skillet firmly, flip over so that the uncooked surface is now on the bottom. Cook until the bottom is golden brown and the eggs are set, about 4–5 minutes longer.

Serves 6.

Frittata di Funghi

Mushroom Frittata

Frittatas can be prepared two ways: on the stovetop, as demonstrated with the frittata alle erbe (page 94), and in the oven, as shown here. If Montasio stagionato is not available, you may substitute any aged cheese such as Parmigiano-Reggiano.

2 tablespoons butter

2 tablespoons olive oil

8 ounces assorted mushrooms (such as porcini, morels, or chanterelles), sliced

1 garlic clove, minced

$^1/_4$ cup chopped fresh Italian parsley

8 eggs

1 cup grated Montasio stagionato

$^1/_2$ teaspoon salt

$^1/_4$ teaspoon ground black pepper

❧ Preheat oven to 325°F. Melt the butter with the olive oil in a 10- or 11-inch nonstick, oven-safe skillet over medium heat. Add the mushrooms, garlic, and parsley; cook and stir until the mushrooms are tender, about 8–10 minutes. Remove from heat.

❧ In a large bowl, whisk the eggs until blended; stir in the Montasio cheese, salt, and black pepper. Pour the mixture into the skillet with the mushrooms. Bake until golden brown, about 25–30 minutes.

Serves 6.

Venzone: Festa della Zucca

The Festa della Zucca occurs annually on the fourth weekend of October in the tiny town of Venzone. Although pumpkins may be the most familiar squash, gourds of all shapes, colors, and sizes are featured in this festival of food, art, music, and dancing. Every year, a contest awards prizes for the largest, heaviest, longest, most beautiful, and most unusual squash. In addition, children participate in a pumpkin-carving contest, while chefs demonstrate their skill in carving intricate floral designs.

The Festa della Zucca not only celebrates the pumpkin, but also transports Venzone back in time. Public squares are illuminated by torches, townspeople dress in medieval costume, and jugglers and fire-eaters perform in the streets. Delegations from Austria, Germany, and Slovenia are presented, and following an ancient Austrian ceremony, the people elect an honorary "Archduke of Pumpkins." Most importantly, the town's taverns and restaurants celebrate the squash with special tasting-menus that include dishes such as pumpkin soup, *frico con la zucca*, *gnocchi di zucca*, puréed squash, and pumpkin cake.

At the festival, exhibits of squash reveal the colorful varieties grown locally, while the elaborate pumpkin carvings demonstrate artistic skill.

Mummies of Venzone

Driving north from Udine, you will find a charming, medieval-walled city—the only one in Friuli—situated unexpectedly at the side of the highway. In Roman times, Venzone was an important post along the ancient Via Giulia Augusta, the last bit of civilization before entering the rough territory of Carnia. Although the town was partially rebuilt following the 1976 earthquakes that devastated its Duomo, Venzone retains much of its medieval character. Stark, gray stone buildings and cobbled streets blend with the surrounding rocky mountains, while an imposing double wall serves to fortify the town against the incursions of contemporary life.

Across from the pointed *campanile* of Venzone's Duomo sits the 13th-century Cappella Cimiteriale di San Michele. This tiny, round crypt houses the result of a peculiar natural phenomenon—corpses mummified by a rare parasitic mold that covered the bodies and blocked decomposition. While the exact age of the mummies has not been determined, the oldest—named Gobbo, meaning "hunchback"—was discovered in 1647 during construction work on the Duomo. Twenty-one mummies were originally uncovered, although only fifteen were salvaged intact from the ruins of the 1976 earthquakes. Five are currently on display, including Gobbo, a mother and daughter, and two noblemen.

The 14th-century Duomo di Sant'Andrea (LEFT)*; the Duomo's campanile, or "bell tower"* (ABOVE)*; medieval stone walls surround the town* (BELOW)*.*

Venzone and nearby Gemona were at the epicenter of the 1976 earthquakes. Many structures, including the Duomo, were painstakingly renovated using original stones that were salvaged from the rubble.

CLOCKWISE FROM ABOVE: *the mummies are housed in the round Cappella Cimiteriale di San Michele; on Venzone's Palazzo Comunale, the Venetian Gothic-style windows and the winged lion of Saint Mark are lasting reminders of the 15th-century Venetian occupation; the Chiesa di San Giovanni Battista still remains in ruins after the earthquakes.*

Earthquakes in Gemona

No one living in Friuli will ever forget the evening of May 6, 1976. For fifty-four seconds, a magnitude 6.4 earthquake shook the region, killing nearly one thousand people and destroying over four thousand homes in an area measuring 2200 square miles. Peaceful Gemona del Friuli, comfortably nestled in the foothills of Monte Chiampon, was at the epicenter of this terrible disaster. People still talk of the unreal stillness that followed the quake, the profound darkness and layers of dust that settled upon the town during the moments after the earth stopped trembling.

Reconstruction was just beginning when, in September of the same year, a second strong earthquake struck the town. One of Gemona's great architectural treasures, the Duomo di Santa Maria Assunta, suffered major damage during both quakes. Ten years of skillful restoration have left the 164-foot-high bell tower, the central rose window, and the 23-foot-high stone relief of Saint Christopher as good as new, but observant visitors may notice that the columns inside the nave are still leaning.

After twenty-five years, the task of rebuilding Gemona was finally completed. Today, the medieval town center appears as unsoiled as a Hollywood movie set with its spotless sidewalks, immaculately clean streets, and freshly painted buildings. But if you wander long enough, you will likely stumble upon some rubble left untouched, a reminder of that fateful spring evening.

The Duomo di Santa Maria Assunta (LEFT); *a 23-foot-high relief of Saint Christopher on the Duomo's façade* (ABOVE); *even today, some ruins still remain standing* (OPPOSITE).

Butterflies of Bordano

The town of Bordano, located in the foothills of the Carnian Alps, is home to the largest tropical butterfly garden in Europe, the Casa delle Farfalle. The microclimate of nearby Monte San Simeone has attracted over 650 native species of butterflies—550 of which are nocturnal—making this town the ideal location for entomological studies.

Inside the Casa delle Farfalle, three greenhouses contain over 400 species of butterflies from Africa, the Amazon, and Indo-Australia. The butterflies are free to fly, surrounded by exotic vegetation in a miniature rainforest setting of vines, rare palms, and colorful orchids. The air is damp, filled with the echoes of mist and fluttering wings. Indigenous birds, reptiles, fish, and other insects complete the realistic ecosystem.

Bordano pays tribute to its butterflies in yet another way. Throughout the town and the neighboring hamlet of Interneppo, artists have decorated houses and public buildings with butterfly murals, transforming the streets into a kaleidoscope of color.

The butterflies inside the Casa delle Farfalle have inspired artists to adorn houses throughout Bordano with butterfly murals—even the town's post office has been decorated.

Arta Terme:
Festa dell'Asparago di Bosco, del Radicchio di Montagna, e dei Funghi di Primavera

Every May, the festival celebrates three bounties of springtime—wild asparagus, mountain radicchio, and mushrooms. Restaurants throughout Arta Terme serve special tasting-menus featuring these local ingredients, while booths display artisanal foods and handmade crafts at the street fair.

CLOCKWISE FROM BOTTOM LEFT: *the town of Arta Terme, as seen from Zuglio on the other side of the Bût River; chanterelle mushrooms for sale; morel mushrooms on display; the festival is held on this wisteria-lined road running through the tranquil hamlet of Piano d'Arta on a hill just above Arta Terme; cooks prepare* frico friabile, *or "deep-fried Montasio cheese," for festival visitors.*

106

Clockwise from above: *the* campanile *towers over stone houses in Piano d'Arta; the famous Terme di Arta spa is housed in an Asian-style pagoda; the festival offers many varieties of* frittelle alle erbe, *or "herb fritters"; mycologists set up a display of wild mushrooms.*

⁊ς

Northern Friuli:
CONTORNI

⁊ς

Pendalons

Potatoes cooked with string beans are typical of the western Carnian valley Val Pesarina. Ristorante Ai Sette Nani—named after the fictional "seven dwarves"—in Prato Carnico serves their pendalons with a topping of crispy pancetta and onion.

12 ounces string beans, cut into
    1-inch-long pieces
1 1/2 pounds white potatoes,
    peeled and cut into 1/4-inch-
    thick slices
1 cup water
1/2 teaspoon ground black
    pepper

. . .

TOPPING:
1 tablespoon olive oil
2 ounces pancetta, chopped
3 tablespoons finely chopped
    onion
1 garlic clove, minced
2 tablespoons chopped fresh
    Italian parsley
2 tablespoons chopped fresh
    chives

⁝ Place a steamer rack inside a large pot; fill with 1 inch of water. Place the string beans on the rack. Bring to a boil over high heat; cover and steam until just tender, about 10–15 minutes.

⁝ Place the potato slices in a large pot, along with 1 cup water; bring to a boil over high heat. Reduce heat to medium-low; cook, covered, until the potatoes are tender, about 20–25 minutes, stirring occasionally as the water begins to evaporate. Remove from heat; coarsely mash the potatoes. Stir in the string beans and black pepper. Season to taste with salt.

FOR THE TOPPING:
⁝ Heat the olive oil in a small skillet over medium heat. Add the pancetta, onion, and garlic; cook and stir until the onion softens and the pancetta is brown and crisp, about 7–8 minutes. Add the parsley and chives; cook and stir until wilted, about 1–2 minutes. Serve the topping over the potatoes.

Serves 4 to 6.

Funghi in Padella

Sautéed Mushrooms

Wild mushrooms may be gathered throughout the forests of Carnia, although this activity is strictly regulated. I once witnessed a couple flaunting a giant porcini they had just picked near Ravascletto—it was the size of a soccer ball. Serve this easy sauté as a filling for frico croccante (page 39) or as an accompaniment to toç in braide (page 52), blècs (page 63), or balote (page 162).

3 tablespoons butter

1 pound assorted mushrooms
    (such as porcini, morels, or
    chanterelles), sliced

1 garlic clove, minced

1 tablespoon chopped fresh
    Italian parsley

1/4 teaspoon ground black
    pepper

☙ Melt the butter in a large skillet over medium heat. Add the mushrooms and garlic; cook and stir until tender, about 7–8 minutes. Stir in the parsley and black pepper. Season to taste with salt.

Serves 4.

Cavucin

Butternut Squash Purée

This delicious purée can be prepared with any type of winter squash, such as butternut, acorn, or pumpkin. You may also serve it as a first-course soup; just add extra water to achieve the desired consistency. If ricotta affumicata is not available, you may substitute ricotta salata.

1 large butternut squash (about 2 to 3 pounds), peeled, seeded, and cut into 1-inch cubes

4 tablespoons butter

2 garlic cloves, minced

2 tablespoons all-purpose flour

1/4 cup water, plus extra as needed

1/2 teaspoon ground cinnamon

1/4 teaspoon ground black pepper

Pinch ground cloves

. . .

1/2 cup grated ricotta affumicata

Ground cinnamon

  Place a steamer rack inside a large pot; fill with 1 inch of water. Place the squash on the rack. Bring to a boil over high heat; cover and steam until tender, about 10–15 minutes. Transfer to a large bowl; mash well.

  Melt the butter in a large pot over medium-low heat. Add the garlic; cook and stir until it begins to soften, about 3 minutes. Add the flour; cook and stir until the butter begins to brown, about 3–5 minutes. Stir in the mashed squash, 1/4 cup water, cinnamon, black pepper, and cloves. Reduce heat to low; cook until the water is absorbed, about 2–3 minutes, stirring occasionally. (If the squash is too thick, add more water as necessary.) Season to taste with salt. Serve topped with grated ricotta affumicata and a sprinkle of cinnamon.

Serves 4 to 6.

Architecture of Carnia

In the mountainous territory of Carnia, isolated for centuries by a harsh terrain and the consequent lack of roads, villages have been able to maintain a sense of character, a charm that is preserved through their traditional architectural style. Even after the 1976 earthquakes destroyed many towns, houses were typically rebuilt to their original design. This style evolved from the numerous civilizations that have made Carnia their home and has always been a matter of practicality rather than aesthetics.

The Romans introduced the use of stone, brick, and vaulted arches, their peasant homes having only one story. During the late medieval period, families began to add on to their houses, building upper floors out of the plentiful wood from the forests. In some areas, straw and wooden shingles were gradually replaced by bricks or tiles. It was around this time that the homes of each valley began to assume their own individual characteristics.

Forni di Sopra and Sauris are home to Carnia's most recognizable structure—the stone house with an external wooden balcony and stairway. This type of house reflects the influence of immigrants from Bavaria and Tyrol and is often shared duplex-style by two families. The houses consist of two or three floors plus an attic, the base constructed of masonry and the upper floors of wood. In hilly Sauris, homes are often built into the slopes with a storage cellar partially below ground. In peasant homes, the living quarters and stable once shared the same roof, with the stable and kitchen on the ground floor and the hayloft and bedrooms on the second. The exterior stairway was the only access to the upper floors, with the water closet typically located on the balcony. Today, such homes have been modernized with an additional interior staircase and bathroom.

Decorative woodwork adorns homes in Forni di Sopra (LEFT AND FAR LEFT); *homes in Sauris, Paularo, and Forni di Sopra display the external wooden balconies characteristic of these towns* (ABOVE, TOP, AND OPPOSITE).

On these houses, the traditional roof is made of two gently sloping eaves. The rectangular, wooden shingles overlap one another on the roof's framework without requiring any nails—a method employed mainly in areas with little wind or rain. In autumn, families place wide planks over the roof to keep the shingles down and to help support the weight of the snow. The most recognizable element of these houses is the abundant external woodwork—numerous grates, trellises, and galleries that were traditionally used to dry hay. This woodwork often features intricate designs carved by Carnia's master carpenters.

In contrast, the homes of the Val Degano include little or no external woodwork and contain an internal staircase. The roof usually consists of four eaves, two having a fairly steep incline plus

two smaller eaves on the house's short sides. The shingles in this valley typically resemble fish scales—flat slabs of terracotta with a rounded bottom—and are often painted emerald green.

The houses of central Carnia and the Valle del Bût have a distinct Venetian influence, characterized by a series of arches—a portico at ground level and an open loggia on the upper floors. The purpose of this loggia is not merely decorative but serves as both a sheltered place to work and an open area to dry clothes (or vegetables such as corn and beans).

Throughout Carnia, the homes of well-to-do families are somewhat grander, often four stories high. Like the buildings of central Carnia and the Friulian plains, there is less external woodwork, and the stable is separate from the living quarters.

High in the pastures of Carnia are tiny stalls called *stavoli*. With a masonry base and a hayloft made of wood, *stavoli* are designed to shelter both families and cattle during the summer months of Alpine grazing. In a room to the side is the kitchen, and there is a small bunk for sleeping upstairs. Today, many *malghe* have built more accommodating quarters, but the hills—especially around Sauris—are peppered with these old huts.

A stavolo *in the hills near Ravascletto* (BELOW LEFT); *a crucifix adorns this tiny house in Sauris* (BOTTOM LEFT); *a typical Sauris home* (BELOW RIGHT); *this green-shingled house in Prato Carnico appears as quaint as any storybook cottage* (OPPOSITE).

Forni di Sopra

Forni di Sopra—Carnia's westernmost town—borders the Parco Naturale delle Dolomiti Friulane, a nature reserve profuse with flora and fauna.

CLOCKWISE FROM TOP LEFT: *overlooking the Dolomites; the town's Vecchio Municipio, or "old town hall," is now used for temporary exhibits during tourist season; the typical architecture of this region features multiple wooden balconies, which are always bedecked with flowers during the spring and summer months; enjoying an afternoon bicycle ride; Chiesa di San Giacomo; every balcony offers a magnificent view.*

OPPOSITE: *clouds part over the majestic Dolomite range.*

Forni Avoltri: Festa dei Frutti di Bosco

CLOCKWISE FROM BOTTOM RIGHT: *assorted jellies and preserves for sale; slices of* crostata alla marmellata *made with blackberry jam; frutti di bosco, or "fruits of the forest," include raspberries, blackberries, blueberries, red currants, and gooseberries; the town of Forni Avoltri nestled in the foothills of the Austrian Alps.*

OPPOSITE, CLOCKWISE FROM TOP LEFT: *townspeople in medieval costume parade through the streets; the tiny, pink Chiesetta di Sant'Antonio; wild strawberries; one of many jam-filled desserts offered at the festival; Forni Avoltri's spring water is bottled and sold throughout Friuli under the label "Goccia di Carnia."*

Monte Santo di Lussari

Among the towering, snow-capped peaks of the Giulian Alps, one mountain stands out like a precious gem. Near the 5870-foot summit of Monte Santo di Lussari, a pristine 14th-century sanctuary looks out over the forested valleys below. Legend says that in 1360 a shepherd knelt to pray atop this mountain and discovered hidden in the brush a wooden statue of the Madonna and Child. The patriarch of Aquileia soon ordered a small chapel built on that very spot. Over time, the Santuario di Monte Lussari has come to symbolize a spiritual union of the region's three Alpine peoples—Latins, Slavs, and Germans. For centuries, pilgrims from neighboring countries have journeyed to this religious site. The year 1860, marking the sanctuary's fifth centennial, saw at least one hundred thousand visitors.

Today, the mountain's ski slopes attract equally sizeable crowds. A *telecabina*, or "ski lift," carries passengers from the village of Camporosso at its base to Borgo Lussari at the summit, where they may glide down the ski run, dig into a plate of *goulasch* in one of the village's rustic taverns, or simply admire the panoramic views across the Valcanale and Tarvisio basin.

Skiing down the slopes (ABOVE); *the* telecabina *carries visitors up and down the mountain* (BELOW LEFT); *the village of Camporosso* (BELOW RIGHT); *views of Borgo Lussari and its breathtaking surroundings* (OPPOSITE).

Laghi di Fusine

Just outside Tarvisio near the hamlet of Fusine are two glacial lakes, Lago Infe-
riore and Lago Superiore, both part of the Parco Naturale dei Laghi di Fusine.
These views are of the smaller—though "superior" in altitude—Lago Superiore
at the foot of Monte Mangàrt, one of the tallest peaks in the Giulian Alps.

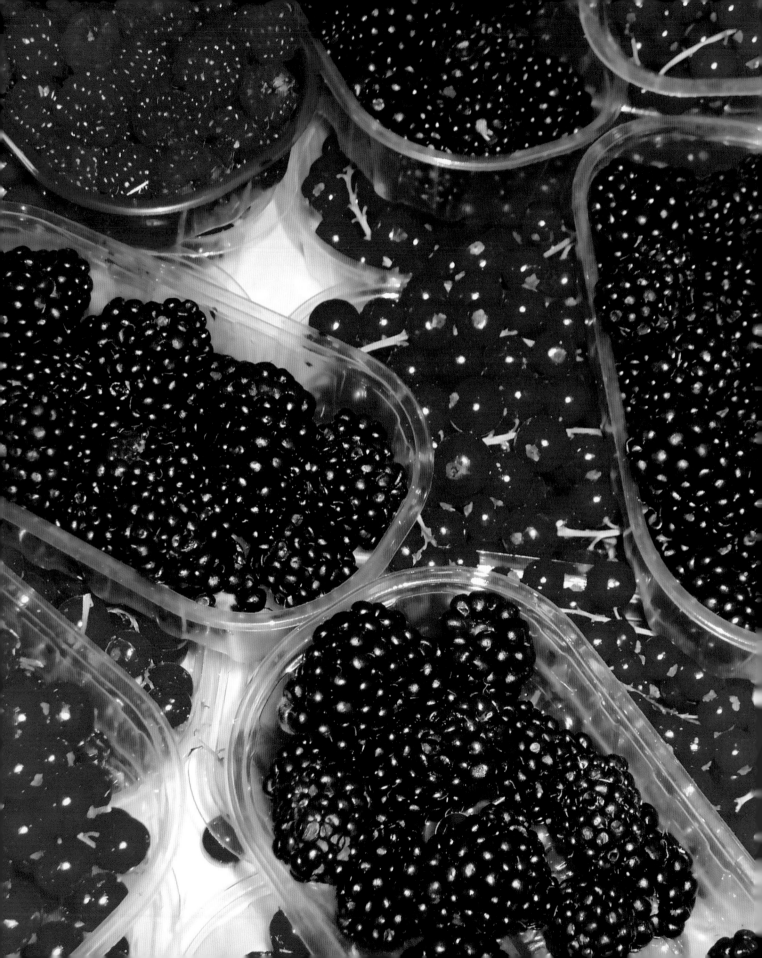

Northern Friuli: DOLCI

Crostata alla Marmellata   *Mixed Berry Jam Tart*

The dessert table at Forni Avoltri's Festa dei Frutti di Bosco showcases many cakes and tarts made with wild berries from the surrounding forests—this jam tart is one of my favorites. To save time, or if fresh berries are not available, you may substitute 2½ to 3 cups prepared jam.

MARMELLATA:

1 cup fresh blackberries

1 cup fresh raspberries

1 cup fresh blueberries

1 cup sliced fresh strawberries

1 medium apple, peeled, cored, and grated (or puréed in a food processor)

2 ½ cups sugar

. . .

DOUGH:

2 cups blanched slivered almonds

3 cups all-purpose flour

1 cup sugar

1 teaspoon freshly grated lemon peel

½ teaspoon salt

¼ teaspoon ground cinnamon

¼ teaspoon ground cloves

1 cup (2 sticks) unsalted butter, cut into cubes

2 eggs

FOR THE MARMELLATA:

❧ Place the blackberries, raspberries, blueberries, strawberries, and apple in a large pot, mashing slightly with a spoon. Cook over medium heat until the berries soften and release a little of their juice, about 5 minutes. Stir in the sugar. When the liquid begins to boil, reduce heat to low; cook until thickened, about 45 minutes, stirring occasionally. (When the jam is ready, a small amount of syrup will hold its shape when cooled. To test, dip a spoon into the liquid; as it cools, the syrup will thicken and coat the spoon.) Transfer the jam to a medium bowl; cool to room temperature.

FOR THE DOUGH:

❧ Finely grind the almonds in a food processor. Transfer to a large bowl; stir in the flour, sugar, lemon peel, salt, cinnamon, and cloves. Blend in the butter, a little at a time, until crumbly. Add the eggs; mix until the dough forms a solid mass. Refrigerate for 1 hour.

❧ Preheat oven to 350°F. Divide the dough into two parts, about two-thirds for the bottom crust and one-third for the lattice top. (Keep the reserved third of dough refrigerated until ready to use.) Roll the dough on a lightly floured sheet of waxed paper to form a 10- by 15-inch rectangle. Invert the dough onto a greased 10- by 15-inch baking sheet. (Any rough or broken areas may be easily patched.) Spread the jam over the dough, leaving a ½-inch border on all sides. Roll out the reserved third of dough on a lightly floured surface. Cut into ¾-inch-wide strips; arrange the strips over the jam to make a lattice crust. Bake until the crust is golden brown, about 30 minutes.

Serves 8 to 12.

Torta di Mele

Apple Cake

This rustic cake makes good use of Carnia's abundant apples. Instead of a firm, crisp apple like Granny Smith, I prefer using one that will soften while baking, such as Fuji, Golden Delicious, or McIntosh.

1 1/4 cups all-purpose flour

2 teaspoons baking powder

Pinch salt

1/2 cup (1 stick) unsalted butter, softened

3/4 cup sugar

2 eggs

1/4 cup grappa or rum

1 medium apple, peeled, cored, and thinly sliced

. . .

Confectioners' sugar (optional)

Ground cinnamon (optional)

&ℭ Preheat oven to 350°F. In a medium bowl, combine the flour, baking powder, and salt. In a large bowl, beat the butter and sugar until light and fluffy; beat in the eggs and grappa. Stir in the flour mixture.

&ℭ Spread the batter into a greased 9-inch springform pan. Making a decorative circular pattern, set the apple slices into the batter. Bake until a wooden pick inserted near the center comes out clean, about 50 minutes. Cool 15 minutes before removing from the pan. Serve warm, sprinkled with confectioners' sugar and cinnamon, if desired.

Serves 6 to 8.

Esse di Raveo

"S" Cookies

These crisp, S-shaped cookies were created in 1920 by baker Emilio Bonanni in the Carnian town of Raveo. While the original esse di Raveo is now distributed throughout Friuli, many bakeries produce similar cookies.

3 ½ cups all-purpose flour

1 teaspoon baking powder

Pinch salt

1 ¼ cups sugar

1 cup (2 sticks) unsalted butter, melted

2 eggs

1 egg yolk

1 teaspoon vanilla extract

☙ In a medium bowl, combine the flour, baking powder, and salt. In a large bowl, beat the sugar, melted butter, eggs, egg yolk, and vanilla extract until thick and pale in color, about 5 minutes. Stir in the flour mixture. Refrigerate for 1 hour.

☙ Preheat oven to 350°F. Working in batches, roll the dough into a ½-inch-diameter rope. Cut into 4-inch-long sections and form each into an S shape. Flatten each cookie to ⅛-inch thickness and place on a baking sheet lined with parchment paper. (A solid spatula or flat pastry cutter works well to flatten the cookies; place waxed paper over the cookie to prevent sticking. Keep the unused dough refrigerated until ready to use.) Bake until the edges are golden brown, about 10–12 minutes.

Makes about 5 dozen.

Pane di Zucca

Butternut Squash Bread

This bread is one of numerous baked goods featured at Venzone's Festa della Zucca. You may use any type of squash, such as butternut, acorn, or pumpkin—even canned pumpkin works well.

1 small butternut squash (about
  1 to 1½ pounds), halved
  lengthwise

1 package active dry yeast (2¼
  teaspoons or ¼ ounce)

¼ cup sugar, divided

½ cup warm water (100° to
  110°F)

2 eggs

2 tablespoons unsalted butter,
  melted

1 teaspoon salt

3¾ cups all-purpose or bread
  flour

⅓ cup raisins

⅓ cup coarsely chopped
  walnuts

. . .

1 egg, beaten to blend

€ Preheat oven to 375°F. Place the squash halves on a baking sheet. Bake until tender, about 40–45 minutes. When the squash is cool enough to handle, remove and discard the seeds and membrane. Scoop out enough flesh to measure 1 cup. (Reserve any extra for another use.) Place in a small bowl; mash well. Cool to room temperature.

€ In a large bowl, dissolve the yeast and a pinch of sugar in ½ cup warm water. Let rest until foamy, about 10 minutes. Whisk in the remaining sugar, mashed squash, eggs, melted butter, and salt. Gradually stir in the flour until the dough forms a solid mass; stir in the raisins and walnuts. Using a mixer with a dough hook attachment, knead for 10 minutes. (It may be necessary to occasionally scrape the ball of dough off the hook.) Transfer the dough to a lightly floured surface; knead briefly by hand. (The dough should be smooth and elastic.) Form the dough into a ball; cover loosely with plastic wrap or a kitchen towel and let rise until doubled in size, about 1½ hours.

€ On a lightly floured surface, divide the dough into six equal sections; roll each into a 12-inch-long rope. Form three ropes into a braid, tucking under the loose ends; repeat with the remaining three ropes. Place the braided loaves on a baking sheet. Cover loosely with plastic wrap or a kitchen towel and let rise for 30 minutes.

€ Preheat oven to 350°F, placing a pan filled with water on the bottom rack to create steam. Brush the loaves with beaten egg. Bake until golden brown, about 30–35 minutes.

Makes 2 loaves.

CENTRAL FRIULI:
Hills and Plains

A pocket of agriculture and industry, central Friuli is characterized by low, flat plains with an occasional hill town rising out of the monotonous countryside. The cities of Udine and Pordenone are industrial centers, their suburban sprawl expanding at an ever-increasing rate. Much of the landscape has been tarnished with factories and manufacturing plants, although endless fields of corn and barley may still be seen lining the highways.

As Friuli's most centrally located city, Udine makes an ideal base for exploring the region. Its lovely Piazza della Libertà gives the impression of a miniature Venice. Designed in the 15th and 16th centuries to demonstrate allegiance to the region's new rulers, this portico-lined square features replicas of such Venetian landmarks as the pink- and white-striped Palazzo Ducale, the blue- and gold-faced clock tower, and the winged lion of Saint Mark.

The Venetian influence is perceptible throughout Friuli—in its architecture, its language, and its cuisine. Nowhere is this more evident than in the province of Pordenone, which borders the Veneto region to the west and extends eastward to the Tagliamento River.

The town of Sacile, located just west of Pordenone, has a particularly Venetian air. The heart of the old town was built at a fork in the Livenza River, creating a small network of canals and

Vineyards near the town of Cormòns (ABOVE); *Udine's Piazza della Libertà* (OPPOSITE).

bridges. Since the year 1274, the town has celebrated a festival of songbirds called the Sagra dei Osei. Eastward near the town of Codroipo lies the Villa Manin, Friuli's largest *palazzo*. Originally the summer residence of Ludovico Manin, the last Doge of Venice, this palace was also home to Napoleon Bonaparte during the peace negotiations for the Treaty of Campoformido. Farther north are the towns Spilimbergo, famous for its mosaic school, and Maniago, known for its skilled knife craftsmen.

Pordenone province boasts several unique cured meats. The Val Cellina and Val Tramontina valleys are known for their *pitina*—a salami made from ground mutton that has been seasoned with herbs, dredged in cornmeal, and smoke-cured using juniper wood. This preparation developed out of necessity when pig intestines were not available for stuffing sausages.

These mountains north of Pordenone are also home to a type of salted cheese called Asìno. Produced in the *malghe* of Val Cellina and Val d'Arzino, this cheese is used to stuff the traditional cornmeal dumplings called *balote*.

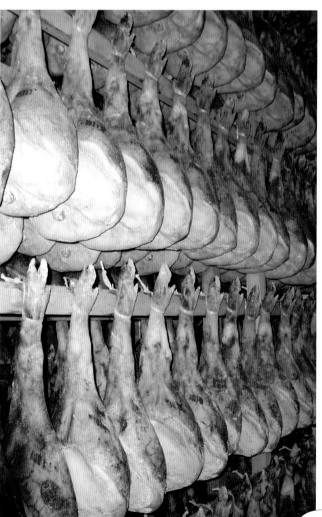

Cured *petti d'oca* (goose breast) and *petti d'anatra* (duck breast) were created by the region's modest Jewish population. Produced today in the southern plains called Bassa Pordenonese, they remain a kosher alternative to the more traditional pork *salumi*.

Then there is the ubiquitous *baccalà*, or "salt cod." A holdover from the centuries of Venetian rule, *baccalà* is popular throughout central and southern Friuli. Other types of preserved fish are served as well, smoked herring and trout in particular. Friultrota, in the town of San Daniele del Friuli, is perhaps the region's most well-known producer of smoked trout, the fish being especially plentiful in Friuli's rivers and lakes.

San Daniele is also home to Friuli's most renowned pork product, *prosciutto di San Daniele*. The dry climate and fresh breezes of this quiet hill town are said to make the perfect environment for salt-curing ham. A drive along the "Strada dei Castelli e del Prosciutto" circles

Latteria Sociale produces cheese in Cividale (ABOVE); *prosciutto ages at Prosciuttificio Il Camarin in San Daniele* (LEFT); *gubana on display in a bakery window in Udine* (OPPOSITE, TOP); *dried corn is used to make polenta* (OPPOSITE, BOTTOM LEFT); *large batches of polenta are prepared in giant cauldrons* (OPPOSITE, BOTTOM RIGHT).

through many of Friuli's ancient hill towns and will provide you with ample opportunity to sample prosciutto, cheese, and wine in tasting rooms along the way.

Frugal by necessity, the Friulians waste nothing. When a pig is slaughtered, every part not eaten immediately is cured in the forms of bacon, sausage, salami, ham, and *lardo* (cured fat). The less desirable parts are often disguised. *Musetto* is made with parts of the pig's head combined with skin and fat, similar to the *cotechino* sausage found elsewhere in Italy. The lungs, liver, and sweetbreads are used to make *marcudela*, while *zilidina* is a gelatin made from discarded parts such as feet and ears.

Until modern times, most Friulians were farmers. Their cuisine was a diet of poverty, consisting primarily of hearty grains and vegetables, especially those with a long shelf life like potatoes. Beans, barley, rice, and corn could easily be dried for lengthy storage. During cold winter months, Friulians subsisted on polenta, made from stone-ground dried corn, and *orzo e fagioli*, a barley and bean soup. Turnips were preserved through fermentation in grape skins to make *brovada*, the most typical of winter side dishes. Today, the white asparagus of Tavagnacco is one of the most celebrated of Friuli's crops. Every May, the town honors the vegetable with the popular Festa degli Asparagi.

The region's Slavic influence is especially apparent in eastern Friuli, home of its signature dessert, *gubana*. Filled with raisins, nuts, and spices, this spiral cake originated in Cividale, a small town located on the emerald green Natisone River and the site of an important 6th-century Lombard civilization.

The hills of Friuli are covered with lush vineyards, reminiscent of Tuscany or even California's Napa Valley. The town of Cormòns, located in the province of Gorizia near the Slovenian border, is at the heart of Friulian wine country. Here, the Collio zone and the Colli Orientali zone to the north are known for producing some of Italy's best white wines—particularly Tocai Friulano. While the Collio has become famous for its white wine blends, the Colli Orientali is recognized for cultivating many native grapes, including Schioppettino, Verduzzo, and Picolit. Though less renowned, the Grave del Friuli zone, stretching through the center of Pordenone and Udine provinces, produces more wine than any other zone in Friuli.

All of these local products—plus many more from other parts of Friuli—are featured at the region's premier gastronomic festival, Friuli DOC, held in Udine every September.

San Daniele's Duomo di San Michele Arcangelo (RIGHT)*; Palmanova's central piazza shares the star shape of the town's surrounding fortress walls* (BELOW)*; the town of Cividale is situated on the banks of the Natisone River* (OPPOSITE)*.*

142

Central Friuli:
ANTIPASTI

Asparagi con Prosciutto

Asparagus with Prosciutto

This appetizer makes use of the white asparagus from Tavagnacco, as well as the famed prosciutto di San Daniele. Green asparagus may be used if white is not available; any aged cheese such as Parmigiano-Reggiano may be substituted for the Montasio stagionato.

1 pound white asparagus, tough ends trimmed

4 ounces prosciutto di San Daniele, thinly sliced

2 tablespoons olive oil

1 tablespoon grated Montasio stagionato

ᘓ Peel the asparagus, starting 1½ inches from the top and running the length of the spear. Place a steamer rack inside a large pot; fill with 1 inch of water. Place the asparagus on the rack. Bring to a boil over high heat; cover and steam until just tender, about 5 minutes.

ᘓ Preheat oven to 350°F. Divide the asparagus into six piles. Wrap each bundle of asparagus with one or two slices of prosciutto; place in a greased baking dish. Drizzle with the olive oil and sprinkle with the Montasio cheese. Bake until the cheese melts, about 15 minutes.

Serves 6.

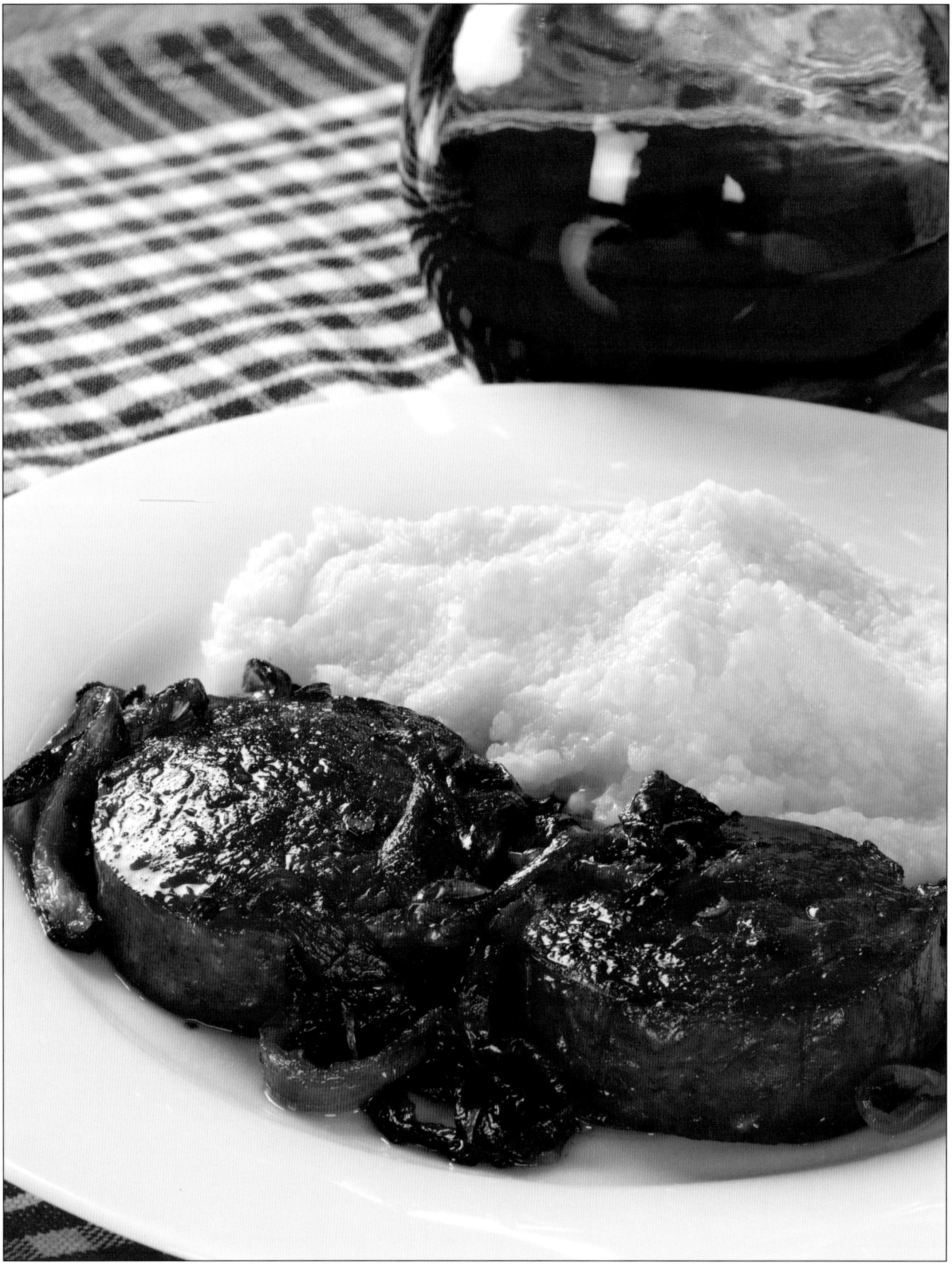

Salame all'Aceto

Salami Cooked in Vinegar

Salami cooked with onions and vinegar is served throughout central Friuli, as well as in the northern mountains. In the province of Pordenone, pitina (a salami made from mutton that has been dredged in cornmeal and smoked) is often used, although any type of salami will work. The dish is typically accompanied by polenta (page 196).

2 tablespoons olive oil

½ medium yellow onion, thinly sliced

8 ounces salami (about 2 inches diameter), sliced into eight ½-inch rounds

¼ cup red wine vinegar

   Heat the olive oil in a large skillet over medium heat. Add the onion; cook and stir until it begins to soften, about 8–10 minutes. Add the salami slices; cook until brown, about 3–5 minutes on each side. Add the vinegar. Reduce heat to low; simmer until most of the liquid has evaporated, about 5 minutes.

Serves 4.

Udine: Friuli's Venetian Gem

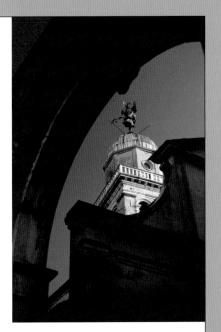

In the center of Udine, the winged lion of Saint Mark perches atop a lofty column, surveying what was once Venetian territory. A lacy, pink *palazzo* dominates the square, while two bronze moors strike the hour above a blue and gold clock tower. Everywhere you look, the city's streets reveal clues to its Venetian past. In fact, there are even a few canals flowing through town.

Along with most of Friuli and parts of Venezia Giulia, Udine was conquered by Venice in 1420 and remained under Venetian rule until Napoleon's 1797 invasion. To demonstrate the city's allegiance to the lagoon republic known as "La Serenissima," architects were instructed to replicate certain Venetian buildings and monuments.

It is no coincidence then that the two columns that tower over Piazza della Libertà bear a striking resemblance to those in Venice's Piazza San Marco. The first is crowned by the symbol of the Venetian Republic, the winged lion of Saint Mark. Although Saint Theodore stands atop the second column in Venice, Udine honors judicial might with a female statue holding a sword and the scales of justice.

Lining the elevated piazza is the Porticato di San Giovanni, a long stretch of arcades in the center of which nestles Udine's most recognizable monument, the Torre dell'Orologio, or "clock tower." Inspired by the zodiac signs on Venice's famous clock, a golden sun radiates from a brilliant blue clock face, while the winged lion makes another appearance below the clock.

Adjacent to the Torre dell'Orologio, a large, domed arch houses the Tempietto di San Giovanni. Originally designed as a church, this structure provided shelter for wounded soldiers during Napoleon's invasion and the subsequent struggle for liberation. In the spirit of victory after Italy's unification, the chapel was transformed into a war memorial.

At the south corner of the Porticato, there is a bronze *disco solare*. A sundial of sorts, this disk casts a ray of sunlight on a precisely calculated point on the wall every spring and fall equinox at twelve o'clock noon.

Across the piazza is the Loggia del Lionello, a small-scale version of Venice's Palazzo Ducale. Adorned with filigree and statuettes, the pink- and white-striped building is supported by a graceful Gothic arcade and features the characteristic trilobed, arched windows.

The hilltop Chiesa di Santa Maria di Castello is Udine's oldest church (ABOVE); the Tempietto di San Giovanni in the center of the Porticato is now a war memorial (FAR LEFT); the bronze disco solare functions as a sundial (LEFT).

Near the border of the raised terrace are the statues of Hercules and Cacus. Known locally as Florean and Venturin, they were originally owned by the scoundrel Count Lucio, who was condemned to death in 1717 by Venice's Council of Ten. The Republic confiscated the count's property and destroyed most of his belongings, but these two statues were auspiciously salvaged.

Another winged lion can be found standing guard over the Arco Bollani. Designed by the architect Palladio, this arch leads to a neat cobblestone path that winds up the hill to Udine's *castello*. Now a massive museum complex, the castle has at times housed the patriarch as well as the Venetian military.

Throughout Udine, street names offer hints to the city's Venetian history. Via Manin was named after Doge Ludovico Manin, the final ruler of the Republic, while Via Rialto was named after Venice's famous bridge. At one time, a series of canals—called *rogge*—flowed through Udine, one of which ran alongside the once important Via Rialto. Most of the canals have since been filled in, but a few still exist today, such as the ones on Via Zanon and Via Ciconi.

The Casa Veneziana was originally built on Via Rialto, but in 1929, the immense stone *palazzo* was reconstructed in Piazza XX Settembre to make way for a new municipal building. The palace's dull, gray

The Statue of Peace was commissioned by Napoleon Bonaparte (TOP LEFT); the Loggia del Lionello is a small-scale version of Venice's Palazzo Ducale (TOP RIGHT); a winding cobblestone path leads to the castle, which today houses the Civic Museums (RIGHT); the Arco Bollani was designed by Palladio (FAR RIGHT).

façade is marked by arched Gothic-style windows, Udine's coat of arms, and a crest of the winged lion.

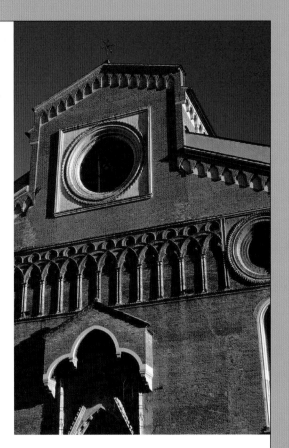

Venetian artists are also well represented here. The Civici Musei, or "civic museums," inside the castle contain paintings by Carpaccio and, most notably, Tiepolo. The Museo Diocesano displays Udine's largest group of works by this 18th-century painter, including portraits of the patriarchs of Aquileia in the museum's Throne Room and exquisite floor-to-ceiling frescoes in the Galleria del Tiepolo. Udine's Duomo di Santa Maria Annunziata and the Oratorio della Purità also house Tiepolo masterpieces.

While many cultures have left their mark on Udine over the last millennium, none define this tranquil city so well as the Venetian Republic. Earthquakes, fires, and countless wars have demolished many historical buildings and works of art, but the spirit of Venice continues to shine through.

The Casa Veneziana (TOP LEFT); the Duomo di Santa Maria Annunziata (TOP RIGHT); Chiesa di San Giacomo in Piazza Matteotti (BELOW LEFT); Trattoria Alla Ghiacciaia overlooks a willow-shaded canal (BELOW CENTER); along the canal on Via Zanon (BELOW RIGHT); the winged lion of Saint Mark perches atop a column near the statue of Hercules in Piazza della Libertà (OPPOSITE).

Osteria Al Vecchio Stallo

During my very first visit to Friuli, my friend Steno Dondè treated me to dinner at Osteria Al Vecchio Stallo. At that time, I had no familiarity with Friulian cuisine, but Steno wanted me to experience authentic regional cooking at its best. Ever since that first meal of *cjalsòns* and *frico con polenta*, this unassuming, hole-in-the-wall restaurant has held a truly special place in my heart.

One of the oldest in Udine, this *osteria* is housed in a 17th-century building that once served as a stable and rest stop for deliverymen. Until the arrival of automobiles, goods were transported long distances via horse and cart. Carters would stop midway along their journey for a meal and a respite. Leaving their horses to be cared for in the stable, they would then continue their route using new horses. On the way back, the borrowed horses would be returned for the original ones.

In the early 1900s, the stall was closed and converted into a section of the dining room. The *osteria* persisted with marginal success for decades, then saw a revitalization in 1985 under new management by the three Mancini brothers—Enzo, Maurizio, and Mario. Their objective was to preserve the traditional cuisine of Friuli, while giving it the elegance and style that modern tastes have come to expect. Al Vecchio Stallo exudes the warmth and hospitality so characteristic of Friulians, making guests feel just like family.

The dining room retains the atmosphere of an old-world tavern—wood-beamed ceilings, hardwood floors, red-checked tablecloths, and walls cluttered with colorful paintings, newspaper clippings, period photographs of Udine, and memorabilia of all sorts. In warm weather, diners can sit outside in the courtyard under a canopy of grapevines.

During my frequent solo travels, I usually find myself dining alone, and this is one restaurant where I always feel at home. The atmosphere is comfortable, the clientele an assortment of crusty, old men drinking at the bar, families with rambunctious toddlers, young couples sporting the latest fashion trends, and inevitably a particular *signora* at the same corner table every night.

The food is simple—what some might describe as peasant fare—but still tasty and completely satisfying. The prices are inexpensive, a huge bargain for such generous portions. Their *stinco di maiale* (braised pork shank) is gigantic, as are the sardines in *sarde in saor*. Chef Mario Mancini rotates his menu daily, some dishes being served only on certain days, such as savory, herb-filled *cjalsòns* on Sundays or creamy, salty *baccalà* on Fridays. Their numerous variations of gnocchi can be a bit doughy at times, but you can't go wrong with *frico*, *orzo e fagioli*, or *salame all'aceto*. For dessert, order the *gubana*—it comes soaked in grappa.

Central Friuli: PRIMI

Orzo e Fagioli

Barley and Bean Soup

This hearty soup is perfect for a cold winter's evening in Friuli. Triestini also prepare a version of orzo e fagioli that uses smoked pork in place of the pancetta.

8 ounces dried borlotti
   (cranberry) beans

2 ounces pancetta, chopped

1 medium yellow onion,
   chopped

1 medium white potato, peeled
   and cut into 1/2-inch cubes

1 carrot, chopped

1 celery stalk, chopped

1 garlic clove, minced

1/4 cup chopped fresh Italian
   parsley

1 tablespoon chopped fresh
   basil

1 tablespoon chopped fresh
   rosemary

1 tablespoon chopped fresh
   sage

1/2 teaspoon ground black
   pepper

1 bay leaf

3 tablespoons olive oil

6 cups water, divided

2/3 cup pearl barley

. . .

Olive oil
Freshly ground black pepper

❧ In advance, place the beans in a medium bowl and cover with water. Let soak for at least 12 hours, or overnight; drain.

❧ Place the beans in a large pot, along with the pancetta, onion, potato, carrot, celery, garlic, parsley, basil, rosemary, sage, black pepper, bay leaf, olive oil, and 4 cups water. Bring to a boil over high heat. Reduce heat to low; simmer, covered, for 1 1/2 hours.

❧ Meanwhile, place the barley in a medium bowl and cover with water. Let soak for 1 hour; drain.

❧ After the soup has simmered for 1 1/2 hours, remove about one-fourth of the soup and purée in a blender or food processor. Add the purée back to the pot, along with the barley and remaining 2 cups water; return to a boil over high heat. Reduce heat to low; cook, covered, until the barley is tender, about 1 1/2 hours longer, stirring occasionally. Remove the bay leaf; season to taste with salt. Serve with a drizzle of olive oil and a sprinkle of freshly ground black pepper.

Serves 6.

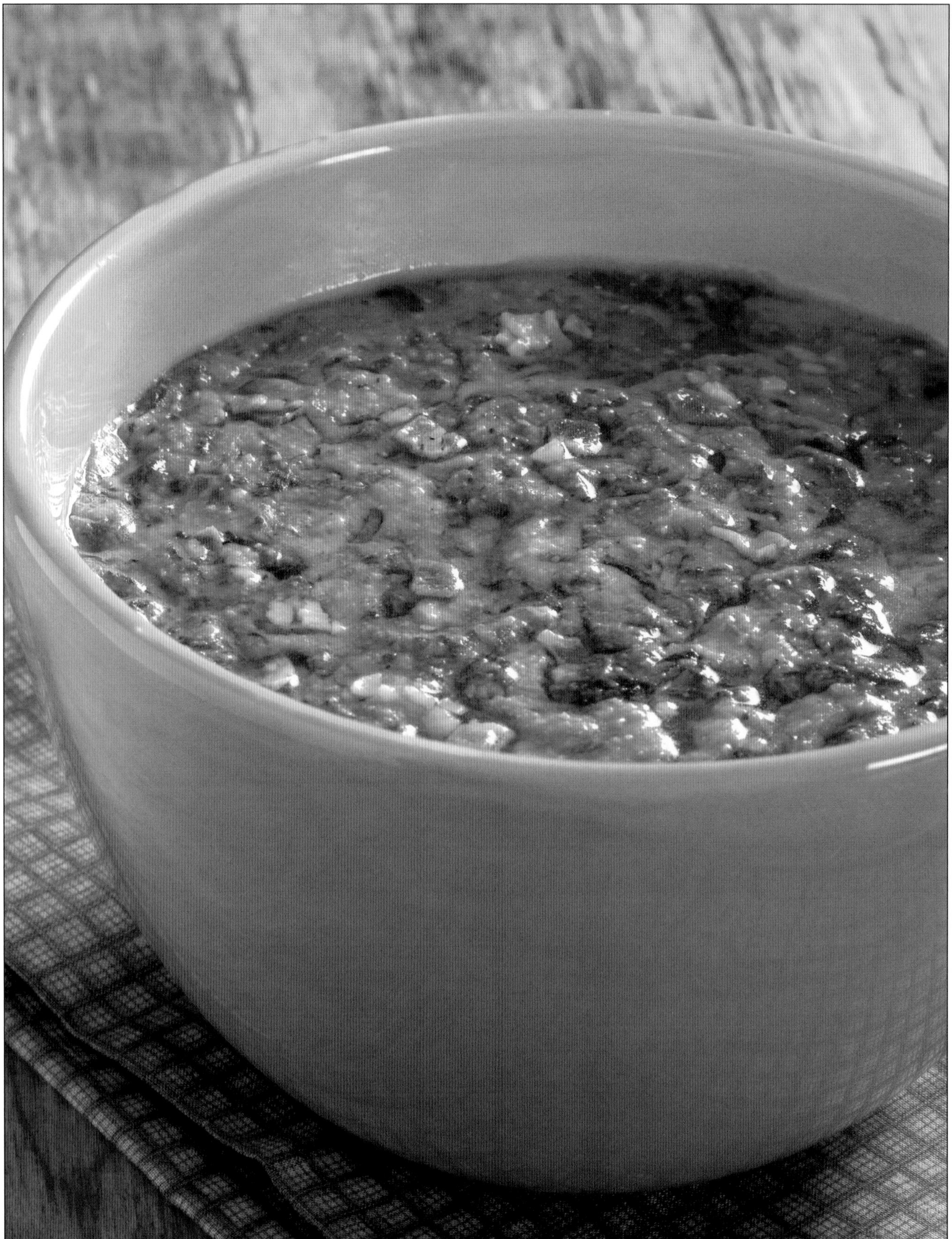

Paparòt

Spinach and Cornmeal Soup

This savory soup is typical of central Friuli's home cooking, especially in the province of Pordenone.

1 pound fresh spinach leaves

1 tablespoon butter

2 ounces pancetta, chopped

2 garlic cloves, minced

4 cups beef or vegetable broth

$1/2$ cup finely ground cornmeal

$1/4$ cup all-purpose flour

$1/2$ teaspoon ground black
  pepper

&} Place the spinach (plus 1–2 tablespoons water if using packaged, prewashed spinach) in a large pot over medium-low heat. Cook, covered, until wilted, about 10 minutes, stirring occasionally. Remove the spinach; chop coarsely.

&} Melt the butter in a large pot over medium heat. Add the pancetta and garlic; cook and stir until brown and crisp, about 5 minutes. Add the beef broth; bring to a boil over high heat. In a medium bowl, combine the cornmeal and flour; whisk in about 1 cup of the hot broth. Reduce heat to low; gradually add the cornmeal mixture to the pot, along with the chopped spinach and black pepper, whisking thoroughly to prevent lumps. Cook, covered, for 30 minutes, stirring occasionally. Season to taste with salt.

Serves 4.

Balote

These cornmeal balls originated in the town of Clauzetto, located in the mountains north of Pordenone. Cooks typically use a salted cheese like the local Asino, which comes in two varieties: "classico" (standard semi-soft) and "morbido" (very soft, somewhat like cream cheese). According to local tradition, when a young man wanted to propose marriage, he would present an offering of balote to the potential bride's family; if the balote were immediately placed on the fogolâr to roast, it was understood that he had the family's approval. Since Asino cheese is difficult to find outside this region, I have found that a combination of cream cheese and ricotta salata captures both the flavor and texture needed for this dish. As an alternative, you can substitute eight ounces of Montasio fresco, cut into twelve cubes. Balote are often served with sautéed mushrooms (see funghi in padella on page 113).

FILLING:

4 ounces cream cheese

4 ounces ricotta salata, grated
   (about 1 1/4 cups)

. . .

POLENTA:

4 cups water

1 cup coarsely ground cornmeal

1 teaspoon salt

FOR THE FILLING:

&) In a small bowl, combine the cream cheese and ricotta salata. Divide the mixture into twelve equal parts, rolling each into a small ball. Refrigerate until ready to use.

FOR THE POLENTA:

&) Bring 4 cups water to a boil in a medium pot over high heat. Stir in the cornmeal and salt. When the water returns to a boil, reduce heat to low; cook and stir until soft, about 25 minutes. Pour immediately into a 9- by 13-inch baking dish; spread evenly. Let cool for 15 minutes, or until just cool enough to handle.

TO PREPARE:

&) Preheat oven to 350°F. Slice the polenta into twelve equal portions. Scoop out a portion of polenta and roll into a rough ball. Flatten slightly, place one cheese ball in the center, and smooth the polenta over to enclose the cheese. (The polenta will be very sticky, so work gently.) Place the finished polenta balls in a greased baking dish. Bake until heated through, about 25 minutes.

Serves 4.

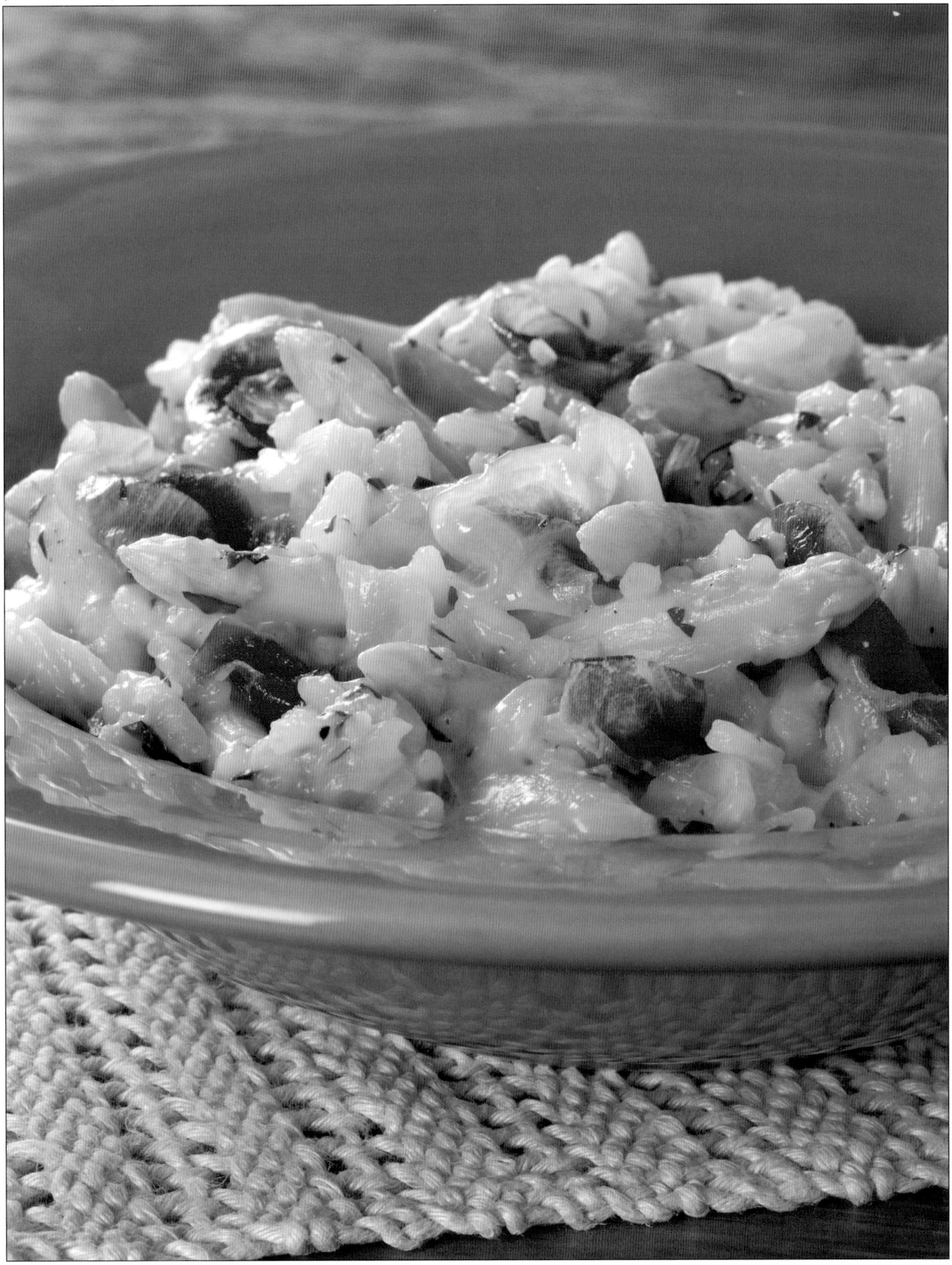

Risotto con gli Asparagi

Risotto with Asparagus

This springtime risotto uses Tavagnacco's white asparagus, as well as prosciutto di San Daniele. If Montasio stagionato is not available, you may substitute any aged cheese such as Parmigiano-Reggiano.

1 pound white asparagus, tough
    ends trimmed

4 tablespoons butter

1 medium yellow onion,
    chopped

1 cup Arborio (Italian short-
    grain) rice

1/2 cup dry white wine

3 1/2 cups chicken broth, heated

4 ounces prosciutto di San
    Daniele, thinly sliced and cut
    into 1-inch pieces

1 cup grated Montasio
    stagionato

1/4 cup chopped fresh Italian
    parsley

⁖ Peel the asparagus, starting 1 1/2 inches from the top and running the length of the spear; cut into 2-inch-long pieces. Place a steamer rack inside a large pot; fill with 1 inch of water. Place the asparagus on the rack. Bring to a boil over high heat; cover and steam until just tender, about 5 minutes.

⁖ Melt the butter in a large pot over medium-low heat. Add the onion; cook and stir until soft and translucent, about 20 minutes. Add the rice; cook and stir for 5 minutes to allow the rice to absorb the butter. Add the white wine; cook and stir until the liquid has been absorbed, about 3 minutes. Add 1/2 cup warm chicken broth; cook and stir until the rice has absorbed most of the liquid. Continue stirring in broth, 1/2 cup at a time, until the rice is cooked, about 25 minutes; remove from heat. Stir in the asparagus, prosciutto, Montasio cheese, and parsley. Season to taste with salt and black pepper.

Serves 4.

Tagliolini al Prosciutto

Tagliolini Pasta with Prosciutto

This simple, yet elegant, pasta dish can be found on menus throughout the hill town of San Daniele where the famous prosciutto is produced.

12 ounces dried tagliolini,
   tagliatelle, or fettucine pasta
1 cup heavy cream
8 ounces prosciutto di San
   Daniele, thinly sliced and cut
   into 1-inch pieces
2 teaspoons poppy seeds

ɤ Bring a large pot of lightly salted water to a boil over high heat. Add the pasta; cook until just tender, about 10–12 minutes. Drain and place in a large serving bowl.

ɤ Warm the cream in a small saucepan over medium-high heat. (Do not bring to a boil.) Pour over the cooked pasta; toss to coat. Stir in the prosciutto and poppy seeds. Season to taste with salt.

Serves 4 to 6.

Prosciutto di San Daniele

The Celts were the first culture to use salt in preserving pork, and their arrival in the hill town of San Daniele del Friuli around 400 BC marks the origin of this celebrated ham. Throughout Roman and medieval times, *prosciutto di San Daniele* became a valuable commodity. Later, during several centuries of Venetian rule, San Daniele enjoyed periods of relative independence thanks to generous donations of prosciutto to the Doges of Venice.

Though not produced in such mass quantities as the widely distributed *prosciutto di Parma*, prosciutto from San Daniele is considered by many to be more delicate and flavorful due to the unique climate where salty Adriatic breezes intermingle with fresh Alpine air. The nearby Tagliamento River acts as a natural ventilation system, helping to circulate the warm and cool winds while maintaining a low humidity.

Originally, only black Friulian pigs were used, but during a period of near extinction in the 1960s, swine from Lombardy were shipped and secretly delivered in the dark of night. Today, the product's origin is guaranteed by the European Union and strictly regulated by a local consortium. The law allows swine to be raised in certain regions throughout Italy, but they must be of particular breeds, no younger than nine months, and weigh at least 350 pounds. Although the pigs are heavier than average, their meat is leaner due to a strict diet. Producers tout their hams' nutritional benefits—a fat content of only 3 to 5 percent, much of which is monounsaturated.

Before the process was industrialized, pigs were slaughtered just once a year, in late autumn. A distinctive feature of *prosciutto di San Daniele* is that the foot is left intact, purportedly aiding in the drainage of excess liquid. After the leg is branded with the DOP (Denominazione d'Origine Protetta) mark, the lengthy curing process begins with a coating of sea salt. By tradition, the salting time is in direct proportion to the leg's weight. For example, a leg weighing eleven kilograms (the required minimum) would be salted for eleven days. The salt content of *prosciutto di San Daniele*—a mere 5 to 6 percent—is lower than many other Italian hams, which makes the meat sweeter by comparison.

Halfway through the salting phase, the legs are washed and then massaged with fresh salt. After the salting period, the legs are cleaned of excess salt, then pressed for several days to remove moisture. Not only does pressing give the prosciutto its characteristic guitar shape, but it affects both taste and texture by merging the fat with the lean meat.

After a three-month resting period, the legs are washed and dried, then covered with a paste of lard, flour, and salt in order to protect them from excessive dehydration. They are now left to cure for a minimum of eight months. While the initial salting takes place under refrigeration, this final maturing phase exposes the hams to San Daniele's natural climate. Temperature and humidity are controlled by simply opening or closing storeroom windows.

The entire curing process takes a minimum of twelve months. The prosciutto is finally deemed ready when it passes the ultimate test—an expert inspector inserts a horse-bone needle into the meat and judges its quality based on the aroma released.

Plates of *prosciutto di San Daniele* are served in practically every restaurant in the region, but to experience this delicious treat at its source, spend an afternoon visiting the town's numerous tasting rooms. Or join the hundreds of thousands of visitors who flock to this tiny town every summer for Aria di Festa, a grand celebration of San Daniele's renowned prosciutto.

Alessio Prolongo in the refrigeration room at Prosciuttificio Prolongo (LEFT) *and testing the quality and readiness of his prosciutto using a horse-bone needle* (OPPOSITE, TOP); *prosciutto curing in Prosciuttificio Il Camarin* (ABOVE) *and in Prosciuttificio Prolongo* (OPPOSITE, BOTTOM).

169

San Daniele del Friuli

San Daniele's Chiesa di Sant'Antonio Abate happens to be dedicated to the patron saint of pork butchers. Inside this 15th-century church—often called the "Sistine Chapel of Friuli"—is a vibrant fresco cycle by the Renaissance artist Martino da Udine, also known as Pellegrino da San Daniele (ABOVE); Ristorante Alle Vecchie Carceri is housed in a former Austrian prison and offers updated and artfully plated versions of local specialties (RIGHT).

OPPOSITE, CLOCKWISE FROM TOP LEFT: *prosciutto, salami, and lardo, or "cured pork fat," for sale in a local food shop; the rose window of Chiesa di Sant'Antonio Abate; the campanile of Chiesa di San Daniele in Castello; prosciutto and other local products on display in a store window; Chiesa di San Daniele in Castello sits in a shady park overlooking the Friulian countryside.*

Lombard Treasures of Cividale

Lined with narrow cobblestone streets and perched above the emerald green Natisone River, Cividale del Friuli has been a site of historical importance throughout many civilizations. In fact, it was the town's original Roman name, Forum Iulii, that evolved linguistically into the name of the region, Friuli.

Julius Caesar founded Forum Iulii in 50 BC, and it remained one of the region's principal towns for several centuries of Roman rule. During the 6th century AD, King Alboino led his band of fierce Lombard warriors across central Europe and into northern Italy, effortlessly occupying Forum Iulii in 568. The king then gave the town to his nephew Gisulfo, establishing the first of three Lombard duchies in Italy. In 776, Forum Iulii was sacked by King Charlemagne's Franks, who renamed the town Civitas Austriae. Over time, the two appellations were combined into the town's present name, Cividale del Friuli.

Of all the cultures that have left their mark here, Cividale is most often associated with the Lombards, as the town is one of the few places in Italy where one can still view tangible evidence of this early medieval civilization. Situated on a cliff overlooking the river, the Tempietto Longobardo is Cividale's most significant Lombard monument. Inside this tiny church are faded frescoes, intricately carved wooden choir stalls, and six female saints in high relief poised above a grapevine-motif arch. Experts consider these statues to be among the finest surviving works from this period.

Many more Lombard relics are housed in the Museo Archeologico Nazionale, including a coin collection, eating utensils, swords and other weaponry, ivory ornaments, gold brooches, and jeweled necklaces. The sarcophagus of Duke Gisulfo is also displayed, along with countless artifacts from Roman, paleo-Byzantine, medieval, and Romanesque periods. The Duomo di Santa Maria Assunta houses another museum, the Museo Cristiano. Its most notable 8th-century treasures include the altar of the Lombard duke Ratchis and the octagonal baptistery built for Patriarch Callisto.

Cividale: Mittelfest

The end of the cold war and the subsequent collapse of the Communist bloc sparked an ironic sense of unity in countries throughout Central Europe. Along with freedom and individuality came a feeling of collective identity, a desire to tear down boundaries that separated East from West. Mittelfest, held annually in Cividale del Friuli since 1991, celebrates this convergence of Central European cultures with an international festival of the arts.

According to producers, the goal of Mittelfest is to revive unity through celebrating diversity. Performers from more than a dozen countries, including Austria, Hungary, Poland, Albania, Bulgaria, Romania, Czech Republic, and Slovakia, as well as the countries that constitute the former Yugoslavia, present a week-long program of theater, music, dance, and puppetry events. In addition to outdoor stages, venues include church naves, town squares, and even the windows and terraces of ancient *palazzi*.

PONTE DEL DIAVOLO

The "Devil's Bridge" was named after a legend in which the townspeople of Cividale made a pact with the Devil. The Devil agreed to build the bridge overnight in exchange for the first soul to cross it. The next day, however, the townspeople outwitted the Devil by sending across a cat instead of a human.

Cividale on the banks of the emerald green Natisone River (ABOVE); *Caffè Longobardo in Piazza Paolo Diacono* (FAR LEFT); *views of the Ponte del Diavolo* (LEFT AND OPPOSITE, BOTTOM); *Chiesa dei Santi Pietro e Biagio, located in the town's ancient Borgo Brossana neighborhood* (OPPOSITE, TOP).

173

Central Friuli:
SECONDI

Braciole di Maiale al Latte   *Pork Chops Cooked in Milk*

Braising meat in milk is a common technique in Friuli, and pork loin or ribs may also be prepared this way. (Used independently, the term "maiale al latte" means "suckling pig" and does not necessarily refer to cooking the pork in milk.) Don't worry if the milk curdles a bit while cooking—this only adds delicious texture to the sauce.

4 bone-in pork chops (about 8 ounces each)
¼ cup all-purpose flour
1 tablespoon butter
1 cup whole milk

℥ Sprinkle the pork chops with salt and black pepper; dredge in flour.

℥ Melt the butter in a large, deep skillet over medium-high heat. Place the pork chops in the skillet; cook until brown, about 5–6 minutes on each side. Pour in the milk. Reduce heat to medium-low; cook, covered, until the pork is done (150°F on a meat thermometer), about 8–10 minutes. Transfer the pork chops to serving plates.

℥ Increase heat to medium-high; cook the sauce until thick and reduced by half, about 5 minutes, stirring occasionally. Season to taste with salt and black pepper. Spoon the sauce over the pork chops.

Serves 4.

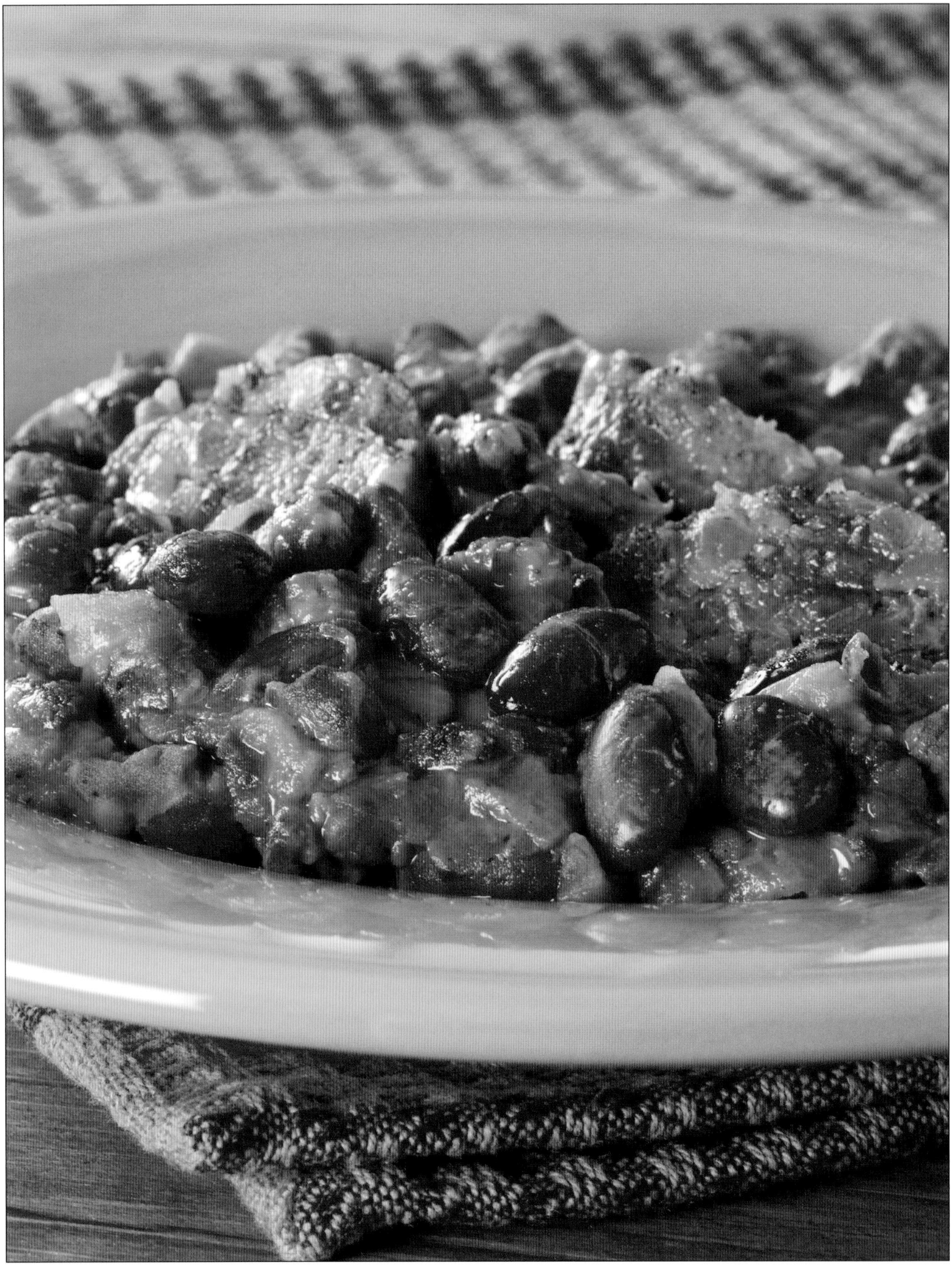

Musetto e Fagioli

Sausage and Beans

Musetto is named after one of its main ingredients, pig's snout ("muso" in Italian), which gives the sausage a sticky, gelatinous texture. The snout is minced along with a bit of lean meat, pig skin, and lard, then mixed with white wine and various spices, such as cinnamon, coriander, nutmeg, cloves, and pepper. The sausage requires an especially long cooking time to tenderize all those fatty, cartilaginous bits. Cotechino, a similar sausage from the Emilia-Romagna region, may be substituted for the musetto.

8 ounces dried borlotti
   (cranberry) beans
1 pound musetto sausage
3 cups water
3 tablespoons butter
3 tablespoons olive oil
1 medium yellow onion,
   chopped
1 tablespoon chopped fresh
   sage
$\frac{1}{2}$ teaspoon ground black
   pepper

ɗ In advance, place the beans in a medium bowl and cover with water. Let soak for at least 12 hours, or overnight; drain.

ɗ Bring a large pot of water to a boil over high heat. Prick the musetto several times with a toothpick and place in the water. Reduce heat to medium-low; simmer for 2 hours. Remove the musetto; peel off and discard the skin. Cut the musetto into $\frac{1}{2}$-inch-thick slices.

ɗ Meanwhile, place the beans in a large pot, along with 3 cups water; bring to a boil over high heat. Reduce heat to low; simmer, covered, for 1 hour.

ɗ Melt the butter with the olive oil in a large skillet over medium-low heat. Add the onion; cook and stir until soft and translucent, about 15–20 minutes. After the beans have simmered for 1 hour, add the cooked onion to the pot, along with the sage and black pepper. Cook, uncovered, until the beans are tender and all liquid has been absorbed, about 1 to 1½ hours longer, stirring occasionally. Season to taste with salt. Stir in the musetto slices.

Serves 4.

Petti d'Anatra ai Frutti di Bosco

Duck Breasts with Berry Sauce

Duck is widely served throughout central Friuli, particularly in the province of Pordenone. This recipe makes use of the wild berries that grow in the region, as well as spices from overseas.

SAUCE:

1 tablespoon olive oil

1 cup assorted fresh berries
   (such as blueberries,
   raspberries, blackberries,
   and sliced strawberries)

¼ teaspoon ground cinnamon

¼ teaspoon ground cloves

. . .

4 duck breasts (about 10 to 12
   ounces each)

1 tablespoon fresh thyme
   leaves

. . .

Assorted fresh berries
   (optional)

FOR THE SAUCE:

  Heat the olive oil in a small saucepan over low heat. Add the berries, cinnamon, and cloves; cook until the berries soften, about 10 minutes. Remove from heat. Strain the sauce, discarding the pulp; return the strained juice to the saucepan.

TO PREPARE:

  Preheat oven to 375°F. Sprinkle the duck breasts with salt, black pepper, and the thyme. Place skin-side down in a large, oven-safe skillet over medium heat; cook until the skin is golden brown, about 8–10 minutes. Turn the breasts over; transfer the skillet to the oven. Bake until medium-rare, about 7–10 minutes. Transfer the duck breasts to a plate and let rest for 5 minutes.

  During its resting time, the duck will release some cooking juices; add these to the saucepan with the berry sauce. Warm over medium heat, about 1–2 minutes.

  Slice each duck breast into ¼-inch-thick slices. Serve with the berry sauce; garnish with extra berries, if desired.

Serves 4.

Baccalà

Salt Cod Stew

This Friulian preparation of salt cod closely resembles baccalà alla Vicentina, a dish from the adjacent Veneto region. In the town of Vicenza, after which the dish is named, baccalà is usually baked, while in Friuli, it is more commonly cooked on the stovetop, as shown here. Baccalà is typically served with polenta (page 196). If Montasio stagionato is not available, you may substitute any aged cheese such as Parmigiano-Reggiano.

1 pound dried salt cod

¼ cup all-purpose flour

¼ cup olive oil

1 medium yellow onion, chopped

2 garlic cloves, minced

1 cup dry white wine

1½ cups whole milk

¼ cup chopped fresh Italian parsley

3 canned anchovies, chopped

½ teaspoon ground black pepper

¼ teaspoon ground cinnamon

¼ cup grated Montasio stagionato

ᴆ In advance, place the salt cod in a large bowl and cover with water. Refrigerate for 48 hours, changing the water about every 12 hours; drain.

ᴆ Remove any bones or skin from the fish; cut into 2-inch pieces. Dredge in flour.

ᴆ Heat the olive oil in a large, deep skillet over medium-low heat. Add the onion and garlic; cook and stir until the onion is soft and translucent, about 20 minutes. Add the white wine; bring to a boil over high heat. Reduce heat to low; simmer for 10 minutes. Stir in the milk, parsley, anchovies, black pepper, and cinnamon. Place the fish in the skillet; sprinkle with the Montasio cheese. Bring to a boil over high heat. Reduce heat to low; cook, covered, until the sauce has thickened and the fish flakes easily when tested with a fork, about 20 minutes, stirring occasionally. Season to taste with salt.

Serves 4 to 6.

Asparagi con Uova

Asparagus with Egg Salad

In Friuli, egg salad is frequently served with white asparagus from Tavagnacco. You may substitute green asparagus if white is not available.

4 eggs

2 tablespoons olive oil

2 tablespoons red wine vinegar

. . .

1 pound white asparagus, tough
   ends trimmed

₧ Place the eggs in a medium saucepan and cover with water. Bring to a boil over high heat; immediately remove from heat and let rest, covered, for 10 minutes. Remove the eggs and place in a bowl of cold water. When the eggs are cool enough to handle, remove and discard the shells. Coarsely chop the eggs.

₧ In a small bowl, whisk together the olive oil and vinegar; stir in the chopped eggs. Season to taste with salt and black pepper. Refrigerate until ready to serve.

₧ Peel the asparagus, starting 1 1/2 inches from the top and running the length of the spear. Place a steamer rack inside a large pot; fill with 1 inch of water. Place the asparagus on the rack. Bring to a boil over high heat; cover and steam until just tender, about 5 minutes. Serve with the egg salad.

Serves 4.

Furlan

Friuli's native tongue, Furlan, is a Romance language belonging to the Rhaetian family, which also includes Ladin (spoken in the Dolomites) and Romansh (spoken in southern Switzerland). Furlan—called "Friulano" in Italian—evolved from Latin and Celtic roots during the late Middle Ages and was subsequently influenced by Italian, German, and Slavic cultures.

A victim of modern times, Furlan had become practically obsolete when the language saw a significant revival during the mid-20th century. As part of an initiative to preserve the region's heritage, Furlan was recognized by the government as an official language in 1999.

Today, an estimated six hundred thousand Italians speak Furlan. There are two writing systems, using either French or Slavic lettering, as well as four distinct dialects. The Furlan spoken around Udine is considered the standard form, while the dialect spoken in western Friuli shows a Venetian influence. The people of Carnia have their own dialect, although there are variations from valley to valley. Interestingly, the Furlan dialect of southeastern Friuli most closely resembles the Italian language.

A Furlan menu with an artistic rendition of Friulian specialties adorns a wall at Osteria Alla Terrazza in Cividale (LEFT); throughout Friuli, street names are often given in both Italian and Furlan (BELOW).

Pitina

Since the early 19th century, *pitina*—also called *peta* and *petuccia*—has been prepared in the mountainous areas of Val Tramontina and Val Cellina in the northern part of Pordenone province. Like all cured meats, *pitina* was originally created as a way of preserving the meat, in this case mutton, goat, or game such as chamois or venison. The conventional method of sausage-making, which involved stuffing pig intestines with ground meat, was impractical due to the scarcity of swine in these hills. So instead, the meat was seasoned with salt, pepper, garlic, herbs, and red wine, then rolled into balls and dredged in cornmeal. This simple preparation required no special equipment, so it was feasible to make *pitina* by hand in these isolated mountain villages.

Once prepared, these meatballs were placed above a *fogolâr* to smoke for several days, typically using juniper wood to give the *pitina* its distinctive smoky flavor. They were then relocated to a cool, dry place to age for several months. Today, only a few artisans still prepare *pitina* from wild game. Most butchers use a combination of mutton, pork, beef, and goat, adding pork fat to soften the texture and, occasionally, mushrooms or truffles for extra flavor.

Pitina may be used in the dish *salame all'aceto* (page 149) or simply served as part of an antipasto platter with cheese and bread.

Pitina *from Macelleria Bier in the Val Tramontina* (RIGHT)*; the slogan on a box of* pitina *from Jolanda de Colò reads: "There exists a taste that, beyond the palate, touches the soul and traverses time"* (BELOW).

Villa Manin

Friuli's largest *palazzo*, the Villa Manin, stands along a stretch of highway in Passariano, a village just southeast of Codroipo. Set amid cornfields and vineyards, the palace was originally the summer residence of Ludovico Manin, the last Doge of Venice.

During the 1797 signing of the Treaty of Campoformido, which ceded much of northern Italy to Austria, this palace was briefly home to Napoleon  Bonaparte, whose diminutive bed is on display in the Napoleon Room. In contrast to its interior décor, painted in typical 17th-century *trompe l'oeil*, the villa is currently used for rotating exhibitions of contemporary art.

To complement the palace's monolithic dimensions, the vast courtyard was modeled after Rome's Piazza San Pietro, with a semi-circular colonnade at the opposite end. To the rear of the villa lie forty-seven acres of gardens, complete with mythological statues, fountains, and fishponds.

189

Sacile: Sagra dei Osei

Located at the western edge of Pordenone province, Sacile was once dubbed the "Garden of the Serenissima," suggesting a resemblance to the region's former capital, Venice. Built at a fork in the Livenza River, the town sits amid a small network of canals and bridges, shaded by willow trees and Venetian-style *palazzi*. Once a year, Sacile's peaceful streets transform into a chirping, chattering marketplace with its festival of songbirds, the Sagra dei Osei.

One of the oldest festivals in Italy, the Sagra dei Osei was first held on August 2, 1274, under the name Mercato di San Lorenzo. With only a few interruptions, this annual event has survived for centuries. The name was officially changed to Sagra dei Osei in 1907, along with the formation of an organizational committee and promotional campaign.

On the morning of the festival, thousands of songbirds—including nightingales, blackbirds, finches, and larks—celebrate daybreak with their spirited melody. Later, prizes are awarded by a panel of ornithologists. Originally limited to Sacile's main piazza, the exhibit has gradually outgrown the confines of the town center. Today, the heart of the festival is located in a nearby park, while the piazza remains the showplace for exotic species of birds and their rainbow of plumes.

In keeping with the tradition of the original market of San Lorenzo, the Sagra dei Osei also features an exhibit of farm animals, where vendors can sell or trade pigs, chickens, and rabbits. The festival concludes with a bird-calling competition, perhaps the most popular attraction of the day.

The hexagonal Chiesa della Madonna della Pietà (ABOVE)*; this stone* palazzo *is typical of the architecture in Pordenone province* (FAR LEFT)*; Duomo di San Nicolò on the Livenza River* (LEFT AND OPPOSITE)*.*

Pordenone

Established during the Middle Ages as a port on the Noncello River, Pordenone was acquired by the Venetian Republic in 1514. Today, the city's historic center retains an atmosphere of Venetian charm, its elegant streets lined with porticoes and painted palaces.

CLOCKWISE FROM TOP LEFT: *Chiesa di San Giorgio features a Doric column as its campanile; Palazzo dei Capitani; La Vecia Osteria del Moro offers local cuisine near the old town center; Duomo di San Marco towers over the Palazzo Comunale (also called the Municipio); the frescoes on this palazzo have been restored to their original brilliance; the central tower of the Municipio features a clock with symbols of the zodiac; painted houses line the stylish Corso Vittorio Emanuele; palazzo on Piazzetta San Marco; the Municipio faces the beginning of Corso Vittorio Emanuele; while some palaces have been recently restored, many still have peeling frescoes.*

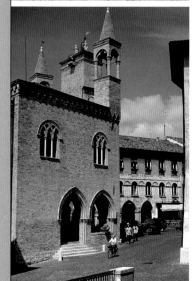

Spilimbergo

Spilimbergo is perhaps best known for its mosaic school, whose works of art are displayed in venues—such as cathedrals, royal palaces, and even airports—all over the world.

CLOCKWISE FROM BOTTOM RIGHT: *a peaceful cobblestone street in the town center; the 16th-century frescoes on the Palazzo Ercole illustrate scenes from the mythical life of Hercules; Duomo di Santa Maria Maggiore; the Duomo's Romanesque Gothic façade; Venetian Gothic windows adorn painted palaces throughout the town; the Palazzo di Sopra is currently home to Spilimbergo's town hall.*

❧❧ ❧

Central Friuli:
CONTORNI

❧❧ ❧

Polenta

Cooked Cornmeal

Maize was originally introduced into Europe by the Spaniards after Columbus brought it back from the Americas, although the grain was initially intended for use only as cattle feed. Recognizing corn's value as a food source for humans, the Venetian Republic soon took over the trade, selling it throughout the Mediterranean—even to their worst enemies, the Turks. Ironically, the Venetians, having forgotten where corn came from, later bought it back from the Turks and reintroduced it to central Europe as "Turkish grain." Even today, corn is known as "granoturco" throughout much of northeastern Italy.

A staple in Friuli since the 16th century and long considered food of the poor, polenta is now the region's ubiquitous side dish, accompanying nearly every meal in restaurants and homes throughout the region. Some families even serve it for breakfast. There are two methods of serving polenta: "morbida" (soft) and "alla piastra" (grilled). You may use either yellow or white cornmeal in this recipe.

4 cups water

1 cup coarsely ground cornmeal

1 teaspoon salt

2 tablespoons butter

. . .

3 tablespoons olive oil, divided
    (for grilling)

❦ Bring 4 cups water to a boil in a medium pot over high heat. Stir in the cornmeal and salt. When the water returns to a boil, reduce heat to low; cook and stir until soft, about 25 minutes. Stir in the butter.

For grilled polenta:

❦ Pour the hot polenta immediately into a greased 9- by 13-inch baking dish; spread evenly. Refrigerate for 1 hour, or until firm. Slice into twelve rectangles.

❦ Preheat grill (or heat a large skillet over medium-high heat). Brush one side of the polenta slices with 1 1/2 tablespoons olive oil; place the slices oil-side down on the grill. Cook until grill marks are golden brown, about 10–12 minutes. Brush the top surface of the polenta slices with the remaining 1 1/2 tablespoons olive oil; turn the slices over. Cook until grill marks are golden brown on the reverse side, about 8–10 minutes.

Serves 6.

Brovada

Pickled Turnips

Pickled turnip, one of Friuli's most typical side dishes, is especially popular in the central plains around Udine, although for many modern-day Friulians, brovada is an acquired taste. Following an ancient Roman recipe dating as far back as the 3rd century AD, turnips are marinated for at least one month in grape "marc" (the solid matter that remains after grapes are pressed, containing skin, seeds, pulp, and stems). In Carnia, where the climate is not conducive to growing grapes, the residue from distilling apples or pears may be used instead. Traditionally, the turnips are fermented whole, then sliced using a special grater; in this recipe, they are sliced beforehand to hasten the process. This version also marinates the turnips for just a few days in a mixture of wine and vinegar; for a more acidic flavor, you may increase the marinating time to several weeks or even a month. Brovada may be eaten raw, boiled, or sautéed, as shown here, and is often served with musetto, a mildly spiced sausage made from pig's snout.

1 pound turnips, peeled and
   sliced into 1/8-inch julienne
   strips
1 cup dry red wine
1 cup red wine vinegar
    • • •
2 tablespoons butter
1 tablespoon olive oil
1/2 medium yellow onion, thinly
   sliced
2 garlic cloves, minced
3/4 cup beef broth
1 tablespoon chopped fresh
   Italian parsley
1 tablespoon chopped fresh
   sage
1/2 teaspoon ground black
   pepper

ಶಿ In advance, combine the turnips, red wine, and vinegar in a medium bowl, making sure that the turnips are completely submerged in the liquid. Refrigerate for 48 hours; drain.

ಶಿ Melt the butter with the olive oil in a large skillet over medium-low heat. Add the onion and garlic; cook and stir until the onion begins to soften, about 10 minutes. Add the drained turnips, beef broth, parsley, sage, and black pepper; cook until the turnips are tender, about 30 minutes, stirring occasionally. Season to taste with salt.

Serves 4 to 6.

Rape Dolci

Sweet Turnips

Similar turnip dishes are also served in Trieste, where lard replaces the butter, and in Carnia, where vinegar is often added for a sweet-and-sour flavor.

4 tablespoons butter

2 pounds turnips, peeled and
  cut into ½-inch pieces

3 tablespoons sugar

& Melt the butter in a large skillet over medium heat. Add the turnips and sugar; cook and stir until tender, about 20 minutes. Season to taste with salt and black pepper.

Serves 4.

Wines of the Collio

The Collio and Colli Orientali del Friuli constitute the heart of Friuli's wine country. These two wine zones, which are sometimes referred to collectively as the Collio Goriziano, are reminiscent of Tuscany's rolling hills or California's lush Napa Valley. The word *colli*, meaning "hills," epitomizes this landscape where the grapes have more sun exposure than in the low-lying plains. Though the centrally located Grave del Friuli zone is the region's largest wine producer—chiefly of Merlot—the wines from the Collio and Colli Orientali are regarded to be Friuli's best. In fact, most experts agree that the white wines from this region are the most superb in all of Italy.

The Collio lies in Gorizia province, along the Slovenian border and separated from the Colli Orientali by the Judrio River. This zone is most famous for its white wines, Tocai Friulano in particular. Although this grape is not believed to be native to Friuli, it has been produced there for centuries. Recently, the European Union delivered an unpopular verdict regarding the name Tocai: of the three European wines having a historical claim on the name—Tocai Friulano, Tokai-Pinot Gris from France, and Hungarian Tokaj—only the Hungarian wine has been allowed to continue using its name. Despite much local protest, Tocai Friulano is now officially called merely Friulano.

Also popular are Collio's white wine blends, which usually contain at least two of the following: Tocai, Malvasia Istriana, and Ribolla Gialla, as well as occasionally Sauvignon Blanc, Pinot Bianco, or Pinot Grigio. Perhaps the Collio's most famous blend is the Vino della Pace, which is produced from 540 grape varieties selected from every continent. This "wine of peace" is bottled and sent to political and religious leaders around the world.

The town of Cormòns is home to one of the region's most noted wine bars, the Enoteca di Cormòns. Also the seat of the Collio's wine-producing consortium, this bar makes a great place to taste regional wines along with the locally smoked *prosciutto D'Osvaldo*. Every September, Cormòns hosts the Festa Provinciale dell'Uva, a wine festival featuring music, theater, and cultural events, along with the obligatory wine tasting.

The Colli Orientali lies to the north of the Collio in Udine province and also borders on Slovenia. Many native grapes are grown here, including the reds Refosco, Schioppettino, and Pignolo, and whites Ribolla Gialla, Verduzzo, and Picolit. While the versatile and abundant Verduzzo grapes can be vinified as either a dry or sweet wine, Picolit is one of the rarest and most precious dessert wines ever made.

Produced exclusively in the Valli del Natisone near the town of Cividale, Picolit is believed to have

been cultivated since Roman times. A fragile and high maintenance variety, the grapevine is extremely low yielding due to a condition called "floral abortion," where many buds die before maturing into grapes. With a golden color, honeyed fragrance, and subtle hints of almond, dried fruit, and spice, Picolit is what Italian experts call a "meditation wine," meaning that it is best savored on its own without any food.

During the 18th century, winemaker Count Fabio Asquini of Fagagna developed an unrivaled appreciation for Picolit. With the idea that a diminutive package would increase the wine's appeal, he commissioned special half-size bottles from the glassblowers in Murano. These he then exported to Venice where Picolit soon became the drink of choice for Doge Manin and his court. Asquini proved himself to be a marketing genius, able to manipulate the laws of supply and demand to his advantage. He had held back part of his inventory, thus creating the illusion of limited supply. Then, when reports of this magnificent wine reached Vienna, he was able to ship some to the emperor. (It was a fortuitous decision to expand his clientele base, for the Venetian Republic was soon to collapse.) Before long, Asquini was sending Picolit to the king of France, the tsar of Russia, and even the pope, but following Asquini's death, Picolit nearly disappeared from production.

An epidemic of the *phylloxera* fungus ravished vineyards throughout 19th-century Europe. Then, after winemakers had successfully replanted, the two world wars caused even further devastation. Several grapes were facing extinction when they were rescued during the 1970s. A scholar named Walter Filiputti found two surviving vines of Pignolo in an abbey in Rosazzo and was able to nurse them back to health, while winemaker Paolo Rapuzzi did the same for the failing Schioppettino grape.

During these periods of revival, Friulians replanted not only native grapes—as did most of Europe—but foreign varieties as well. With a long history of inter-mingling cultures and openness to foreigners, it was only natural that Friuli be one of the first regions in the world to do so. During the late 19th century, Friuli was the first region in Italy to produce Merlot and was among the first to have Cabernet Franc, Cabernet Sauvignon, Sauvignon Blanc, Chardonnay, Pinot Blanc, Pinot Gris, Pinot Noir, and Traminer. Today, these non-natives are produced as 100 percent varietal wines, as well as mixed in Friuli's popular blends.

Wine tasting (OPPOSITE) *and local vintages on display* (ABOVE) *at Enoteca di Cormòns; vineyards in the hills of the Collio* (RIGHT).

Cormòns

Clockwise from above: *a panoramic view of Cormòns and the surrounding plains; at the D'Osvaldo family home, Lorenzo D'Osvaldo produces a popular smoked prosciutto; the Enoteca di Cormòns doubles as the town's tourist office; Chiesa di Santa Caterina is also known as "Rosa Mistica" after its altar statue of the Madonna and Child holding a rose made of precious stones (the stones were stolen by raiding French troops in 1812).*

CLOCKWISE FROM ABOVE: *local wines, cheeses, and* salumi, *including* prosciutto D'Osvaldo, *may be sampled inside the Enoteca di Cormòns; the campanile of Duomo di Sant'Adalberto; the surrounding Collio countryside is blanketed with vineyards; Chiesetta della Beata Vergine del Soccorso overlooks Cormòns from the slopes of Monte Quarin.*

La Subida

Situated in the heart of the Collio is one of Friuli's most esteemed restaurants, Trattoria Al Cacciatore de La Subida (known to locals simply as La Subida). On the outskirts of Cormòns, surrounded by rolling hills and lush vineyards, La Subida serves impeccable dishes inspired by the nearby border where Friulian and Slovenian cultures merge.

Opened at Christmastime in 1960 by Slovenian Joško Sirk and his wife, Loredana, La Subida was originally a small *osteria* and inn, which soon became a popular gathering spot for hunters. A recreational *cacciatore* (hunter) himself, Sirk takes great pride in the land and has built a small

complex of apartments adjacent to his restaurant, complete with tennis courts, children's playground, horse stables, and swimming pool. For Sirk, building these rustic farmhouses has been an obsessive hobby and his primary passion—the realization of a longtime dream. "Subida isn't a hotel with all the creature comforts," he admitted, "and it's not even very entertaining," but he hopes it to be an ideal place for vacationers to spend a relaxing and invigorating holiday.

To the Sirk family, Trattoria Al Cacciatore is not just a restaurant—it is their home, filled with special belongings, mementos, and memories. Daughters Tanja and Erika have grown up here and now help out in the dining room. Joško and Loredana are always there as well, interacting with their guests, even joining them at the table. After a while, dining at La Subida is like dining with family.

The Sirks look at their cuisine as a slice of life, a part of their culture and heritage. The menu leans toward the Triestine—*jota* and *gnocchi di susine*, for example—but also offers a variety of Friulian dishes, including *frico*, frittata, and *orzotto*. They specialize in the Slovenian pastas *mlinci* and *zlikrofi*, as well as wild game, which is roasted or grilled to perfection. The *stinco di vitello*, carved tableside, simply melts in one's mouth. While their food remains authentic, each dish is refined to an exquisite level through added touches such as fried sage leaves, elderberry flower syrup, and herb-infused sorbets.

The best way to experience this slice of culture is with La Subida's multi-course tasting menu. After an aperitif and some light snacks under the lime tree or inside by the *fogolâr*, diners will feast on an appetizer, two or three first courses, two meat dishes, a palate-cleansing sorbet, and a dessert that inevitably includes a plate of homemade biscotti. This must all be accompanied, of course, by local Collio wine from Joško's cellar.

Loredana and Joško Sirk (OPPOSITE, TOP)*; Trattoria Al Cacciatore* (RIGHT AND OPPOSITE, BOTTOM) *is considered by many critics to be one of Friuli's best restaurants; the* fogolâr *keeps diners warm on cold winter evenings* (BELOW)*.*

Central Friuli:
DOLCI

Gubana

Derived from the Slovene word *guba*, meaning "wrinkle" or "fold," the name *gubana* is suggestive of the swirls and spirals in this sumptuous pastry. Filled with a mixture of dried fruit, nuts, and spices, *gubana* may be prepared with either a yeast-based dough (*gubana delle Valli del Natisone*) or puff pastry (*gubana Cividalese*). While literary sources date similar recipes to the Middle Ages and perhaps even the Romans, the first document to mention *gubana* by name was written in 1576. Since puff pastry required equipment and knowledge only available to the upper classes, *gubana delle Valli del Natisone* was the version typically prepared by peasants living in the valleys around

the Natisone River, while *gubana Cividalese* was the aristocrat's pastry of choice in the prominent city of Cividale. Originally baked only for holidays such as Christmas and Easter, *gubana* may now be enjoyed throughout the year. Bakeries such as Pasticceria Ducale in Cividale specialize in both types of *gubana*, as well as the dried fruit- and nut-filled cookies called *strucchi*.

Gubana Cividalese, gubana delle Valli del Natisone, *and* strucchi *for sale in the bakeries of Cividale* (RIGHT AND BELOW).

Gubana Filling

This filling is used in the following three recipes: gubana delle Valli del Natisone (page 212), gubana Cividalese (page 215), and strucchi (page 216).

1 cup raisins

1/2 cup grappa or rum

1 cup coarsely chopped walnuts

1/2 cup blanched slivered
     almonds

3/4 cup finely crushed biscotti or
     amaretti cookies

1/2 cup diced candied orange
     peel

1/4 cup pine nuts

4 tablespoons unsalted butter,
     melted

3 tablespoons sugar

1 1/2 teaspoons ground cinnamon

1 egg

ಶ Place the raisins in a large bowl; add the grappa and let soak for 30 minutes.

ಶ Finely grind the walnuts and almonds in a food processor; add to the bowl of raisins. Stir in the crushed biscotti, candied orange peel, pine nuts, melted butter, sugar, cinnamon, and egg.

Gubana delle Valli del Natisone

*Dried Fruit and
Nut Spiral Cake*

This type of gubana originated in the Natisone valleys but may now be found in bakeries throughout Friuli. Locals often serve the pastry soaked in grappa.

DOUGH:

*3 ½ teaspoons active dry yeast,
divided*

⅓ cup sugar, divided

*½ cup warm water (100° to
110°F), divided*

*2 ⅔ cups all-purpose flour,
divided*

1 egg

1 egg yolk

*4 tablespoons unsalted butter,
diced and softened*

1 teaspoon salt

1 teaspoon vanilla extract

. . .

*Gubana Filling (see recipe on
page 211)*

1 teaspoon sugar

FOR THE DOUGH:

⁂ In a small bowl, dissolve 2 teaspoons yeast and a pinch of sugar in ¼ cup warm water. Let rest until foamy, about 10 minutes. Stir in ½ cup flour. Cover and let rise for 30 minutes.

⁂ Transfer the mixture to a large bowl. Stir in 1 cup flour, 1 tablespoon sugar, the egg, and egg yolk. Cover and let rise for 1 hour.

⁂ In a small bowl, dissolve the remaining 1 ½ teaspoons yeast and a pinch of sugar in the remaining ¼ cup warm water. Let rest until foamy, about 10 minutes. Add to the bowl of risen dough, along with the remaining flour and sugar, butter, salt, and vanilla extract; mix well. Using a mixer with a dough hook attachment, knead for 10 minutes. (It may be necessary to occasionally scrape the ball of dough off the hook.) Transfer the dough to a lightly floured surface; knead briefly by hand. (The dough should be smooth and elastic.) Form the dough into a ball; cover loosely with plastic wrap or a kitchen towel and let rise for 1 ½ hours.

TO PREPARE:

⁂ Preheat oven to 350°F, placing a pan filled with water on the bottom rack to create steam. On a lightly floured surface, roll the dough to a 14- by 20-inch rectangle. Spread the filling over the dough, leaving a 1-inch border on all but one short side. (The filling will be sparse in places; just cover the dough as evenly as possible.) Starting with one long side, roll up jelly roll style. Place the roll seam-side down on a sheet of parchment paper. Beginning with the end that has the filling spread to the edge, form the roll into a spiral. Transfer the spiral, along with the parchment paper, to a baking sheet. Cover loosely with plastic wrap or a kitchen towel and let rise for 30 minutes.

⁂ Sprinkle the top of the spiral with 1 teaspoon sugar. Bake until golden brown, about 45 minutes.

Serves 12 to 16.

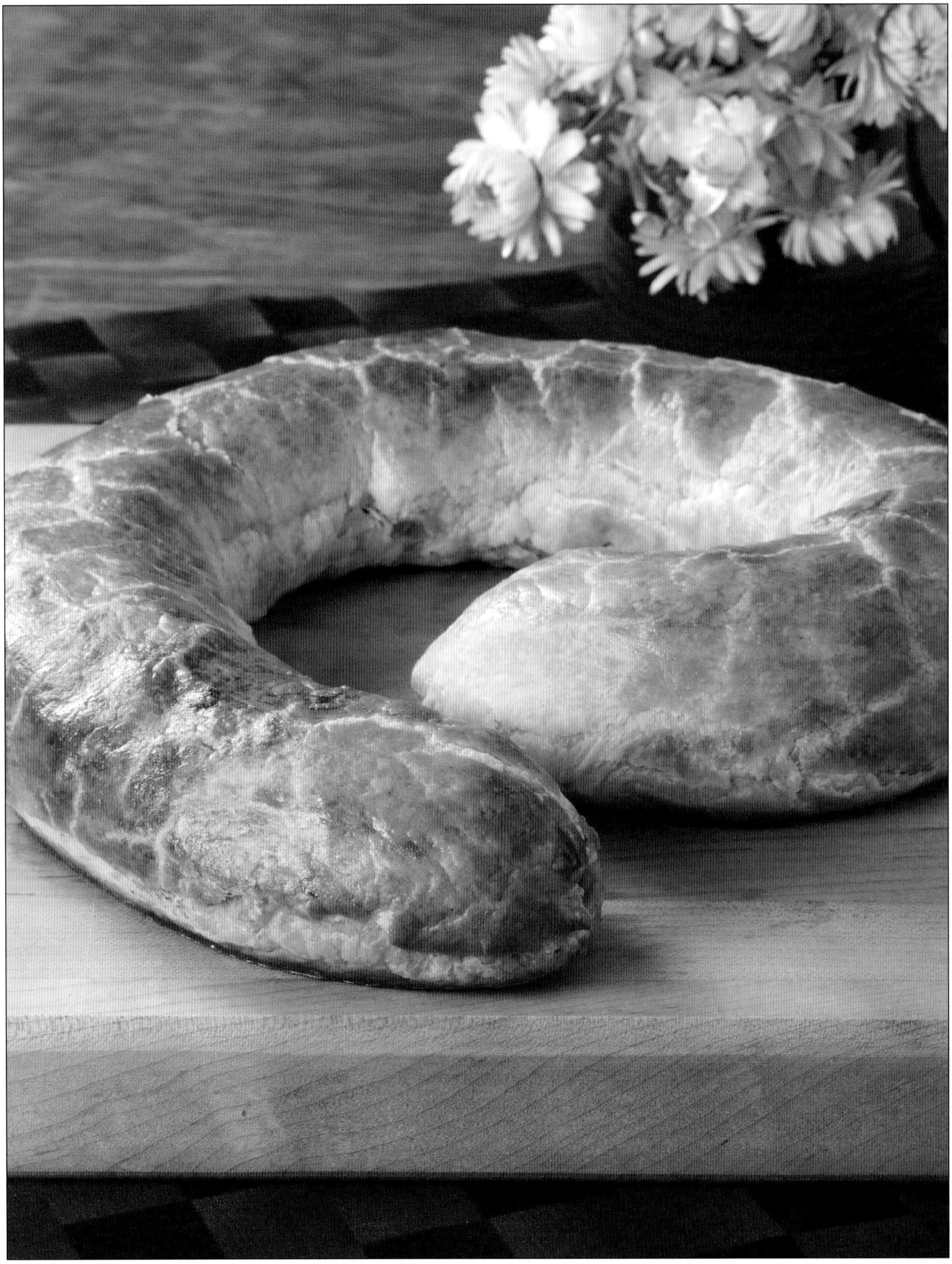

Gubana Cividalese

Cividale-Style Pastry Spiral

This recipe for puff pastry dough is also used for presnitz (page 325) and strucolo de pomi (page 329).

PUFF PASTRY DOUGH:

3/4 cup plus 2 tablespoons all-purpose flour

1/4 teaspoon salt

1/2 cup (1 stick) unsalted butter, divided and softened

1/4 cup cold water

. . .

Gubana Filling (see recipe on page 211)

1 egg, beaten to blend

FOR THE DOUGH:

ೞ In a large bowl, combine the flour and salt. Cut 2 tablespoons butter into cubes; blend into the flour mixture. Add 1/4 cup cold water; mix until crumbly. Transfer the dough to a lightly floured surface and knead briefly. Flatten the dough to a 1/2-inch-thick disk. Wrap in plastic wrap; refrigerate for 30 minutes.

ೞ Unwrap the dough and place on a lightly floured surface; roll to a 7-inch square. Roll the corners of the square away from the center to form four flaps, leaving a 3-inch square in the center at the original thickness. Beat the remaining 6 tablespoons butter with a rolling pin to form a 3-inch square; place in the center of the dough. Fold the flaps over to enclose the butter; turn the dough folded-side down. Roll to a 6- by 9-inch rectangle; fold in thirds (like a letter). Rotate the dough 90°. Roll again to a 6- by 9-inch rectangle; fold in thirds again. (This completes two "turns.") Wrap in plastic wrap; refrigerate for 30 minutes.

ೞ Repeat rolling and folding the dough for two more turns. Wrap and refrigerate for 30 minutes. Repeat rolling and folding the dough for two final turns. (This completes a total of six turns.) Wrap and refrigerate for at least 1 hour before using.

TO PREPARE:

ೞ On a sheet of waxed paper, form the filling into a 12-inch log. Wrap securely in the waxed paper and refrigerate for 1 hour, or until ready to use.

ೞ Preheat oven to 400°F. On a lightly floured surface, roll the dough to a 10- by 13-inch rectangle. Unwrap the filling and place along the center of the dough. Wrap the dough around the filling, tightly sealing all seams. Gently roll and stretch the dough into a 2 1/2-foot-long rope. Coil into a loose spiral and transfer to a baking sheet lined with parchment paper. Brush the surface of the dough with beaten egg. Bake until golden brown, about 25–30 minutes.

Serves 10 to 12.

Strucchi

Dried Fruit- and Nut-Filled Cookies

These sweet bites were most likely named after the Slovenian dumplings called "štruklji." Their origin dates back to the 15th century, when Martino da Como, chef for the patriarch of Aquileia, documented a recipe for fritters filled with dried fruit and nuts. Historians believe these were a precursor to modern strucchi as well as gubana. While strucchi are sometimes baked, this fried version is more traditional.

DOUGH:

6 cups all-purpose flour

6 tablespoons sugar

1 tablespoon freshly grated lemon peel

1 teaspoon salt

2 cups (4 sticks) unsalted butter, cut into cubes

4 eggs

2 teaspoons vanilla extract

• • •

Gubana Filling (see recipe on page 211)

Vegetable oil

Sugar

FOR THE DOUGH:

In a large bowl, combine the flour, sugar, lemon peel, and salt. Blend in the butter, a little at a time, until crumbly. Add the eggs and vanilla extract; mix until the dough forms a solid mass. Refrigerate for 1 hour.

TO PREPARE:

Working in batches, roll the dough on a sheet of waxed paper to ⅛-inch thickness. Cut the dough into 1- by 1½-inch rectangles. Place ½ teaspoon filling in the center of one rectangle; cover with another rectangle, sealing the edges tightly. (Keep the unused dough refrigerated until ready to use.)

Pour 1½ inches of vegetable oil into a large pot. Heat the oil to 365°F. Working in batches, carefully place the strucchi in the hot oil; fry until golden brown, about 1–2 minutes. Remove from oil; drain on paper towels. Sprinkle with sugar.

Makes about 10 to 11 dozen.

Southern Friuli:
Adriatic Coast

An exotic crossroads of culture, the Adriatic Coast was for centuries Europe's gateway to the East. Emperors and writers alike traveled here to bask in its stunning beauty. Today, modern hotel resorts line the region's few sandy beaches. Elsewhere, sailboats bob and sway in countless harbors, while city dwellers catch rays on concrete waterfront promenades. Perched high on the coastline's craggy cliffs, villas and castles provide a majestic view of the sparkling, sapphire waters.

From pastel fishing villages to Trieste's busy port, the sea is a way of life here. For both merchants and fishermen, the Adriatic Sea has long been a major source of prosperity. Throughout the last two millenniums, ships regularly transported goods between Europe and Asia, contributing to the success of the Roman, Venetian, and Austro-Hungarian empires. In addition to promoting a lucrative international trade, the Adriatic has long supplied its people with a bounty of fresh seafood. The fish caught in the waters off Friuli have not only provided economic sustenance but have significantly shaped the region's cuisine as well.

While the coastline of Friuli-Venezia Giulia spans three of the region's four provinces, it is precisely the use of local seafood that unifies the cuisine. Along the western shores that border the

Castello di Miramare perches on a promontory overlooking the sea (ABOVE); *the bronze statue* Le Sartine dei Bersaglieri—*meaning "the soldiers' seamstresses"—on the waterfront across from Trieste's Piazza dell'Unità* (OPPOSITE).

Veneto, the Venetian influence is especially noticeable in typical dishes using salt cod, sardines, crab, langoustines, and squid.

The Venetian lagoon extends eastward into Friuli, where tiny, thatched fishermen's huts, called *casoni*, are scattered among the marshy islands. In the province of Udine, Marano Lagunare—originally a Venetian settlement and today a quiet fishing village—rests peacefully amid the lagoon. Nearby, the seaside resort of Lignano Sabbiadoro sports the region's largest beach—with a comparably sizeable holiday crowd.

Just a few miles inland lies the ancient Roman town of Aquileia, known for its vibrant mosaics. The city was revitalized as a center of commerce during the Middle Ages when it was rebuilt by Patriarch Poppone. During both Roman and patriarchal times, the coastal town of Grado functioned as Aquileia's seaport. Today, Grado is located in a tiny sliver of Gorizia province. The surrounding lagoons reap plentiful seafood that is used in the vinegar-laced *boreto alla Gradese*.

Aside from the abundance of seafood, the most distinguishing characteristic of the cuisine in southern Friuli is the pervasive Germanic influence. This is perhaps more evident in Venezia Giulia than in the rest of the Friuli region, due to its lengthy Austro-Hungarian heritage. From dumplings to desserts, the food has a distinct Austrian flavor. Although Gorizia is not a coastal city, it is part of Venezia Giulia and will be included in this section because of the marked similarities between its cuisine and that of Trieste.

Gorizia has often been compared to Berlin, having also been split into two cities following World War II. The Slavic half, Nova Gorica, was at that time situated just across the border in Communist Yugoslavia. Today, Gorizia abuts Slovenia, which is now a member of the European Union. This change has brought a significant relaxation of border controls between the two cities. Families who had been separated for decades are now free to cross the border and reunite. Cultural and culinary elements have crossed borders as well. For example, Slavic dishes such as *cevapcici* are frequently served in Gorizia's counterpart to the Italian *osteria*—the *gostilna*.

The province of Trieste is exclusively coastal, stretching from the Castello di Duino southeastward to the Istrian peninsula, where the town of Muggia is the final stop before crossing into Slovenia. This skinny finger of Italian land extends entirely into foreign territory, isolated from the rest of Friuli by the rocky Carso plateau. Like the Carnians, the people of the Carso uphold a unique culture preserved by their imposed isolation.

Due to this geographical separation, as well as their city's political history, the Triestine people possess an identity somewhat disconnected from other Italians. As the chief port of the Austro-Hungarian Empire from the late 14th century until the end of World War I, Trieste has only revealed a noticeable Italian personality during the last hundred years. While Italian is now the official language, most residents also speak German or Slovene.

Throughout history, ethnic diversity has been key to the city's allure and fusion of cuisines. Especially during the Hapsburg reign, immigrants arrived in Trieste from all over the map. Austrians, Hungarians, Italians, Slavs, Jews, and Greeks lived side by side in relative peace. The prosperity of this period allowed for a sense of contentment among the people, and foreigners were embraced as part of the local culture.

While many dishes—such as *liptauer* and *palacinche*—were borrowed directly from various foreign cuisines, others have been given a unique local spin. For example, it is common practice for Triestine cooks to add tomatoes to the Hungarian stew *goulasch*. Still other dishes are considered to be native to Trieste, including *patate in tecia* and *jota*.

Fresh squid for sale in a Trieste fish market (ABOVE); granzievola, or "spiny spider crab" (LEFT).

OPPOSITE, CLOCKWISE FROM TOP LEFT: *whelks; canoce, or "mantis shrimp"; scampi, or "langoustines"; scallops.*

As in the rest of Friuli-Venezia Giulia, pork, potatoes, and polenta remain dietary staples and are often enhanced by foreign ingredients. For centuries, international trade brought exotic spices to the region, and the merchants of Trieste naturally had first pick. Cinnamon, nutmeg, cloves, caraway seeds, and poppy seeds were used extensively in local dishes, as was paprika, a mainstay of Hungarian cooking. The sweet and sour flavor known in Italy as agrodolce was also introduced from abroad. It appears in vinegar-seasoned dishes throughout Friuli and the Veneto, such as *boreto alla Gradese* and *sardoni in savor*.

Established out of the necessities of a bustling seaport and urban center, the buffet has become a long-standing institution in Trieste. Originally a convenient place for workers to grab a quick bite on a midmorning break, this venerable fast-food joint is today a popular spot for the lunchtime crowd, as well as for snackers throughout the day. Typical buffet fare includes pork sandwiches, *liptauer* cheese, and sauerkraut—and often heartier dishes such as soups, stews, or dumplings as well.

Like the Germans, the Triestini have a predilection for beer. The nearby Carso, however, is known for producing superb wines, such as the reds Terrano and Refosco di San Dorligo, and whites Malvasia Istriana and Vitovska. The tiny Carso town of Prosecco has given its name to the native grape Glera di Prosecco, which is thought to be the source of the famed sparkling wine

On a clear day, the Gulf of Trieste can be seen from hiking trails in the Val Rosandra (ABOVE); the modernistic interior of Santuario di Monte Grisa (OPPOSITE).

produced today throughout the Veneto. For a taste of Carso wine, drive along what tourism officials have dubbed the "Terrano Wine Road," from Opicina to Sistiana. Be on the lookout for country houses displaying a cluster of branches over their doors. These are traditional *osmizze* where you can sample not only the local wine but homemade cheese and *salumi* as well.

While they truly love wine and beer, Triestini are even more notorious as coffee drinkers. Claimed by many to be the world's best coffee, Illycaffè got its start in Trieste in the early 1900s. Of the six million cups of Illy espresso or cappuccino that are enjoyed daily around the globe, a good number are imbibed at home in Trieste's old-time cafés. The legendary ones—Caffè San Marco, Caffè Tommaseo, Caffè degli Specchi, and Caffè Tergesteo—date from the 19th to the early 20th century. Authors James Joyce, Sigmund Freud, Italo Svevo, and Umberto Saba were known to be regulars.

Along with their coffee, Triestini often order slices of elegant Viennese cakes, such as the *torta Sacher* and *torta Dobos*. In every bakery counter, strudels ooze a multitude of delicious fruit fillings, while cream- and chocolate-laced pastries abound. Although similar variations are found throughout Friuli, three desserts claim Trieste as their home. *Pinza* is an unembellished sweet loaf, traditionally baked for Easter. *Presnitz* and *putizza* are akin to the spiral-shaped *gubana* found elsewhere in the region, with a similar filling of dried fruit and nuts. These sweets can be sampled in Trieste's oldest bakeries, Pasticceria Bomboniera, Pasticceria Pirona, and Pasticceria Penso.

The beaches at Lignano Sabbiadoro are perpetually crowded in summertime (ABOVE); fave dei morti for sale during All Saints' Day festivities at Pasticceria Penso (RIGHT); the promenade winding around Castello di Miramare offers a spectacular view of the sea (OPPOSITE).

Southern Friuli:
ANTIPASTI

Liptauer

Austrian-Style Cheese Spread

Liptauer is traditionally made from Liptó, a fresh sheep's milk cheese named after the former Austro-Hungarian province of the same name (now part of Slovakia). The cheese is mixed with a variety of savory ingredients that may include onion, anchovies, capers, mustard, pickles, parsley, chives, and caraway seeds, as well as paprika, which colors the dish a vivid pinkish orange. In Trieste, fresh ricotta replaces the Hungarian Liptó cheese and may also be blended with Gorgonzola. In addition, I found that Triestine liptauer was most often white in color, with the paprika sprinkled on top as a garnish. Liptauer is served in many of Trieste's buffets, where it is typically accompanied by rye bread and beer.

1 cup fresh ricotta

1 cup crumbled Gorgonzola

1 tablespoon chopped fresh
    Italian parsley

1 tablespoon chopped fresh
    chives

1 teaspoon minced capers

1 teaspoon prepared mustard

    . . .

Paprika

❦ Purée the ricotta and Gorgonzola in a food processor until smooth; transfer to a medium bowl. Stir in the parsley, chives, capers, and mustard. Season to taste with salt and black pepper. Transfer to a serving bowl; sprinkle with paprika.

Makes about 1 1/2 cups.

Baccalà in Bianco

Salt Cod Purée

Practically identical to the Venetian baccalà mantecato—and often referred to as "bianco" (white) to differentiate it from the "rosso" (red) version on page 284—this addictive spread may be found in buffets throughout Trieste. Serve the baccalà at room temperature with slices of Italian bread.

1 pound dried salt cod

³/₄ cup plus 1 tablespoon olive oil, divided

5 garlic cloves, minced

. . .

Chopped fresh Italian parsley (optional)

🕭 In advance, place the salt cod in a large bowl and cover with water. Refrigerate for 48 hours, changing the water about every 12 hours; drain.

🕭 Remove any bones or skin from the fish; cut into 2-inch pieces. Place the fish in a large pot of water; bring to a boil over high heat. Cook until the fish flakes easily when tested with a fork, about 10–12 minutes. Remove the fish; reserve ¼ cup cooking liquid.

🕭 Heat 1 tablespoon olive oil in a small skillet over medium heat. Add the garlic; cook and stir until soft but not brown, about 1–2 minutes.

🕭 Purée the fish, garlic, and ¼ cup reserved cooking liquid in a food processor. Add ³/₄ cup olive oil, a little at a time, continuing to purée until creamy. Season to taste with black pepper. Transfer to a serving bowl; garnish with chopped parsley, if desired.

Makes about 3 cups.

Sardoni in Savor

Marinated Sardines

This ancient dish evolved out of the necessity to conserve fish and is evidence of the Venetian influence throughout Friuli. Called "sarde in saor" in Venetian dialect—"saor" having derived from "sapore," the Italian word for "flavor"—the dish may also contain raisins or pine nuts. While sardines are used in much of Friuli and the Veneto, European anchovies—known locally as "sardoni barcolani"—are more common in the area around Trieste and the nearby town of Barcola.

6 tablespoons olive oil, divided

1/2 medium yellow onion, thinly sliced

1/4 cup plus 1 1/2 teaspoons all-purpose flour, divided

3/4 cup plus 1 tablespoon water, divided

3/4 cup white wine vinegar

1 bay leaf

1/2 teaspoon salt

1/4 teaspoon ground black pepper

1 pound sardines, cleaned and gutted, heads removed

∞ Heat 2 tablespoons olive oil in a medium saucepan over medium-low heat. Add the onion; cook and stir until soft and translucent, about 15–20 minutes. In a small bowl, combine 1 1/2 teaspoons flour with 1 tablespoon water; stir the mixture into the onion. Add the vinegar, bay leaf, salt, black pepper, and the remaining 3/4 cup water; bring to a boil over high heat. Reduce heat to medium-low; cook for 20 minutes, stirring occasionally. Remove the bay leaf.

∞ Dredge the sardines in the remaining 1/4 cup flour. Heat the remaining 4 tablespoons olive oil in a large skillet over medium heat. Place the sardines in the skillet; cook until golden brown, about 5 minutes on each side. Transfer the sardines to an 8- or 9-inch square baking dish; pour the onion mixture over the sardines. Refrigerate for 24 hours.

Serves 4.

Granzievola alla Triestina
Trieste-Style Crab

Granzievola is Triestine dialect for "granseola"—also known as the European spider crab or spiny spider crab. While some chefs serve granzievola chilled with a simple dressing of lemon juice and olive oil, I have found the preparation shown here to be more characteristic of Triestine cuisine. In restaurants, the appetizer is typically served in an empty crab shell, but you may use small bowls instead.

½ cup olive oil

1 cup dry bread crumbs

¼ cup chopped fresh Italian parsley

1 pound lump crabmeat

1 cup water

¼ cup lemon juice

⁂ Heat the olive oil in a medium saucepan over medium-low heat. Add the bread crumbs and parsley; cook and stir until the bread crumbs begin to turn golden brown, about 5 minutes. Stir in the crabmeat, water, and lemon juice; cook until the crabmeat is warm, about 4–5 minutes, stirring occasionally. Season to taste with salt.

Serves 4.

Capesante Gratinate

Baked Scallops

Throughout the Mediterranean, scallops—as well as clams and mussels—are frequently baked and served in their shells. Scallop shells are oven-safe and may be purchased in gourmet cookware stores; you may also find discarded shells at seafood markets that sell fresh scallops. If shells are not available, use tartlet pans or oven-safe ramekins instead.

¾ cup dry bread crumbs

1 garlic clove, minced

2 tablespoons chopped fresh
    Italian parsley

¼ cup olive oil

· · ·

12 medium scallops (or 6 large
    scallops, halved crosswise)

¼ cup dry white wine

· · ·

1 lemon, cut into wedges

❧ Preheat oven to 425°F. In a small bowl, combine the bread crumbs, garlic, and parsley; stir in the olive oil.

❧ Line two baking sheets with aluminum foil; place twelve 4-inch scallop shells on the baking sheets, bunching the foil to help hold the shells in place.

❧ Place 1 scallop (or scallop half, if using large scallops) in each shell. Drizzle with the white wine, sprinkle with salt and black pepper, and top with the bread crumb mixture. Bake until the topping is golden brown and the scallops are cooked through, about 15 minutes. (If you are using two oven racks, switch the baking sheets halfway to ensure even browning.) Serve with lemon wedges.

Serves 4.

The Golden Age of Hapsburg Trieste

Today, the capital of Friuli-Venezia Giulia occupies a picture-perfect setting, the city practically spilling from the Carso slopes into the Gulf of Trieste. On a clear day, the azure sky echoes the domes of Trieste's most recognizable landmarks, while the hilltop Castello di San Giusto stands watch over the dark sea, its distant horizon, and an ever-constant flow of ships. For centuries, Trieste has witnessed the arrival and departure of merchant vessels, the city's port serving as a lifeline in transporting goods throughout the Mediterranean and the Orient.

Trieste's prominence as a port city began even with its earliest civilizations. Founded originally by proto-Veneto tribes as a cluster of fortified settlements on what is now San Giusto hill, the area became a Roman colony around 178 BC. In ancient times, the city—called Tergeste from the root *terg*, meaning "market"—developed into a thriving commercial center, and its strategic waterfront location soon attracted hordes of barbarian invaders.

Trieste was able to sustain its independence during the Middle Ages, but as the expanding Venetian Republic sought to gain a monopoly on the Adriatic Sea trade, the autonomous port city was unable to hold out much longer. In 1382, weary from more than a century of constant warfare with "La Serenissima," Trieste finally placed itself under the protection of the Hapsburgs of Austria. It was during this lengthy reign that Trieste enjoyed its true golden age, a period of growth, wealth, and prosperity.

Trieste's most lucrative years began in 1719, when Emperor Charles VI declared the city a free port. As customs barriers were lifted, large numbers of merchants arrived from all over Europe and the Mediterranean. This spawned an unprecedented population boom, which in turn stimulated urban development. Over the next two centuries, countless *palazzi* were designed in the baroque, neoclassical, neo-Renaissance, and art nouveau styles. Churches built during this period—including the Serbian Orthodox San Spiridione, the Greek Orthodox San Nicolò, and the Jewish Synagogue—reflected the mix of cultures and ethnicities that coexisted in relative harmony.

The Serbian Orthodox church of San Spiridione (FAR LEFT); the former Lloyd Triestino building now houses Friuli's regional government offices (LEFT); the waterfront along Piazza dell'Unità (BELOW); Trieste's Municipio (OPPOSITE, TOP); the Palazzo del Governo (OPPOSITE, BOTTOM).

During the early 19th century, a new grid of streets was laid adjacent to San Giusto hill. Named the Borgo Teresiana after the beloved empress Maria Theresa, this district was square and linear, more Viennese in character than the winding roads of ancient Tergeste. Canals connecting the Borgo to the waterfront were an efficient means of conveying goods to and from the docks; only one—the Canale Grande—remains today. Between San Giusto and the Borgo Teresiana lies Trieste's largest square, Piazza dell'Unità d'Italia. Overlooking the sea, the piazza is bordered on three sides by ornate Viennese-style palaces that currently house the city and regional government offices. In and around Piazza dell'Unità, a few original coffee houses still linger. Modeled after those found in cosmopolitan Vienna and Budapest, they evoke a sense of nostalgia for life in 19th-century Trieste.

It was in these coffee houses, perhaps over a cup of espresso and a slice of *torta Dobos*, that political revolutionaries plotted during the Irredentist movement that followed the 1861 unification

of Italy. Trieste did unite with Italy after World War I, although the city hung in limbo for more than a decade following World War II, occupied in turn by Germany, Yugoslavia, and a joint British-American government.

In 1954, Trieste ultimately rejoined with Italy, marking the beginning of a new era—one that acknowledges its Hapsburg roots but also looks toward a prosperous Italian future. Today, as the countries of Eastern Europe gradually seek to enter the European Union, Trieste is experiencing a cultural and economic resurgence as the center of a flourishing region.

CLOCKWISE FROM TOP RIGHT: *the colorful neo-Renaissance façade of Palazzo Gopcevich; in the 14th century, two parallel churches were joined to create the cathedral of San Giusto; the Faro della Vittoria lighthouse; remains of a Roman basilica at the Castello di San Giusto; an ancient Roman amphitheater.*

OPPOSITE: *the Canale Grande leads to the neoclassical Chiesa di Sant' Antonio Nuovo.*

Buffet Da Pepi

Best described as an old-world fast-food counter, the buffet emerged from the habit of Trieste's dockworkers and shopkeepers to take a quick midmorning snack, or *rebechin* (from the Italian *ribeccare*, meaning "to pick at"). Conveniently located near Trieste's seaport, train station, markets, and office buildings, buffets have served satisfying Mitteleuropean food for several centuries.

Said to be the oldest still in existence, Buffet Da Pepi was established in 1897 by Pepi Klajnsic and moved to its current location in 1903. After numerous changes of ownership, the buffet ended up in the hands of another Pepi—Pepi Tomazic. During World War II, the buffet suffered much damage from fires and looting, and inevitably it was forced to close down. Sadly, Tomazic was killed in a bombing, but his widow eventually reopened the buffet with much success, thus helping to preserve a long-standing Triestine tradition.

Ask any resident of Trieste where to eat and he will no doubt mention Buffet Da Pepi. Boiled pork sandwiches, *liptauer* on rye bread, and hard-boiled eggs make an ideal *rebechin* eaten standing at the counter with a glass of wine or beer. For a heartier meal, sit at one of the few small tables and order the *piatto misto*. You will be served a pig-shaped platter of assorted types of pork, including ham, bacon, sausage, and tongue, accompanied by sauerkraut, mustard, and freshly grated *cren* (horseradish).

While Buffet Da Pepi specializes in pork, many buffets serve a variety of local dishes, including *jota*, *goulasch*, *gnocchi di pane*, and *baccalà in bianco*. *Parsuto in crosta*, a large ham baked in a crust, is traditionally prepared at home for Easter but may be found in Trieste's buffets year round.

The piatto misto con kraut *makes a hearty lunch* (ABOVE); *the serving counter at Buffet Da Pepi is laden with pork, assorted sausages, hard-boiled eggs, and other typical buffet fare* (OPPOSITE).

Castello di Miramare

For the most dramatic view, the Castello di Miramare is best approached by boat. The starkly whitewashed castle perches on the tip of a promontory just north of Trieste, its wedding-cake façade glistening against sea and sky. Even on an overcast day, the castle makes a stunning picture, the gray skies a particularly fitting backdrop for this most tragic of castles.

Archduke Maximilian, brother of the Hapsburg emperor Franz Joseph, decided to settle in Trieste after being appointed Rear Admiral in the Austro-Hungarian Navy. He chose the headlands of Miramare as the site for his new home, which was built by Karl Junker according to the archduke's detailed designs. In 1860, Maximilian moved into the castle with his young wife, Carlotta of Belgium. They lived there only a few short years before their happiness came to an unfortunate end.

As an attempt to counter the growing strength of the United States, an imperial plan was devised in 1864 to re-establish a European power in North America. Napoleon III of France offered

Maximilian a position as emperor of Mexico, which the archduke reluctantly accepted. Just three years later, Maximilian was captured and executed by Mexican rebels. Carlotta, who had returned to Miramare only months earlier, was devastated. She moved into the Castelletto, a smaller villa on the castle grounds, where she went mad from grief. Legends tell of many subsequent house-guests—dukes, emperors, and generals—who have met a similarly tragic fate, thus giving Miramare a reputation for cursing anyone who sleeps under its roof.

Today, the castle is open for visitors to explore the couple's lavish apartments, all featuring the original 19th-century decorations and furnishings. Of note are Maximilian's study (designed in the style of a ship's cabin), library, and music room (where Carlotta often played the piano). During the 1930s, the castle's second floor was home to Duke Amadeo d'Aosta, who refurbished his apartment in the so-called Rationalist style of the day.

At the time Maximilian selected his castle's location, the landscape was practically barren. His goal was to transform this rocky Carso ter-

rain into a lush garden, rich with rare and exotic vegetation. Today, Miramare stands amid fifty-four acres of perfectly manicured gardens, complete with statues, ponds, and walking paths. Within the grounds is the Parco Tropicale, a garden filled with numerous species indigenous to South America, Africa, and Southeast Asia. Here, tropical plants and trees are home to butterflies, parrots, hummingbirds, flamingoes, bats, and reptiles.

Miramare's fairytale-like façade (ABOVE LEFT); *the castle grounds encompass fifty-four acres of lush gardens and walking paths* (ABOVE RIGHT); *the promenade behind the castle offers an incomparable view of the sea* (BELOW LEFT); *boats from Trieste drop passengers at the harbor of Grignano, one of three entrances to the park* (BELOW RIGHT); *the castle perches on a rocky promontory overlooking the sea* (OPPOSITE, TOP); *perfectly manicured gardens inside the park* (OPPOSITE, BOTTOM).

Southern Friuli:
PRIMI

Minestra di Bobici

Corn and Bean Soup

Originally a specialty of the Istrian peninsula, this tasty soup is now popular in Trieste—where bobici is dialect for "corn"—as well as in the villages of the Carso. The sweet corn and salty pancetta provide lots of flavor, making this one of my all-time favorite soups.

4 ounces dried borlotti (cranberry) beans

¼ cup olive oil, divided

1 medium yellow onion, chopped

2 garlic cloves, minced

4 ounces pancetta, chopped

6 cups water

1½ pounds white potatoes, peeled and cut into ½-inch cubes

2 ears corn, or about 2 cups whole kernels

½ teaspoon ground black pepper

& In advance, place the beans in a small bowl and cover with water. Let soak for at least 12 hours, or overnight; drain.

& Heat 2 tablespoons olive oil in a large pot over medium heat. Add the onion, garlic, and pancetta; cook and stir until the onion softens and the pancetta is brown and crisp, about 15 minutes. Add the beans and 6 cups water; bring to a boil over high heat. Reduce heat to low; simmer, covered, for 2 hours.

& Add the potatoes to the pot; return to a boil over high heat. Reduce heat to medium; cook until the potatoes are tender, about 25 minutes.

& Shave the corn kernels off the cobs using a sharp knife; rub the blunt edge of the knife over the cobs to extract their milky liquid. Add the corn kernels and the liquid to the pot, along with the black pepper; cook 10 minutes longer, stirring occasionally. Remove from heat; stir in the remaining 2 tablespoons olive oil. Season to taste with salt.

Serves 4 to 6.

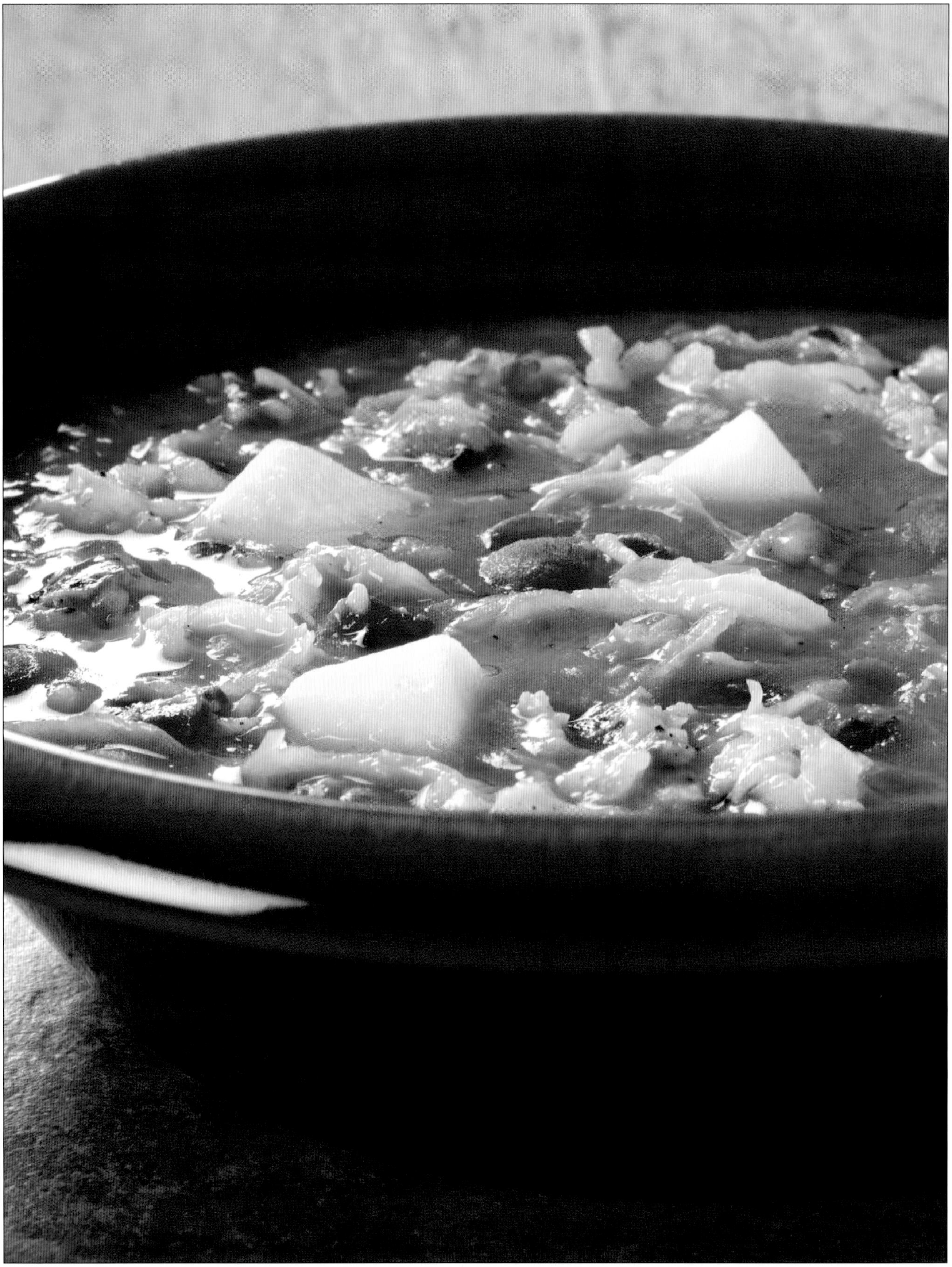

Jota

This soup—also spelled "iota"—is considered to be one of Trieste's native dishes. A similar soup is made in Carnia using brovada in place of the sauerkraut.

8 ounces dried borlotti
   (cranberry) beans
2 bay leaves
8 cups water
1 pound white potatoes, peeled
   and cut into ½-inch cubes
2 tablespoons olive oil
2 ounces pancetta, chopped
2 garlic cloves, minced
2 tablespoons all-purpose flour
1 teaspoon caraway seeds
2 cups sauerkraut
½ teaspoon ground black
   pepper

⁜ In advance, place the beans in a medium bowl and cover with water. Let soak for at least 12 hours, or overnight; drain.

⁜ Place the beans in a large pot, along with the bay leaves and 8 cups water; bring to a boil over high heat. Reduce heat to low; simmer, covered, for 2½ hours.

⁜ Meanwhile, place the potatoes in a medium pot filled with water; bring to a boil over high heat. Cook until just tender, about 15 minutes. Drain the potatoes and divide into two portions; mash half the potatoes, leaving the other half in cubes.

⁜ Heat the olive oil in a large skillet over medium heat. Add the pancetta and garlic; cook and stir until brown and crisp, about 5 minutes. Add the flour and caraway seeds; cook and stir 1 minute longer. Add the sauerkraut and black pepper; cook and stir until thickened, about 4–5 minutes.

⁜ After the beans have simmered for 2½ hours, remove half the beans, plus a little of the liquid; purée in a blender or food processor. Add the puréed beans back to the pot, along with the sauerkraut mixture and potatoes; return to a boil over high heat. Reduce heat to low; cook for 20 minutes, stirring occasionally. Remove the bay leaves; season to taste with salt.

Serves 6.

Brodeto alla Triestina

Trieste-Style Seafood Stew

This fish soup is virtually indistinguishable from the numerous varieties of "zuppa di pesce" found throughout the Mediterranean, including Livorno's cacciucco, Ancona's brodetto, and Marseille's bouillabaisse. Aside from the obvious use of locally caught seafood, Trieste's brodeto is unique in one aspect of its preparation—the fish is typically pan-fried before being added to the tomato-based stock.

1 pound fish fillets (such as sea bass or cod), skinned and cut into 2-inch pieces

1/3 cup all-purpose flour

5 tablespoons olive oil, divided

1/2 medium yellow onion, finely chopped

1 garlic clove, minced

1 (15-ounce) can tomato sauce, or 1 3/4 cups

1/2 cup dry white wine

1 1/2 cups water

1/4 teaspoon ground black pepper

12 mussels, scrubbed and debearded

12 clams, scrubbed

4 whole jumbo shrimp

4 ounces squid, bodies sliced into 1/2-inch rings, tentacles left whole

2 tablespoons chopped fresh Italian parsley

· · ·

CROSTINI:

1 small baguette (about 4 ounces), sliced 1/4-inch-thick

6 tablespoons olive oil

1 to 2 garlic cloves, peeled and sliced in half

❧ Sprinkle the fish fillets with salt; dredge in flour. Heat 3 tablespoons olive oil in a large skillet over medium heat. Place the fish in the skillet; cook until the fish flakes easily when tested with a fork, about 2–4 minutes on each side.

❧ Heat the remaining 2 tablespoons olive oil in a large pot over medium-low heat. Add the onion and garlic; cook and stir until soft and translucent, about 15 minutes. Add the tomato sauce, white wine, 1 1/2 cups water, and black pepper. Bring to a boil over medium-high heat. Add the mussels, clams, shrimp, and squid; cook until the shrimp turn pink and the mussel and clam shells open, about 4–5 minutes. (Discard any shells that do not open.) Add the cooked fish fillets, along with the parsley. Season to taste with salt. Serve with crostini.

FOR THE CROSTINI:

❧ Preheat oven to 350°F. Brush both sides of the baguette slices with olive oil; place on a baking sheet. Bake until crisp and golden brown, about 10–12 minutes. Cool to room temperature. Rub the bread with garlic to taste.

Serves 4.

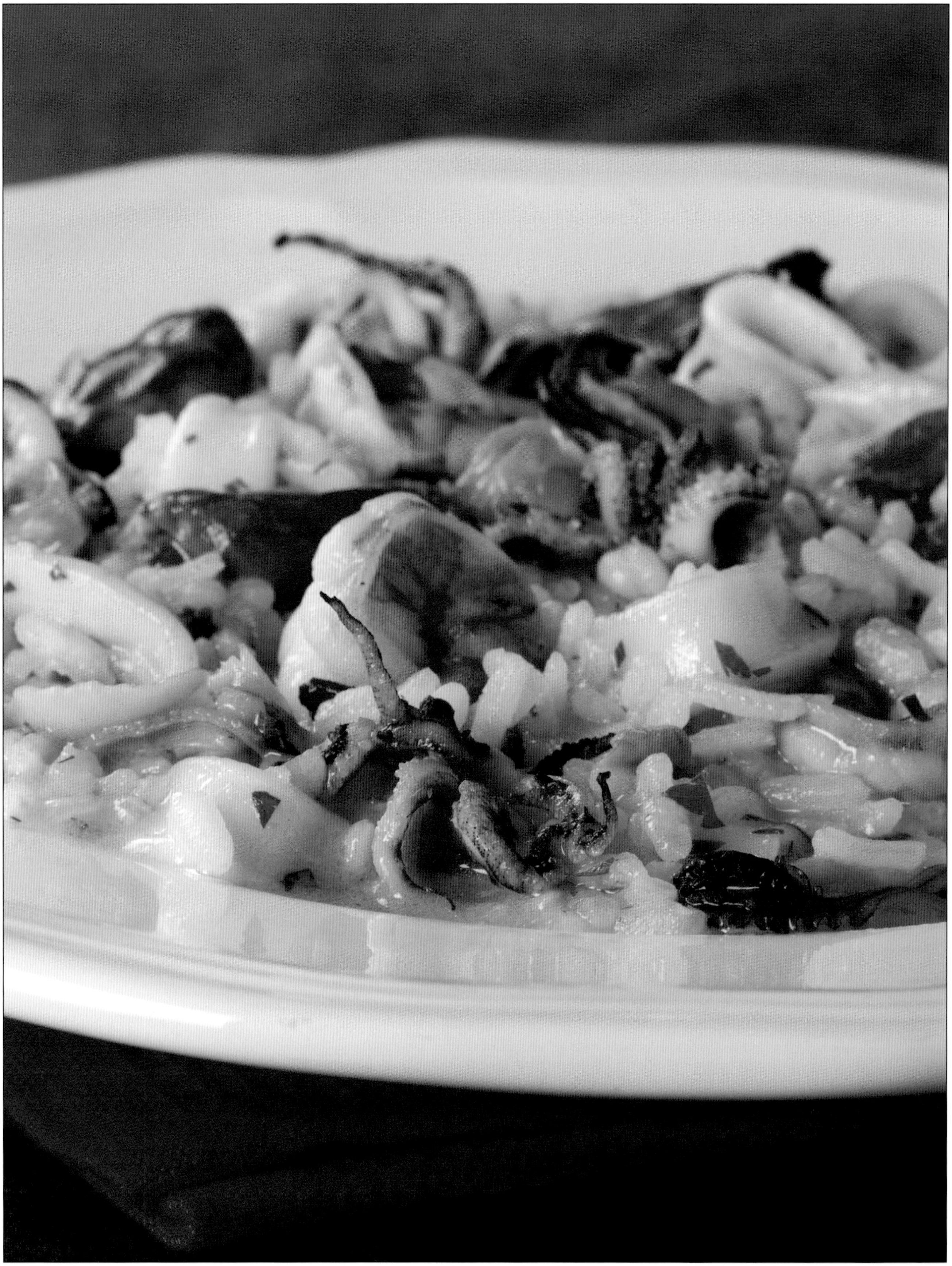

Risotto alla Maranese

Marano-Style Seafood Risotto

This risotto is named after the coastal village of Marano Lagunare, where chefs typically use local wedge shell clams—called "telline" or "arselle"—along with squid, langoustines, and occasionally mussels. In this recipe, inspired by the risotto at Trattoria Alla Laguna, langoustines are replaced by shrimp. If you are able to find telline, the shells are so tiny that it is not necessary to remove them before serving.

1 pound mussels, scrubbed and
    debearded

1 pound clams, scrubbed

½ cup dry white wine

3 tablespoons olive oil

1 garlic clove, minced

8 ounces squid, bodies sliced
    into ½-inch rings, tentacles
    left whole

4 ounces medium shrimp,
    shelled and deveined

¼ cup chopped fresh Italian
    parsley

4 tablespoons butter

1 cup Arborio (Italian short-
    grain) rice

3½ cups fish stock, heated (or
    substitute 2 cups clam juice
    and 1½ cups water)

❦ Place the mussels and clams in a large, deep skillet; pour in the white wine. Cook, covered, over medium heat until the shells open, about 5–10 minutes. Remove the mussels and clams from their shells. (Discard the shells, along with any that do not open.) Reserve the cooking liquid.

❦ Heat the olive oil in a large skillet over medium heat. Add the garlic; cook and stir until it begins to turn golden brown, about 2 minutes. Add the squid and shrimp; cook until the shrimp turn pink and the squid turns opaque, about 3–4 minutes. Stir in the mussels, clams, reserved cooking liquid, and parsley.

❦ Melt the butter in a large pot over medium-low heat. Add the rice; cook and stir for 5 minutes to allow the rice to absorb the butter. Add ½ cup warm fish stock; cook and stir until the rice has absorbed most of the liquid. Continue stirring in stock, ½ cup at a time, until the rice is cooked, about 25 minutes. Stir in the seafood mixture. Season to taste with salt and black pepper.

Serves 4.

Gnocchi di Susine
Plum-Filled Gnocchi

These fruit-filled dumplings of Austro-Hungarian origin are typically served as a first course, although their sweetness lends easily toward dessert. Italians normally use their small native plums, which are pitted and then wrapped in the dough whole; if using standard red or black plums, they may be cut into smaller pieces, as shown here. Fresh plums are most commonly used, although prunes may be substituted when plums are out of season. Alternatively, the gnocchi may be filled with apricots or cherries.

DOUGH:

2 pounds white potatoes,
    peeled and quartered

4 cups all-purpose flour

4 teaspoons salt

1 egg

. . .

½ cup sugar, divided

6 medium plums (about 1 to
    1 ¼ pounds), pitted and cut
    into 8 wedges each

. . .

½ cup (1 stick) butter

¼ cup dry bread crumbs

Ground cinnamon

Sugar

FOR THE DOUGH:

⁖ Place the potatoes in a large pot filled with water; bring to a boil over high heat. Cook until tender, about 20–25 minutes. Drain the potatoes and place in a large bowl; mash well. Cool to room temperature. Add the flour, salt, and egg; mix thoroughly to form a soft dough.

TO PREPARE:

⁖ Roll the dough into four dozen balls. Flatten each into a 3-inch circle; sprinkle with ½ teaspoon sugar and top with a plum wedge. Wrap the dough around the plum and seal tightly. (At this point, the sugar will begin to draw the juice out of the plums; placing the filled gnocchi on a wooden board will help prevent them from getting soggy.)

⁖ Bring a large pot of lightly salted water to a boil over high heat. Working in batches, place the gnocchi in the water, taking care not to overcrowd the pot. Once the gnocchi have risen to the surface, cook until the dough is tender, about 10 minutes longer; remove them promptly with a slotted spoon.

⁖ Melt the butter in a large skillet over medium heat. Add the bread crumbs; cook and stir until golden brown, about 3–4 minutes. Add the gnocchi and toss to coat with bread crumbs. Divide the gnocchi among serving dishes. Drizzle with the excess butter and bread crumbs; sprinkle with cinnamon and sugar.

Serves 6.

VARIATION:

⁖ Substitute 1 pound dried plums (about four dozen) and use ¼ cup sugar. Fill the cavity of each dried plum with ¼ teaspoon sugar. Form four dozen balls of dough. Make an indentation in the dough, place a dried plum inside, and wrap the dough around, sealing tightly. Cook and serve as described above.

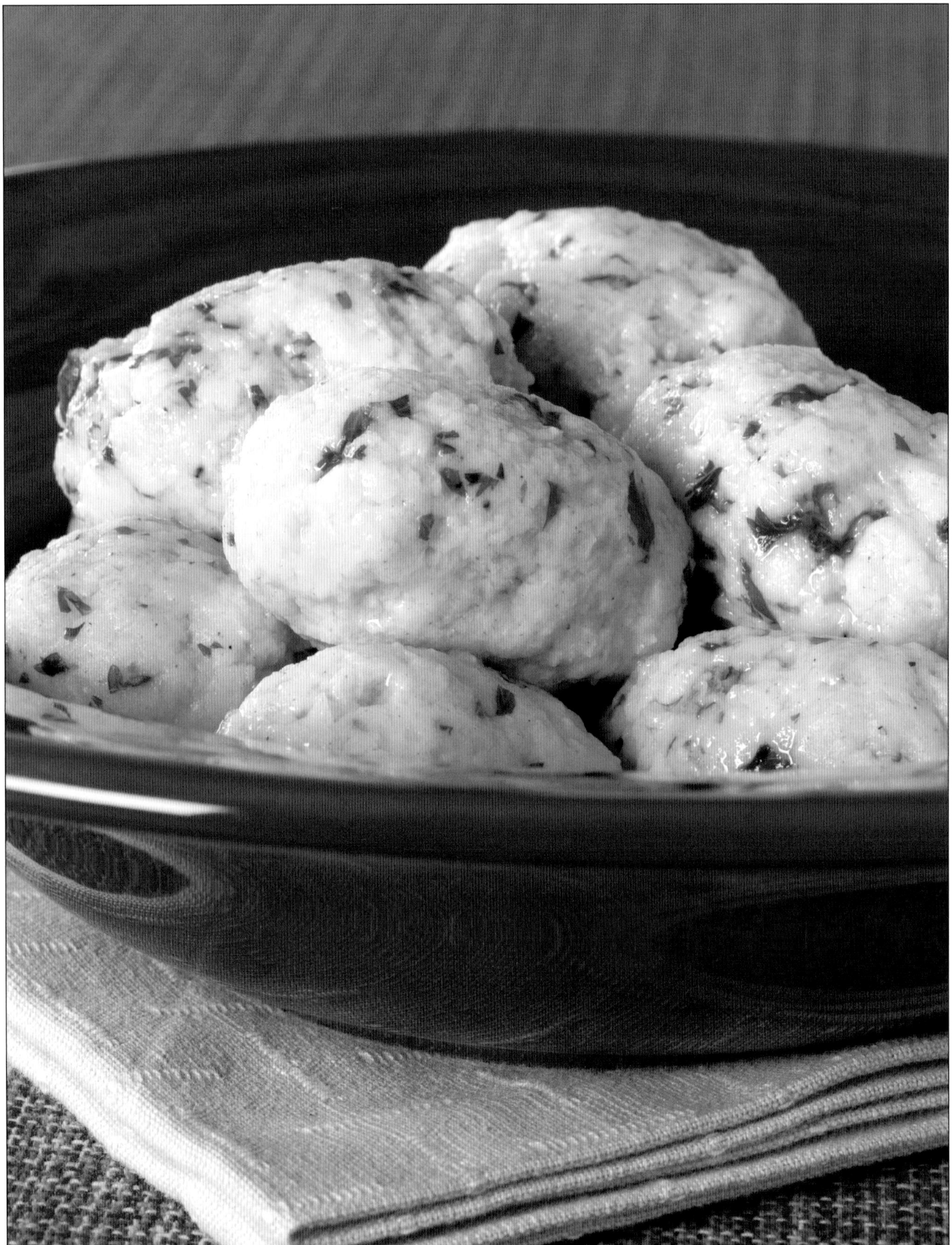

Gnocchi di Pane

Bread Gnocchi

These bread-based dumplings are similar to Austria's knödeln and may be served with either beef broth or the pan sauce from a braised meat such as stinco di vitello (page 275). They also make a fine accompaniment to goulasch (page 272). If Montasio stagionato is not available, you may substitute any aged cheese such as Parmigiano-Reggiano.

1 pound Italian bread or
    baguette

2 ounces pancetta, chopped

1 cup whole milk

2 eggs

1 cup grated Montasio
    stagionato

½ cup all-purpose flour

½ cup chopped fresh Italian
    parsley

1 teaspoon salt

½ teaspoon ground black
    pepper

. . .

1½ cups beef broth, heated

 Slice the crust off the bread. (Discard the crust, or reserve for another use.) Tear the bread into ½-inch pieces and place in a large bowl.

 Place the pancetta in a small skillet over medium heat; cook and stir until brown and crisp, about 5 minutes. Add the pancetta (including the excess oil in the skillet) to the bowl of bread, along with the milk, eggs, Montasio cheese, flour, parsley, salt, and black pepper; mix well. Form the dough into 2-inch oblong balls.

 Bring a large pot of lightly salted water to a boil over high heat. Working in batches, place the gnocchi in the water, taking care not to overcrowd the pot. Once the gnocchi have risen to the surface, cook until the dough is tender, about 15 minutes longer; remove them promptly with a slotted spoon. Serve with the warm beef broth.

Serves 6.

Strucolo de Spinaze
Spinach-Filled Pasta Roll

Strucolo means "strudel" in the Triestine dialect, although restaurants may also refer to it as a "rotolo" or "rollata." Common throughout the Carso region, this dish may be prepared with either a basic pasta dough, as shown here, or a potato-based gnocchi dough. The strucolo is typically served with a few spoonfuls of beef broth or, if available, sugo d'arrosto (pan sauces from a roasted or braised meat). If Montasio stagionato is not available, you may substitute any aged cheese such as Parmigiano-Reggiano.

FILLING:

1 pound fresh spinach leaves

1 cup fresh ricotta

3/4 cup grated Montasio stagionato

1 teaspoon salt

1/2 teaspoon ground black pepper

1/2 teaspoon ground nutmeg

. . .

DOUGH:

3/4 cup semolina flour

1 egg

1 tablespoon olive oil

1/4 teaspoon salt

. . .

1/2 cup beef broth, heated

FOR THE FILLING:

  Place the spinach (plus 1–2 tablespoons water if using packaged, prewashed spinach) in a large pot over medium-low heat. Cook, covered, until wilted, about 10 minutes, stirring occasionally. Drain the spinach thoroughly, squeezing out all excess liquid. Coarsely chop the spinach and place in a large bowl; cool to room temperature. Stir in the ricotta, Montasio cheese, salt, black pepper, and nutmeg. Refrigerate for 1 hour, or until ready to use.

FOR THE DOUGH:

  In a medium bowl, combine the flour, egg, olive oil, and salt. Transfer the dough to a clean surface; knead until the flour is fully incorporated and the mixture becomes smooth and elastic, about 10 minutes. (If the dough is too dry or crumbly, lightly moisten your fingers with water during kneading until you reach the desired texture.) Cover with plastic wrap and let rest for 30 minutes.

TO PREPARE:

  Roll the dough to form a 12- by 18-inch rectangle. Spread the spinach mixture over the dough, leaving a 1-inch border on all sides. Starting with one short side, roll up jelly roll style, sealing the ends tightly. (Moisten the dough with a little water to help seal, if necessary.) Wrap the strudel inside an 18-inch-square piece of cheesecloth, tying the ends securely with string.

  Bring a large pot of lightly salted water to a boil over high heat. Place the strudel in the water; cook for 1 hour, adding more water as necessary to keep the strudel submerged. (If the strudel is not entirely covered by water, you may turn it over after 30 minutes to ensure even cooking.) Remove the strudel from the cheesecloth. Cut into 1-inch slices; serve with the warm beef broth.

Serves 4 to 6.

Grotta Gigante

Spacious enough to accommodate Saint Peter's Basilica, the Grotta Gigante is the largest tourist-accessible cave in the world. In fact, it has made *The Guinness Book of World Records* with its vast dimensions: 351 feet high, 213 feet wide, and 918 feet long. The cavern is located in the Carso, the rocky plateau that separates Trieste's coastline from neighboring Slovenia and an area rich with caves and underground rivers.

The giant cave was first explored in 1840 by Antonio Federico Lindner, in a search for the subterranean portion of the Timavo River, which was to be used in planning Trieste's aqueduct. In 1908, the Grotta Gigante was made accessible for guided tours, with four thousand candles illuminating the cavern; it was not fully equipped to handle tourism, however, until the installation of electricity in 1957.

Upon entering the Grotta Gigante, a narrow tunnel opens into the enormous cavern. The echo of dripping water fills the silence. Five hundred steps descend past walls covered with curtains of stalactites in shades of white, orange, and brown. The cave's stalagmites are tall and slender with flat tops, the calcite concretions resembling stacks of dishes due to the height from which the water drips. Ruggero Column is the cave's tallest at thirty-nine feet. Other formations have been given names such as the Gnome, the Pulpit, the Mushroom, the Palm, and the Nymphs' Palace.

In the center of the cavern, two pendulums are suspended from the upper roof and encased in long plastic tubes. Geophysicists from the University of Trieste built this structure in 1959 as a project to study the earth's tides. The pendulums are sensitive enough to pick up previously undetectable movement caused by changes in the tide and barometric pressure.

This group of stalagmites is known as the "Nymphs' Palace" (ABOVE).

Risiera di San Sabba

Located in the industrial outskirts just south of Trieste is the Risiera di San Sabba. This former rice-husking plant was taken over by the Nazis during World War II and served as a prison for hostages, political prisoners, and Jews, as well as a transit camp for deportees on their way to Auschwitz. When the Germans fitted the building with a giant gas oven, the Risiera became Italy's only concentration camp to be used for mass exterminations. At least five thousand prisoners are believed to have been executed here between the 1943 German invasion and the liberation of Trieste in 1945.

In 1965, the Risiera di San Sabba was declared a national monument. Inside the austere brick and concrete structure, visitors can view actual prison cells, the death chamber, and a permanent exhibit of photographs and documents. The crematorium was destroyed by the Nazis during their retreat, but some of its remains are still visible along one wall of the stark courtyard. Today, the space where the oven once stood is memorialized with a large steel pavement and serves as a chilling reminder of the horrors of the Holocaust.

Sculptures pay tribute to Holocaust victims in the Risiera's courtyard (BELOW) *and in its exhibition rooms* (ABOVE).

The Carso Plateau

High above Trieste's coastline is a narrow ribbon of jagged rocks eroded by rain and wind, plunging fearlessly into the sea. Called *carso* in Italian, this "karst" landscape of limestone and dolomite conceals an underground world of vast caverns and grottoes, carved by the waters of the Timavo River, which runs below ground for much of its course from Slovenia to the Adriatic Sea. Throughout these miles of subterranean streams and tunnels, centuries of dripping water have sculpted grand stone palaces and carpeted the ground with tall, rocky pillars.

Above ground on the plateau lie acres of evergreen forests and flower-strewn ravines. The land is peppered with large sinkholes, called *doline*, that have been caused by collapsed cave vaults. Here, the warm sea breeze meets the chilling, northeasterly *bora* wind, producing a convergence of Mediterranean and Alpine climates. Oak and spruce mingle with citrus and olive trees, while the landscape is blanketed with vineyards. Only one body of water flows above the plateau—the Rosandra Stream. Slicing through the deep gorge of the Val Rosandra near the Carso's eastern border, these waters once supplied the ancient Roman colony of Tergeste via a seven-mile-long aqueduct.

The Carso comprises over fifty villages and about twenty thousand residents, most of Slavic origin. Isolated by the surrounding terrain, the Carsic people have sustained their own cultural identity and character, one that is unique to Friuli-Venezia Giulia. Street signs are written in both Italian and Slovene, and the Slovenian newspaper *Primorski Dnevnik* is sold throughout the province.

Countless traditional customs are celebrated here, such as the Nozze Carsiche, or "Carsic wedding," which takes place in August every two years. This rite is based on the traditional marriage ceremony of the late 19th century and today attracts thousands of observers. The festivities last four days, beginning with the bachelor and bachelorette parties, followed by the transport of the dowry to the groom's house. The party culminates on Sunday with the wedding ceremony at the Santuario di Monrupino, where around five hundred people participate, all dressed in traditional

costume. This is followed by a bridal procession to the town of Rupingrande, where the bride is given away to the groom's family at the Casa Carsica, an 18th-century Carsic-Friulian house that has been converted into an ethnographic museum. After the ceremony, guests are served a traditional veal stew called *zvacet* at the reception dinner.

Limestone cliffs line the Via Napoleonica, a panoramic path connecting the towns of Opicina and Prosecco (ABOVE); the parish house adjacent to the sanctuary at Monrupino is one of the oldest structures in the Carso (LEFT).

Throughout the Carso countryside, farmhouses open their doors to the public for wine tasting and the sale of other artisanal products. Called *osmizze*, these temporary roadside taverns are indicated by a *frasca*—a leafy cluster of branches hung above the door. Tables are set up inside the courtyard—traditional Carsic homes had stone walls built around a central courtyard as protection from the fierce *bora* winds—and villagers gather to sample the local vintage and feast on homemade cheese and *salumi*. The custom began in 1784 with an imperial decree that allowed peasants to sell their excess wine and produce in an unlicensed restaurant for eight days each year. The word *osmizza* is thus derived from the Slovene word *osem*, meaning "eight."

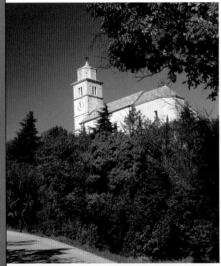

CLOCKWISE FROM TOP RIGHT: *a cluster of branches hangs over the entrance to Azienda Agricola Škerk, a wine producer and osmizza in Prepotto; the contemporary architecture of Santuario di Monte Grisa perches high above the sea; hiking paths in the Val Rosandra provide a stunning view of the surrounding Carso mountains; the obelisk at Opicina was built in 1830 to commemorate a new road connecting Trieste with Austria; autumn colors in the Val Rosandra; the medieval Santuario di Monrupino was built on a hill above the ruins of a prehistoric fort and is the site of the traditional Carsic wedding ceremony.*

Casa Carsica

CLOCKWISE FROM ABOVE: *inside this well-preserved 18th-century house, walnuts and other produce were [stored] in the loft, where older fam-*[...]

flasks, [...] stable; the fogolâr is the heart of the kitchen.

Gorizia: A Tale of Two Cities

After years of being split by the Communist iron curtain, Gorizia has gradually begun to reunite with its Slavic counterpart, Nova Gorica. Centuries ago, the city was home to the powerful counts of Gorizia. From their hilltop castle, they ruled for four centuries a territory that extended from Tyrol to Croatia. In the 16th century, the city was acquired by Austria's Hapsburg monarchy. Except for brief periods of domination by the Venetian Republic and later Napoleon, Gorizia remained Austrian until after World War I, when the region was united with Italy.

Following World War II, Gorizia experienced a similar fate as Berlin. When the Paris Peace Treaty divided the city between Italy and Yugoslavia, fences were literally erected through private gardens, backyards, and driveways, segregating families and neighbors and cutting off farmers from their land. Italy received the best end of the deal, taking the main share of the city and its thirty-seven thousand residents. Yugoslavia was given only the outskirts; however, Communist dictator Josip Tito determined to rebuild those suburbs into a new city that would rival the original, hence the name Nova Gorica, or "new Gorizia."

With the collapse of the Communist bloc—and the subsequent breakup of Yugoslavia—Nova Gorica became part of Slovenia. Today, the city flaunts a progressive character, complete with sporting arenas, casinos, and discotheques. Italian Gorizia, in contrast, abounds with Venetian, Gothic, and Slavic architecture, including the onion-domed church of Sant'Ignazio and a fortified hilltop *castello*, not to mention the winding medieval streets of the city's historical quarter.

In the decades following World War II, border posts began to reopen to local residents in order for them to work and do business in both cities. Many unemployed Slovenians found jobs in Gorizia, while others were lured by the shopping. Italians, on the other hand, ventured across the border to gamble in Nova Gorica's casinos.

When Slovenia joined the European Union in 2004, border controls, military checkpoints, and division walls all but disappeared. Although the comparison has often been made with East and West Berlin, Gorizia and Nova Gorica have no plans to formally reunite into one city, but will sustain their current political jurisdiction and national identities. Even so, most residents already speak both languages, and the cities share many public services, including joint community events and an enhanced bus route. On a cultural level, Gorizia's two faces seem destined to merge now that it is no longer a city divided.

The tiny Chiesa di Santo Spirito is Gorizia's oldest church (BELOW LEFT); *a courtyard inside the Castello di Gorizia* (BELOW RIGHT); *the Chiesa di Sant'Ignazio features characteristic onion-shaped domes* (OPPOSITE).

ഇൻ♋

Southern Friuli:
SECONDI

ഇൻ♋

Goulasch

Hungarian-Style Beef Stew

Derived from the Hungarian word "gulyàs"—meaning "herdsman"—and called "gòlas" in Triestine dialect, goulasch came to Friuli during the reign of the Austro-Hungarian Empire. The dish is prevalent throughout the region, especially in the mountainous area along the Austrian border, where it is prepared in the traditional style using paprika, and in the city of Trieste, where goulasch is commonly made with tomato sauce. While the latter version seems more uniquely Italian, there is still an endless debate among locals as to which version is most authentically Friulian. In Trieste, goulasch may be served with polenta (page 196), gnocchi di pane (page 259), or patate in tecia (page 299).

½ cup olive oil

2 medium yellow onions, thinly
  sliced

2 pounds beef rump roast or
  stew meat, cut into 1-inch
  cubes

1 tablespoon all-purpose flour

1 tablespoon paprika

1 tablespoon chopped fresh
  rosemary

1 tablespoon chopped fresh
  marjoram

1 bay leaf

1 (15-ounce) can tomato sauce,
  or 1 ¾ cups

2 cups water

❧ Heat the olive oil in a large, deep skillet over medium-low heat. Add the onions; cook and stir until soft and translucent, about 25–30 minutes. Sprinkle the beef with salt; add to the skillet with the onions. Increase heat to medium; cook and stir until the beef begins to brown, about 10 minutes. Add the flour, paprika, rosemary, marjoram, and bay leaf; cook and stir 5 minutes longer. Add the tomato sauce and water; bring to a boil over high heat. Reduce heat to low; cook, partially covered, until the beef is tender and the sauce has thickened, about 3 hours, stirring occasionally. Remove the bay leaf; season to taste with salt.

Serves 6.

Stinco di Vitello

Braised Veal Shank

Braised veal shank remains quite popular in the Carso and is typically accompanied by patate in tecia (page 299). Prepared in a similar manner, stinco di maiale (pork shank) is common throughout the rest of Friuli.

1 whole veal shank (about 3 to
    4 pounds)

2 tablespoons olive oil

1 onion, chopped

1 carrot, chopped

1 celery stalk, chopped

2 garlic cloves, peeled

3 sprigs fresh rosemary

3 sprigs fresh thyme

3 sprigs fresh marjoram

1 teaspoon salt

½ cup dry white wine

2 cups beef broth, divided

℠ Preheat oven to 350°F. Sprinkle the veal with salt and black pepper. Heat the olive oil in a large, oven-safe pot over medium-high heat. Place the veal in the pot; cook for 15 minutes, turning to brown each side. Remove from heat; transfer the veal to a plate. Place the onion, carrot, celery, garlic, rosemary, thyme, and marjoram in the pot; sprinkle with 1 teaspoon salt. Place the veal on top of the vegetables; pour in the white wine and 1 cup beef broth. Bake, covered, for 1 hour. Pour in the remaining 1 cup beef broth. Bake, covered, until the meat is tender, about 1 hour longer (it should register at least 170°F on a meat thermometer).

℠ Transfer the veal to a serving platter; let rest for 10 minutes. Strain the pan juices and serve with the veal.

Serves 4.

Cevapcici con Ajvar   *Grilled Sausages with Bell Pepper Sauce*

These tiny, grilled sausages were inspired by the Middle Eastern spiced meat patties brought to the region by the Ottoman Turks. Eaten throughout Slovenia and Croatia, as well as in the provinces of Trieste and Gorizia, they are typically served with chopped onion and a red bell pepper sauce called ajvar (also spelled "haivar").

8 ounces ground beef

8 ounces ground pork

2 tablespoons finely chopped onion

2 garlic cloves, minced

1 teaspoon paprika

1 teaspoon salt

1/2 teaspoon ground black pepper

Dash cayenne pepper

. . .

AJVAR:

1 large red bell pepper

1 small eggplant

1 tablespoon olive oil

1 teaspoon red wine vinegar

1 teaspoon sugar

Dash cayenne pepper

. . .

Finely chopped onion

❧ In a medium bowl, combine the ground beef, ground pork, onion, garlic, paprika, salt, black pepper, and cayenne pepper. Roll the mixture into sausages about 3 inches long and 3/4 inch in diameter.

❧ Preheat grill (or heat a large skillet over medium-high heat). Place the sausages on the grill; cook until done, about 5–6 minutes, turning to brown each side. Serve with ajvar and chopped onion.

FOR THE AJVAR:

❧ Preheat oven to 400°F. Place the bell pepper and eggplant on a baking sheet; bake until the eggplant is tender and the bell pepper skin begins to brown, about 30–40 minutes. When the bell pepper is cool enough to handle, remove and discard the skin, stem, and seeds. Slice open the eggplant and scoop out the flesh. Place the bell pepper and eggplant in a food processor, along with the olive oil, vinegar, sugar, and cayenne pepper; purée until smooth. Season to taste with salt.

Serves 4.

Calamari Ripieni

Stuffed Squid

Popular in many coastal regions of Italy, as well as along the Istrian peninsula, stuffed calamari are featured on menus at the numerous seafood restaurants that line Trieste's waterfront.

¼ cup olive oil, divided

2 pounds squid, tentacles finely chopped and bodies left whole

4 garlic cloves, minced

¼ cup chopped fresh Italian parsley

1½ cups dry bread crumbs

½ teaspoon salt

½ teaspoon ground black pepper

. . .

1 lemon, cut into wedges

⁎ Heat 2 tablespoons olive oil in a small skillet over medium heat. Add the chopped squid tentacles, garlic, and parsley; cook and stir until the squid turns opaque, about 2–3 minutes. Transfer to a medium bowl; stir in the bread crumbs, salt, and black pepper. Carefully stuff the squid bodies with the bread crumb mixture, using a wooden pick to close the opening.

⁎ Preheat grill (or heat a large skillet over medium-high heat). Brush the squid with the remaining 2 tablespoons olive oil. Place the squid on the grill; cook until opaque, about 6–8 minutes, turning halfway to brown both sides. Remove the wooden picks; serve with lemon wedges.

Serves 4.

Boreto alla Gradese   *Grado-Style Fish Steaks with Vinegar*

Not to be confused with the soup brodeto (page 252), this fish dish hails from the coastal town of Grado, where it is prepared with garlic and vinegar and served with white polenta (page 196). Also called "boreto alla graesana" in local dialect, this recipe was adapted from the one at Grado's elegant Tavernetta All'Androna.

2 pounds assorted fish steaks
(such as eel, turbot, bass,
or monkfish), cut 1 to 1½
inches thick
3 tablespoons olive oil
4 garlic cloves, peeled and
slightly crushed
½ cup fish stock or clam juice
½ cup white wine vinegar
* * *
Freshly ground black pepper

ᏯᎧ Sprinkle the fish steaks with salt and black pepper.

ᏯᎧ Heat the olive oil in a large, deep skillet over medium heat. Add the garlic cloves; cook until golden brown, about 5–6 minutes. Remove and discard the garlic. Place the fish steaks in the skillet; cook until golden brown, about 4–5 minutes on each side. Add the fish stock and vinegar; cook until the fish flakes easily when tested with a fork, about 8–12 minutes longer. Divide the fish steaks among serving plates.

ᏯᎧ Increase heat to medium-high; cook the sauce until thick and reduced by half, about 5 minutes. Spoon the sauce over the fish steaks; sprinkle liberally with freshly ground black pepper.

Serves 4 to 6.

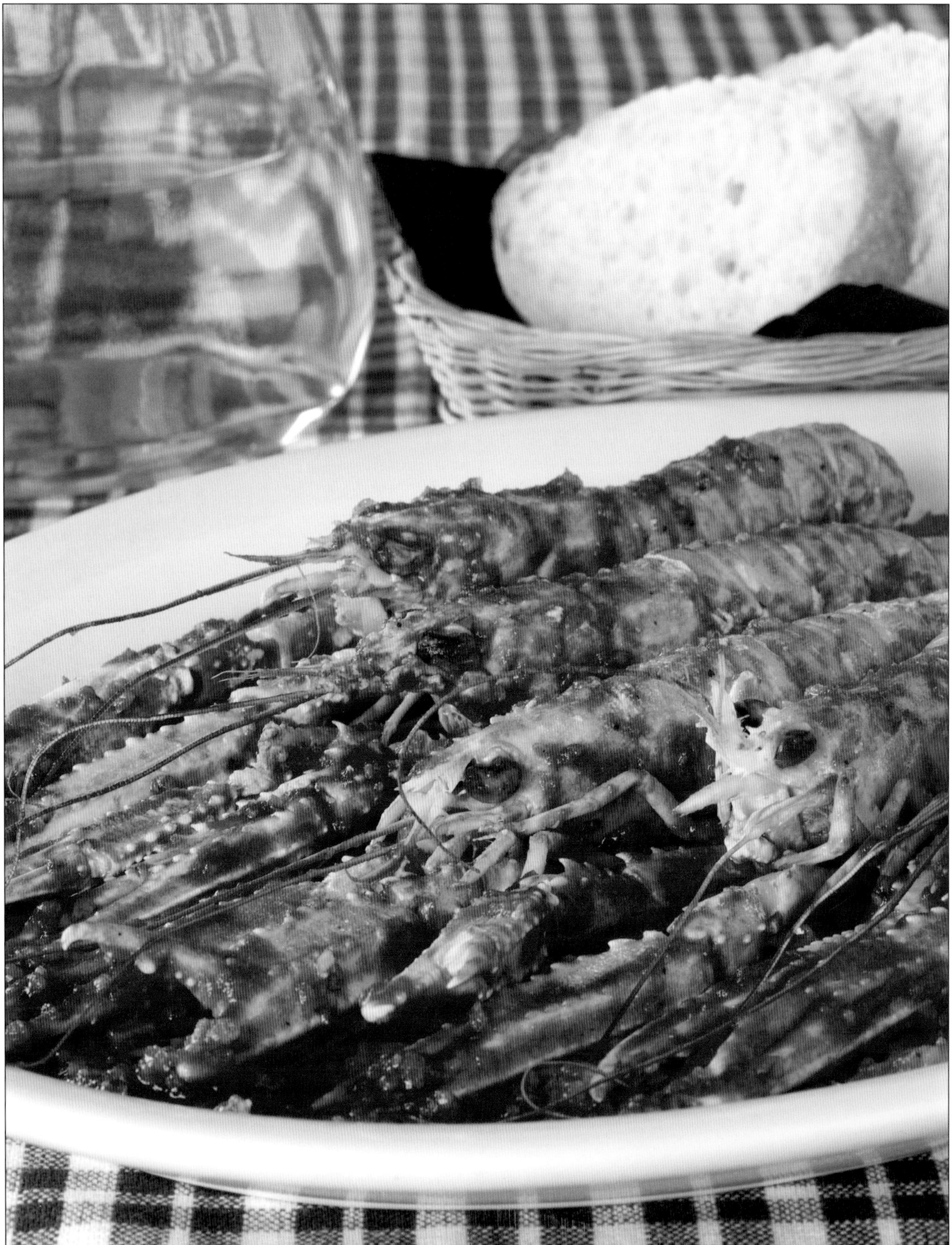

Scampi alla Busara

Langoustines in Tomato Sauce

Scampi—also known as langoustines, Norway lobsters, or Dublin Bay prawns—are found almost exclusively in North Atlantic waters. They are not common in the Mediterranean except for the northernmost Adriatic Sea. In years past, along the route from Istria to Trieste where scampi are plentiful, sailors would cook their meals on board ship in a terracotta or iron pot called a "busara." Canoce (mantis shrimp) may also be prepared in this style, as well as spiny crab, lobster, or even fish. Since langoustines can be tricky to find in the United States—most are imported from Scotland—you may substitute any type of fish or shellfish that you like. Serve with plenty of Italian bread to soak up the sauce.

¼ cup olive oil

1 medium yellow onion, finely
   chopped

2 garlic cloves, minced

3 tablespoons dry bread crumbs

1 (15-ounce) can tomato sauce,
   or 1 ¾ cups

½ cup dry white wine

2 tablespoons chopped fresh
   Italian parsley

½ teaspoon ground black
   pepper

2 pounds whole langoustines

৪০ Heat the olive oil in a large pot over medium-low heat. Add the onion and garlic; cook and stir until the onion begins to soften, about 8–10 minutes. Add the bread crumbs; cook and stir until golden brown, about 2–3 minutes. Stir in the tomato sauce, white wine, parsley, and black pepper. Place the langoustines in the pot; bring to a boil over high heat. Reduce heat to medium-low; cook, covered, until the langoustines turn pink, about 3–5 minutes. Season to taste with salt.

Serves 4.

Baccalà in Rosso

Salt Cod with Tomatoes and Potatoes

Puréed salt cod (see baccalà in bianco on page 231) and Triestine salt cod stews are often referred to by the same name, "baccalà alla Triestina." To add to the confusion, stews by that name may be prepared with either potatoes or tomatoes—or occasionally both, as shown here. For clarity, many cooks label the dish by color, in this case "rosso" (red) for the tomatoes used. Serve the baccalà with polenta (page 196).

1 pound dried salt cod

3 tablespoons olive oil

1 medium yellow onion,
    chopped

2 garlic cloves, minced

1 (28-ounce) can diced
    tomatoes in juice

3 canned anchovies, chopped

½ teaspoon ground black
    pepper

1 bay leaf

1 pound white potatoes, peeled
    and cut into 1-inch pieces

2 tablespoons chopped fresh
    Italian parsley

❧ In advance, place the salt cod in a large bowl and cover with water. Refrigerate for 48 hours, changing the water about every 12 hours; drain.

❧ Remove any bones or skin from the fish; cut into 2-inch pieces.

❧ Heat the olive oil in a large, deep skillet over medium heat. Add the onion and garlic; cook and stir until the onion begins to soften, about 15 minutes. Stir in the tomatoes, anchovies, black pepper, and bay leaf; place the fish in the skillet. Reduce heat to medium-low; simmer, covered, for 30 minutes. Add the potatoes; cook, covered, until the potatoes are tender and the fish flakes easily when tested with a fork, about 30 minutes longer, stirring occasionally. Stir in the parsley. Remove the bay leaf; season to taste with salt.

Serves 4 to 6.

The Rilke Path

Toward the end of the 19th century, Austrian princess Maria von Thurn und Taxis opened her family castle at Duino to numerous figures in contemporary art, music, and literature. One of her favorite guests was the poet Rainer Maria Rilke, who stayed at the castle from 1911 to 1912. It was here that he penned the beginning to his famous *Duino Elegies*.

"Who, if I cried out, would hear me among the angels' hierarchies?" These were the words of inspiration that, like a voice from the wind, called out to Rilke one stormy day while he was wandering along the sea cliffs near the castle. Today, visitors can stroll the same route, called the Sentiero Rilke, or "Rilke path," which stretches just over a mile between the fishing village of Duino and the pretty yacht-filled harbor at Sistiana.

The path begins at the 15th-century Castello di Duino, perched on a promontory overlooking the ruins of the medieval Castello Vecchio. It then follows the meandering coastline, where evergreen shrubs cling to the rock face and precipitous, white limestone cliffs plunge into the sea. At the end of the rocky trail is Sistiana, where white sailboats rest afloat in the sapphire blue bay. All along the Rilke Path, shady pine forests alternate with breathtaking views, each worthy of a poet's inspiration.

Precipitous limestone cliffs plunge into the sea along the Rilke Path (ABOVE); *the trail ends at the Bay of Sistiana* (TOP LEFT); *the Castello di Duino perches on a rocky promontory* (FAR LEFT); *ruins of the medieval Castello Vecchio* (LEFT).

Castello di Duino

The Castello di Duino dates back to the early 15th century, although it is best known as the home of the royal Thurn und Taxis family during the 19th century. Today, the castle houses a museum full of princely memorabilia and is surrounded by lush gardens and romantic pathways lined with cypress trees and statues.

Marano Lagunare

CLOCKWISE FROM ABOVE: *Marano Lagunare's harbor; a quiet street in the old town center; on the lagoon between Marano and Lignano.*

OPPOSITE, CLOCKWISE FROM TOP LEFT: *Trattoria Alla Laguna, also known as Vedova Raddi, offers a prime waterfront location; vividly colored houses are characteristic of this small fishing village; the surrounding marshy wetlands are part of a protected nature reserve.*

Grado

CLOCKWISE FROM ABOVE: *Grado is surrounded by a marshy lagoon; while the Basilica di Sant' Eufemia was built in the 6th century, the bell tower was not added until the 15th century; Grado's beaches are lined with high-rise hotels; a shady courtyard in the town's historic center; boats dock in the Canale della Schiusa; a characteristic stone house.*

OPPOSITE, CLOCKWISE FROM TOP LEFT: *mosaics from a paleo-Christian basilica were discovered in Piazza Biagio Marin; once a major Roman port, Grado is now a popular beach resort; Piazza dei Patriarchi with the 4th-century Basilica di Santa Maria delle Grazie in the background; blossoms in full bloom along the seaside promenade.*

Mosaics of Aquileia

In the marshy, coastal lowlands east of Venice lies Aquileia, a dusty, faded town with an impressive past. Founded as a Roman colony in AD 181, Aquileia soon grew to be the fourth largest city in ancient Italy. Its location along the Natissa River, just north of the port of Grado, established the town as a major crossroads between the Mediterranean and the Orient.

Theodore, one of Aquileia's first bishops, built the city's Basilica Patriarcale in 313, paving the floor with a decorative carpet of mosaics. The church was remodeled by Patriarch Poppone in 1031, and so these intricate works of art became concealed for nearly a millennium. At the beginning of the 20th century, the ancient mosaic pavement was discovered below the nave floor and is thought to be the earliest surviving remnant of any Christian church.

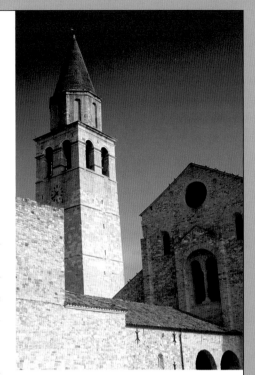

The designs incorporate both Christian and pagan symbols, including animals, birds, trees, flowers, and geometric patterns. Panels represent allegorical scenes, such as the cock fighting the tortoise, as well as portraits of religious figures. The biblical story of Jonah and the Whale is illustrated with numerous sea creatures, its fish motif alluding to the city's proximity to the Adriatic Sea.

More mosaics were uncovered around the bell tower and are on display in the Cripta degli Scavi. Also worth noting is the Cripta degli Freschi, which contains some colorful 12th-century Byzantine-style frescoes. Across the street, the Museo Archeologico Nazionale houses numerous relics from Roman times, including portrait busts, funerary carvings, household items, glassware, bronze objects, amber and precious stones, and a large collection of coins.

Today, the mosaics of Aquileia are one of Friuli's main attractions. It only takes a brief stroll around the city's ancient ruins—along the aqueduct, to the mausoleum, past the forum—to sense what life may have been like in Roman times.

The Basilica Patriarcale di Santa Maria Assunta (ABOVE); *4th-century mosaics inside the basilica* (LEFT).

The Patriarch of Aquileia

In the early 4th century, Christianity arrived in north-eastern Italy, making Aquileia the ecclesiastical center of the region. The next few centuries led to a withdrawal of imperial authority and an increase of power within the church. Bishops began to take on the honorific title of patriarch, thus establishing the patriarch of Aquileia. Following the barbaric invasions of the Huns in 452 and the Lombards in 568, the patriarch was forced to flee to nearby Grado, where the lagoons provided greater military protection. A rival patriarch was founded in Aquileia, which soon transferred to Cormòns, then to Cividale, and later to Udine. Both entities were recognized by the pope and were eventually absorbed by the patriarch of Venice when the Venetian Republic came into power.

In the courtyard of the basilica, a statue of the mythological she-wolf nursing Romulus and Remus, the founders of ancient Rome (RIGHT); *Aquileia's Roman forum* (BELOW).

Southern Friuli:
CONTORNI

Melanzane e Zuchete Apanade

Breaded Eggplant and Zucchini

When Greek immigrants first settled in Trieste, breaded eggplant or zucchini was typically served as a vegetarian main course with tomato sauce and a salad. Today, the dish plays a supporting role as a side dish or even an appetizer. It is offered in many of the city's buffets, to be eaten as a midmorning snack or perhaps with a glass of wine before dinner.

2 small eggplants (about 8 ounces)

2 small zucchini (about 8 ounces)

1 teaspoon salt, divided

½ cup all-purpose flour

3 eggs, beaten to blend

1 ¾ cups dry bread crumbs

¼ cup olive oil, plus extra as needed

 Cut the eggplants and zucchini lengthwise into ¼-inch-thick slices. Arrange the slices in one layer on several plates; sprinkle with ½ teaspoon salt. Let rest for 30 minutes to allow the moisture to be drawn out; pat dry with a towel.

 Prepare three shallow bowls for dredging; place the flour in the first bowl, the eggs in the second, and the bread crumbs mixed with the remaining ½ teaspoon salt in the third.

 Heat ¼ cup olive oil in a large skillet over medium heat. Working in batches, dredge the eggplant and zucchini slices in flour, then egg, then bread crumbs; place in the skillet. Cook until golden brown, about 4–5 minutes on each side. Repeat, adding extra olive oil to the skillet as needed.

Serves 4 to 6.

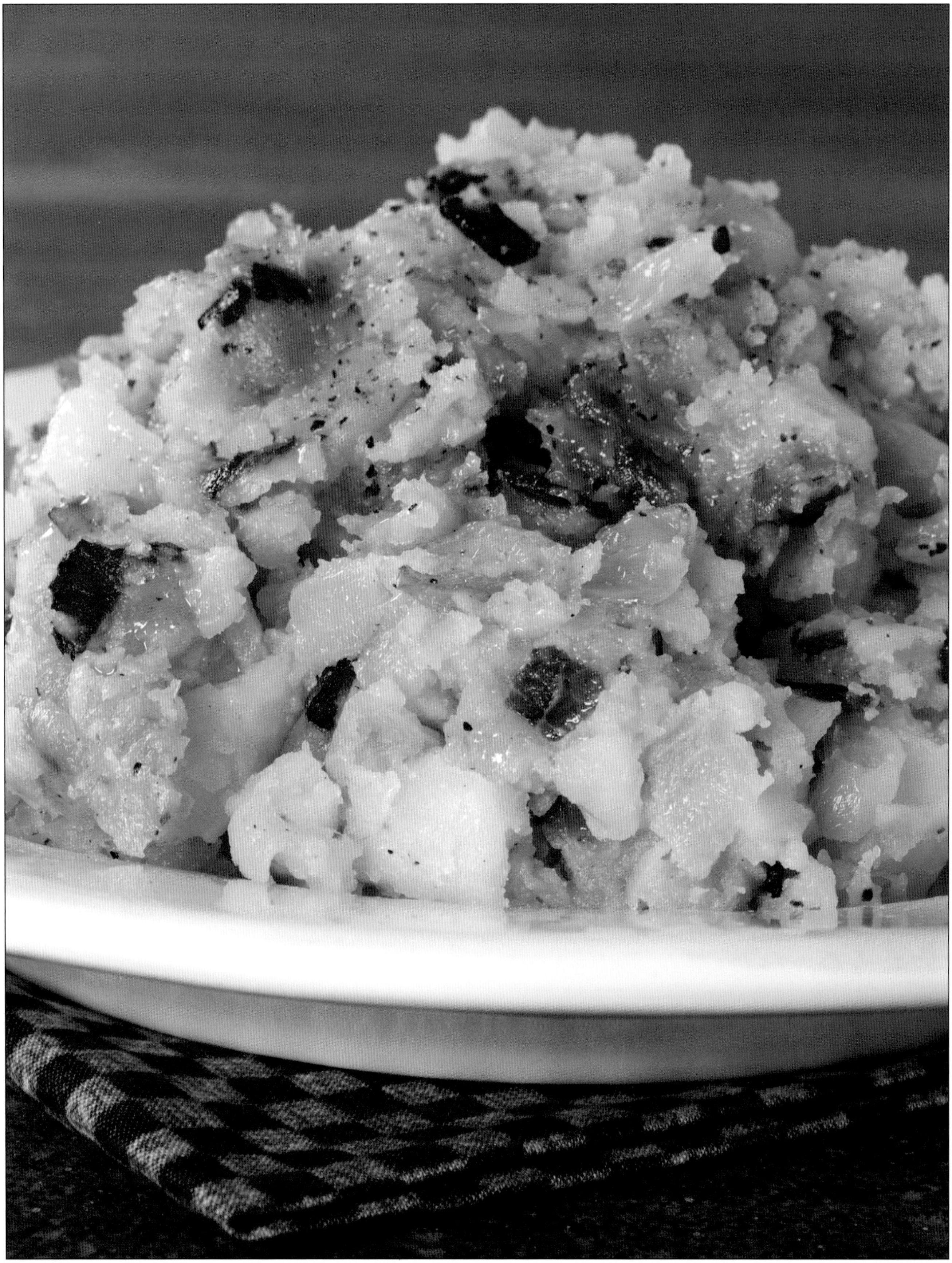

Patate in Tecia

Skillet Potatoes

These potatoes are one of the few dishes considered native to Trieste and can be found in many of the city's buffets as an accompaniment to goulasch (page 272) or boiled pork. They are also typically paired with stinco di vitello (page 275). Trieste's popular method of cooking vegetables "in tecia" refers to the cast-iron skillet traditionally used.

2 pounds white potatoes, peeled and quartered

2 tablespoons olive oil

1 medium yellow onion, chopped

2 ounces pancetta, chopped

½ cup beef broth

½ teaspoon ground black pepper

& Place the potatoes in a large pot filled with water; bring to a boil over high heat. Cook until tender, about 20–25 minutes; drain.

& Heat the olive oil in a large skillet over medium-low heat. Add the onion and pancetta; cook and stir until the onion is soft and golden, about 25–30 minutes. Stir in the potatoes, beef broth, and black pepper, coarsely mashing the potatoes with a spoon. Cook until the liquid has evaporated and the potatoes begin to brown, about 20 minutes, stirring occasionally. Season to taste with salt.

Serves 4.

Peperoni in Tecia

Sautéed Bell Peppers

Ristorante La Tecia in Trieste serves a mixed plate of sautéed vegetables, which may include bell peppers, depending on the season. You may substitute green, yellow, or orange bell peppers—or even use a colorful combination.

1/4 cup olive oil

3 red bell peppers (about 1 1/2
    pounds), seeded and sliced
    into 1/4-inch strips

1 garlic clove, minced

2 tablespoons chopped fresh
    Italian parsley

1/2 teaspoon ground black
    pepper

ಬ Heat the olive oil in a large skillet over medium heat. Add the bell peppers and garlic; cook and stir until tender, about 25–30 minutes. Stir in the parsley and black pepper. Season to taste with salt.

Serves 4.

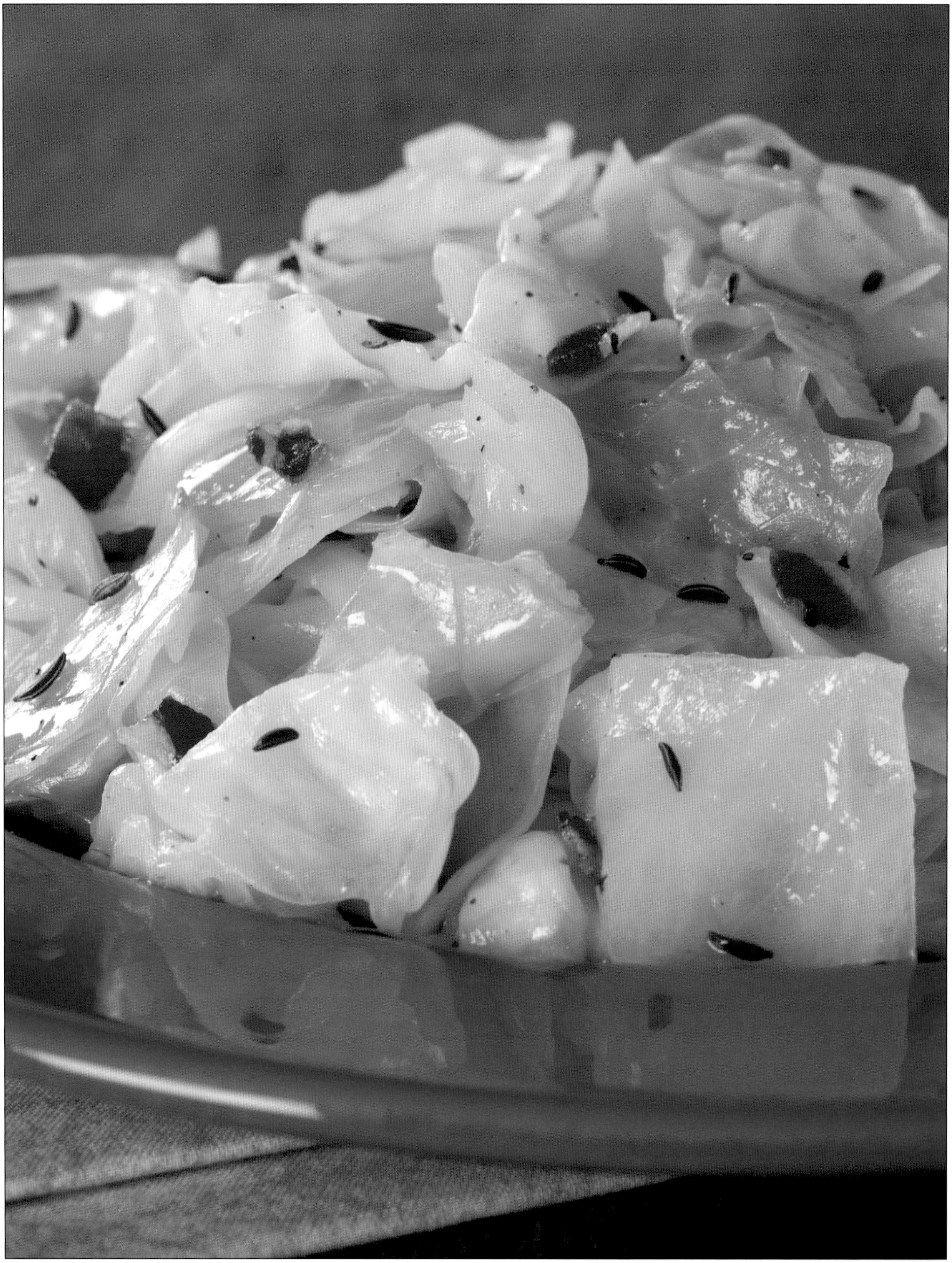

Capuzi in Tecia

Sautéed Cabbage

Capuzi is Triestine dialect for the "cavolo cappuccio" (green cabbage), although savoy or red cabbage may be used instead. The caraway seeds, which flavor many of Trieste's dishes, are a reflection of the region's Austrian roots.

3 tablespoons olive oil

2 ounces pancetta, chopped

2 garlic cloves, minced

1 green cabbage (about 2 to 3 pounds), core removed and sliced into 1-inch pieces

$1/2$ teaspoon caraway seeds

$1/2$ teaspoon ground black pepper

  Heat the olive oil in a large, deep skillet over medium heat. Add the pancetta and garlic; cook and stir until brown and crisp, about 5 minutes. Add the cabbage. Reduce heat to low; cook, covered, until the cabbage is tender, about 40 minutes, stirring occasionally. Stir in the caraway seeds and black pepper. Season to taste with salt.

Serves 6.

Zuchete in Tecia

Sautéed Zucchini

One of many exotic ingredients brought to Trieste from the East, cinnamon plays a role in numerous dishes, both sweet and savory.

¼ cup olive oil

1½ pounds zucchini, sliced into
⅛-inch-thick rounds

3 tablespoons chopped fresh
Italian parsley

¼ teaspoon ground cinnamon

₧ Heat the olive oil in a large skillet over medium heat. Add the zucchini; cook and stir until tender, about 15 minutes. Stir in the parsley and cinnamon; cook 2–3 minutes longer. Season to taste with salt.

Serves 4.

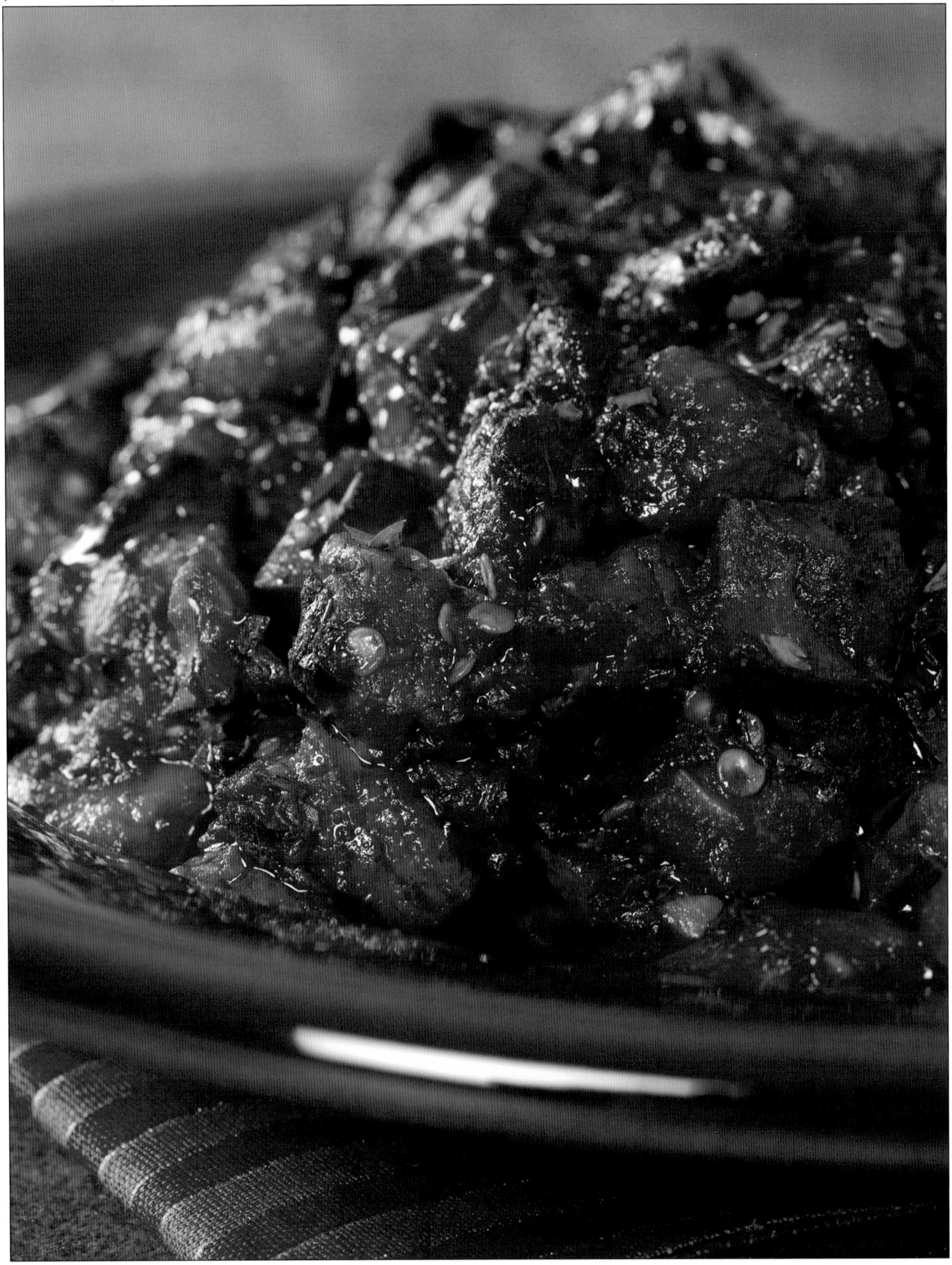

Melanzane in Tecia

Sautéed Eggplant

The tomato sauce in this dish reflects the influence of Greek immigrants in Trieste.

½ cup olive oil

6 small eggplants (about 1½ pounds), cut into ½-inch pieces

2 garlic cloves, minced

1 (8-ounce) can tomato sauce, or 1 cup

¼ cup chopped fresh Italian parsley

½ teaspoon ground black pepper

ঌ Heat the olive oil in a large skillet over medium heat. Add the eggplant and garlic; cook and stir until the eggplant begins to soften, about 5 minutes. Stir in the tomato sauce, parsley, and black pepper. Reduce heat to medium-low; cook and stir until the eggplant is tender, about 10–12 minutes longer. Season to taste with salt.

Serves 4.

Piselli in Tecia

Widely used throughout Friuli, pancetta adds wonderful flavor to these peas.

2 tablespoons olive oil

½ medium yellow onion,
    chopped

2 ounces pancetta, chopped

1 pound shelled fresh or frozen
    peas

1 tablespoon chopped fresh
    Italian parsley

¼ teaspoon ground black
    pepper

ɞ Heat the olive oil in a large skillet over medium heat. Add the onion and pancetta; cook and stir until the onion softens and the pancetta is brown and crisp, about 10 minutes. Add the peas. Reduce heat to medium-low; cook, covered, until the peas are tender, about 8–10 minutes, stirring occasionally. Stir in the parsley and black pepper. Season to taste with salt.

Serves 4 to 6.

Carciofi alla Triestina

Trieste-Style Stuffed Artichokes

Artichokes were considered a delicacy throughout ancient Rome, including the Roman cities of Aquileia and Tergeste. The popularity of the vegetable in Trieste points to the prominence of early Roman civilization in Friuli. Although stuffed artichokes are common in many parts of Italy, this version is regarded as inherently Triestine. If Montasio stagionato is not available, you may substitute any aged cheese such as Parmigiano-Reggiano.

2/3 cup dry bread crumbs

1/4 cup grated Montasio stagionato

1 tablespoon chopped fresh Italian parsley

1 garlic clove, minced

1/2 teaspoon salt

1/4 teaspoon ground black pepper

. . .

6 medium artichokes (about 1 1/2 to 2 pounds)

1 lemon, juiced

2 tablespoons olive oil

❧ In a small bowl, combine the bread crumbs, Montasio cheese, parsley, garlic, salt, and black pepper.

❧ Cut an inch off the top of each artichoke, then cut off the stem to create a flat base. Remove any tough outer leaves. Gently spread open the leaves to remove the thin, yellow leaves in the center. Scrape out the fuzzy inner choke with a small spoon. To prevent browning while preparing the artichokes, place them in a large bowl of cold water mixed with the juice of 1 lemon.

❧ Spoon the bread crumb mixture into the artichoke cavities and between the leaves. Place the artichokes on a steamer rack inside a large pot; drizzle with the olive oil. Fill the pot with water so that the artichokes are halfway submerged; bring to a boil over high heat. Reduce heat to low; cook, covered, until the artichokes are tender, about 20 minutes.

Serves 6.

Muggia

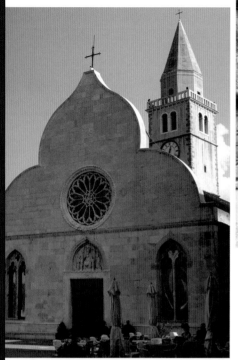

CLOCKWISE FROM BELOW: *Muggia's central square, Piazza Marconi; the Duomo dei Santi Giovanni e Paolo features a Venetian-Gothic trilobed façade with a striking rose window; the winged lion of Saint Mark was added to the Palazzo dei Rettori in the 15th century following the Venetian occupation—his disgruntled expression perhaps symbolizes the town's displeasure with its new government.*

CLOCKWISE FROM ABOVE: *pastel-colored houses line the town's* mandracchio, *or "inner harbor"; the Venetian-style Casa Veneta was built in the 15th century and currently houses an archeological museum; the Palazzo dei Rettori has been rebuilt numerous times since the 13th century and is now home to Muggia's town hall; the 13th-century Basilica di Santa Maria Assunta in the hilltop town of Muggia Vecchia.*

Carnevale Muggesano

Unlike the famous Carnevale di Venezia, Muggia's Carnevale Muggesano does not evoke images of elegant baroque palaces, courtesans waltzing to Vivaldi at a masked ball, or mysterious caped figures drifting past the shadows of the Grand Canal. Instead, Muggia celebrates the absurd and bizarre with townspeople dressed as cartoon characters, farm animals, or even platters of food.

The only town on the Istrian peninsula to remain within the Italian border, Muggia has a distinct Slavic air, as well as a noticeable Venetian character. The harbor, backed by pastel houses, retains the atmosphere of an old-world fishing port. The central focus of Piazza Marconi is the Duomo's Venetian-Gothic trilobed façade. On the orange and yellow Palazzo dei Rettori, the stone relief of the winged lion of Saint Mark—symbol of the Venetian Republic—reveals a clue to Muggia's long tradition of humor and satire. Look closely at the lion's face—the sense of disgust is apparent as he sticks out his tongue at the town's former rulers.

After the battles of World War II had ended, Muggia was reintroduced to the idea of a Carnevale masquerade by a group of friends who dressed up as gauchos and marched through the streets playing music. They named themselves Brivido—meaning "shiver"—after a harrowing boating incident one wet and windy day. As they repeated this annual affair, dressed next as gypsies and later as Apache Indians, the procession grew with more and more people joining in the merriment. Soon a few rival groups had formed, each costumed in its own fantastical theme. By 1954, the parade had blossomed into an official event.

Every year, groups with names such as Bulli e Pupe (ruffians and little girls), Lampo (lightning), Mandrioi (maybeetle), Bellezze Naturali (natural beauty), Trottola (spinning top), and Bora

(northeast wind) choose a theme and design a tractor-pulled float with matching costumes. During the parade, performers dance, play music, and pantomime scenes.

Themes range from the contemporary (comic book superheroes, *The Simpsons* cartoon) to literary (Dante's *Divine Comedy*, the Knights of the Round Table) to geographical (Mexico, Africa, India). A prize is awarded to the most lavish or comical. Not surprisingly, the original group Brivido has won first place most often.

Among the whimsical costumes, however, you will rarely see a masked face. Contrary to the practice of most Carnevale celebrations where anonymity is sacred, the people of Muggia have chosen to expose their individual character. This comes as a natural response in a town that has struggled to assert its identity in the face of domination by so many foreign cultures.

A full week of festivities opens with the "Dance of the Vegetables," when representatives of each group perform

for the public. This is followed by the *megafrittata*, a culinary ritual that begins with townspeople traipsing door to door begging for eggs. The eggs are then used to make what is possibly the world's largest frittata, cooked in a giant thirteen-foot-wide frying pan. For dessert, *frittelle* (doughnuts) and *crostoli* (crispy fritters) are the traditional Carnevale sweets.

On Ash Wednesday, to mark the final day of the celebration, the groups perform a tragicomedy ritual. Following a solemn funeral procession, townspeople throw a lifelike "corpse" of the Carnevale king into the sea.

The Lüganiga Band marches in the Carnevale parade (ABOVE); *festivities continue after dark in Piazza Marconi* (BELOW LEFT); *cooking the* megafrittata *in gigantic "mega"-skillets* (BELOW RIGHT); *floats by the groups Ongia, Mandrioi, and Lampo* (OPPOSITE, CLOCKWISE FROM TOP).

Illycaffè

When it comes to coffee, Illy has practically become a household name. Each day, six million cups of Italy's most famous coffee are enjoyed all around the globe, from Trieste's elegant cafés to homes in 140 countries on five continents.

Illycaffè was founded in 1933 by Hungarian native Francesco Illy, who came to Trieste during World War I as an officer in the Austro-Hungarian army. Following the war, with the city now under Italian rule, he decided to remain in Trieste and open a coffee business. Although he initially dabbled in cocoa production as well, his love of espresso eventually dominated. Using 100 percent Arabica beans, he created a unique espresso blend from nine select varieties.

In 1935, Illy invented the *illetta*, the first automatic coffee maker to substitute compressed air for steam and the predecessor of today's espresso machine. He also developed a new packaging system that filled airtight coffee cans with nitrogen gas in order to prevent oxidation. Having an extended shelf life, these pressurized cans could then be sold throughout the country.

Years later, the business was passed on to Francesco's son, Ernesto Illy, who encouraged the product's export throughout the world. Today, exports comprise over half of Illycaffè's sales—yet the business remains a tight, family-run affair. Ernesto's son Andrea is the current CEO. Another of his sons, Riccardo, is the company's vice-president and perhaps the most prominent member of the Illy family. Riccardo was the mayor of Trieste for two terms during the 1990s and was elected president of Friuli-Venezia Giulia in 2003.

In 1990, continuing the company's legacy of innovation, Illycaffè premiered an exclusive line of china cups created by designer Matteo Thun. Precise measurements of volume, diameter, and thickness were calculated to provide the optimal coffee-drinking experience. Two years later, the first line of decorated cups emerged, the collection entitled "Arts and Crafts." Ever since, Illy has released an annual series of limited-edition cups, with artwork by emerging artists as well as famous names such as Robert Rauschenberg, Federico Fellini, and Francis Ford Coppola.

Pasticceria Penso

My fondest memory of Trieste will always be the day I first stepped into Pasticceria Penso. My timing seems predestined—I arrived on a blustery February morning just as a few dozen chocolate cakes were being pulled from the oven. I was immediately invited back into the cozy kitchen to watch their transformation into *torta Sacher*. The patriarch of the family-run bakery, Italo Stoppar, doused each layer of cake with Maraschino liqueur, then spread on a thick coat of apricot preserves. His son Antonello drizzled the top with dark chocolate ganache, which was soon followed by a garnish of chocolate sprinkles around the sides. This was just the first of many such mornings; the next

year, I arranged for an apartment across the street, so that I could spend countless hours observing their techniques—and sampling every cream-stuffed, chocolate-glazed, fruit-filled morsel I could possibly devour.

The bakery was founded in 1920 by Trieste native Narciso Penso, after he returned from serving in the military during World War I. When he died in 1971, the store was bought by one of his young employees, Italo Stoppar, also from Trieste. Stoppar had begun working at Penso in the 1960s after learning his craft at Pasticceria Colussi and later refining his skills as a pastry chef on the cruise ship Lloyd Triestino.

Today, as Stoppar passes on the trade to his two sons, Lorenzo and Antonello, Pasticceria Penso is truly a family business. Brother-in-law Giovanni also helps out in the kitchen, while Italo's wife, Rosanna, and Giovanni's wife, Silvana, tend to customers. The mood is light, the kitchen functioning like a well-choreographed ballet, each person silently knowing everyone else's next move. Italo's role is both slicer and icer. He can usually be seen preparing the layered cakes and jelly rolls—slicing the cakes into layers, spreading them with buttercream frosting, whipped cream, ganache, or caramel, and finally slicing the sheet cakes into the proper rectangular serving size. His steady hand also garnishes birthday cakes with whipped cream flowers and flourishes, piping special messages in chocolate icing. Lorenzo is in charge of dough, filling tartlet pans with *crostata* crust, rolling puff pastry for strudel and *presnitz*. Antonello handles a little of everything, from applying fruit garnishes to measuring and mixing cake batter, from sorting and grinding almonds for *marzapane* to melting chocolate for ganache.

True to Trieste's multiethnic roots, Pasticceria Penso specializes in the pastries from Austria and Hungary, such as the ever-popular *Sacher* and *Dobos* cakes, as well as the ubiquitous local desserts *presnitz*, *putizza*, and *pinza*. In all, they make around thirty-five different types of pastries, cakes, and cookies, which are purchased by locals for both special anniversary celebrations and as a Sunday post-church ritual. The sturdier pastries—*presnitz*, *putizza*, *pinza*, and *torta Sacher*—are shipped to clients throughout Europe, the United States, and Australia.

While author James Joyce is often noted as having once been a frequent patron of nearby Pasticceria Pirona, Penso's famed customers from the past include writer Italo Svevo and aviator Baron de Banfield. In addition, according to the Stoppars, another former customer worked as a White House chef during the presidency of John F. Kennedy; every time he came home to Trieste for holiday, he would inevitably return to Washington with suitcases loaded full of pastries from Penso.

In a city that clings to heritage and tradition, Pasticceria Penso is surprisingly one of just a few surviving bakeries from its era. The quality of their product is surely what has kept Penso in business for so many years. They use only butter—unlike many modern bakeries that rely on margarine to prolong shelf life—and always top-quality ingredients, from the richest, darkest baking chocolate to the Bulgarian rose oil that flavors the pink *fave dei morti*. Their key to success is perhaps identical to the inherent nature of Trieste itself—classic Viennese precision combined with pure Italian passion.

Italo Stoppar spreads apricot jam on torta Sacher (OPPOSITE, TOP) *while his son Antonello glazes the cake with chocolate ganache* (ABOVE); *the bakery's fruit tart* (BELOW LEFT) *and pastries* (BELOW RIGHT) *taste as delicious as they look; brothers Lorenzo (in foreground) and Antonello hard at work* (OPPOSITE, BOTTOM).

€ 7,90

€ 8,00

Biscotti San Valentino

Etto € 1,30

Biscotti San Valentino

Pezzo € 1,00

❧ ☙

Southern Friuli:
DOLCI

❧ ☙

Putizza

Dried Fruit, Chocolate and Nut Spiral Cake

This rich spiral cake gets its name from the Slovenian pastry called "potica." Trieste's putizza closely resembles central Friuli's gubana delle Valli del Natisone but with a few significant differences—putizza contains chocolate, has a higher filling-to-dough ratio, and is baked in a cake pan rather than as a free-form loaf.

FILLING:

1 cup golden raisins

1/4 cup rum

1 1/2 cups coarsely chopped
　　walnuts

3 ounces semisweet or
　　bittersweet chocolate,
　　coarsely chopped

3/4 cup sugar

3/4 cup finely crushed biscotti or
　　amaretti cookies

3 tablespoons honey

1/4 teaspoon freshly grated
　　lemon peel

1/4 teaspoon ground cinnamon

2 egg whites

· · ·

DOUGH:

1 1/2 teaspoons active dry yeast

3 tablespoons sugar, divided

1/3 cup warm whole milk (100°
　　to 110°F)

1 1/3 cups cake or pastry flour,
　　divided

2 egg yolks

2 tablespoons unsalted butter,
　　melted

1 tablespoon rum

1/2 teaspoon vanilla extract

1/2 teaspoon salt

1/4 teaspoon freshly grated
　　lemon peel

· · ·

1 egg, beaten to blend

FOR THE FILLING:

❧　Place the raisins in a large bowl; add the rum and let soak for 30 minutes. Finely grind the walnuts in a food processor; add to the bowl of raisins. Stir in the chocolate, sugar, crushed biscotti, honey, lemon peel, cinnamon, and egg whites.

FOR THE DOUGH:

❧　In a small bowl, dissolve the yeast and a pinch of sugar in the warm milk. Let rest until foamy, about 10 minutes. Whisk in 1/3 cup flour. Cover and let rise for 30 minutes.

❧　Transfer the mixture to a large bowl. Stir in 1/2 cup flour, 1 tablespoon sugar, and the egg yolks. Cover and let rise for 1 hour.

❧　Stir in the remaining flour and sugar, melted butter, rum, vanilla extract, salt, and lemon peel. Using a mixer with a dough hook attachment, knead for 10 minutes. (It may be necessary to occasionally scrape the ball of dough off the hook.) Transfer the dough to a lightly floured surface; knead briefly by hand. (The dough should be smooth, elastic, and very soft.) Form the dough into a ball; cover loosely with plastic wrap or a kitchen towel and let rise for 1 hour.

❧　Preheat oven to 350°F, placing a pan filled with water on the bottom rack to create steam. On a lightly floured surface, roll the dough to an 11- by 17-inch oval. Spread the filling over the dough, leaving a 1 1/2-inch border on all sides. Starting with one long side of the oval, roll up jelly roll style. Form the roll into a spiral, seam-side down; transfer to a greased 8-inch round cake pan. Cover loosely with plastic wrap or a kitchen towel and let rise for 30 minutes. Brush the top of the spiral with beaten egg. Bake until golden brown, about 45 minutes. Cool 10 minutes before removing from the pan.

Serves 8 to 10.

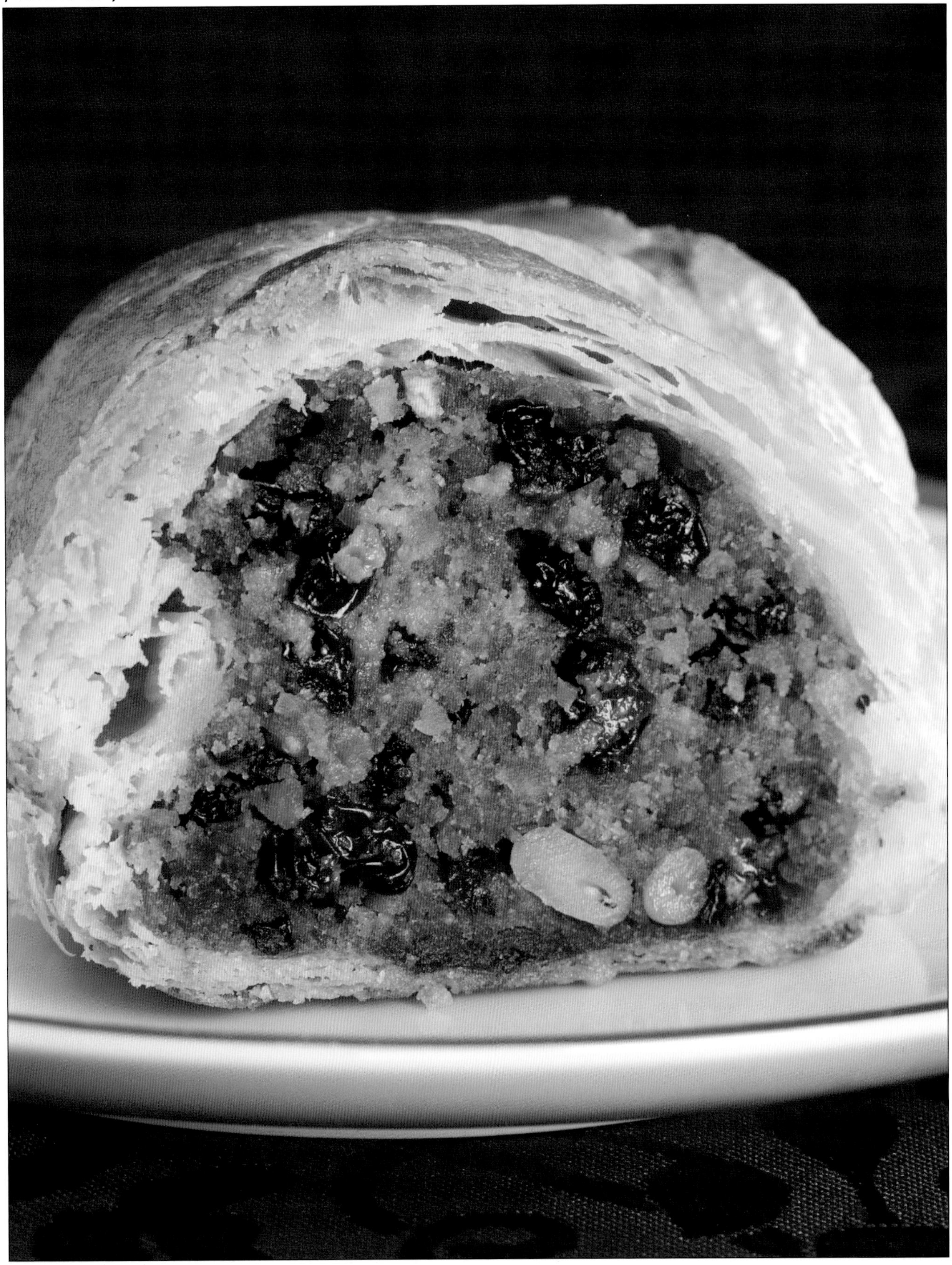

Presnitz

Trieste-Style Pastry Spiral

Named after the Slovenian Easter cake called "presnec," presnitz was first presented to the empress Elisabeth during a mid-19ᵗʰ century visit to Trieste. Today, presnitz is practically synonymous with gubana Cividalese, although it was originally considered a more refined pastry due to Trieste's wealth and the availability of newly imported exotic ingredients. This particular recipe has been adapted from one given to me by Pasticceria Penso.

FILLING:

1 cup dried currants

¼ cup rum

¼ cup Marsala wine

¾ cup coarsely chopped walnuts

½ cup hazelnuts, skinned and toasted (see instructions on page 342)

¼ cup blanched slivered almonds

¾ cup finely crushed biscotti or amaretti cookies

⅓ cup diced candied orange peel

4 tablespoons unsalted butter, melted

3 tablespoons pine nuts

2 tablespoons sugar

1 tablespoon honey

1 teaspoon ground cinnamon

1 teaspoon freshly grated lemon peel

1 egg

. . .

Puff Pastry Dough (see recipe on page 215)

1 egg, beaten to blend

FOR THE FILLING:

ᵭ Place the currants in a large bowl; add the rum and Marsala wine and let soak for 30 minutes.

ᵭ Finely grind the walnuts, toasted hazelnuts, and almonds in a food processor; add to the bowl of currants. Stir in the crushed biscotti, candied orange peel, melted butter, pine nuts, sugar, honey, cinnamon, lemon peel, and egg.

ᵭ On a sheet of waxed paper, form the filling into a 12-inch log. Wrap securely in the waxed paper and refrigerate for 1 hour, or until ready to use.

TO PREPARE:

ᵭ Preheat oven to 400°F. On a lightly floured surface, roll the puff pastry dough to a 10- by 13-inch rectangle. Unwrap the filling and place along the center of the dough. Wrap the dough around the filling, tightly sealing all seams. Gently roll and stretch the dough into a 2½-foot-long rope. Coil into a loose spiral and transfer to a baking sheet lined with parchment paper. Brush the surface of the dough with beaten egg. Bake until golden brown, about 25–30 minutes.

Serves 10 to 12.

Pinza

Easter Bread

Just like the word "pizza," pinza is thought to have derived from the Latin verb "pinsare," meaning "to knead." While this sweet loaf was originally prepared as a special Easter treat, it may now be found in Trieste's bakeries year round. In fact, pinza is common throughout Friuli, where it is often referred to as "focaccia"—not to be confused with the flat Ligurian focaccia. The province of Pordenone claims a similar bread called "pinsa della bassa" that is made with raisins, dried figs, or currants.

2 packages active dry yeast (2 1/4 teaspoons or 1/4 ounce each)

2/3 cup sugar, divided

1/2 cup warm water (100° to 110°F), divided

4 1/2 cups cake or pastry flour, divided

2 eggs

2 egg yolks

4 tablespoons unsalted butter, diced and softened

2 teaspoons salt

1 teaspoon freshly grated lemon peel

1 teaspoon freshly grated orange peel

. . .

1 egg yolk, beaten to blend with 1 tablespoon water

ɞ In a small bowl, dissolve 1 package of yeast and a pinch of sugar in 1/4 cup warm water. Let rest until foamy, about 10 minutes. Stir in 1/2 cup flour. Cover and let rise for 30 minutes.

ɞ Transfer the mixture to a large bowl. Stir in 1 cup flour, 2 tablespoons sugar, 1 egg, and 1 egg yolk. Cover and let rise for 1 hour.

ɞ Dissolve the remaining package of yeast and a pinch of sugar in the remaining 1/4 cup warm water. Let rest until foamy, about 10 minutes. Add to the bowl of risen dough, along with 1 1/2 cups flour, 2 tablespoons sugar, 1 egg, and 1 egg yolk; mix well. Cover and let rise for 1 hour.

ɞ Stir in the remaining flour and sugar, butter, salt, lemon peel, and orange peel. Using a mixer with a dough hook attachment, knead for 10 minutes. (It may be necessary to occasionally scrape the ball of dough off the hook.) Transfer the dough to a lightly floured surface; knead briefly by hand. (The dough should be smooth and elastic.) Form the dough into a ball and place on a baking sheet lined with parchment paper; cover loosely with plastic wrap or a kitchen towel and let rise until doubled in size, about 1 1/2 hours.

ɞ Preheat oven to 350°F, placing a pan filled with water on the bottom rack to create steam. Brush the dough with beaten egg yolk. Cut three 1-inch-deep slits in the dough, starting at the top and stopping about 1 inch from the base. Bake until golden brown, about 40 minutes.

Serves 10 to 12.

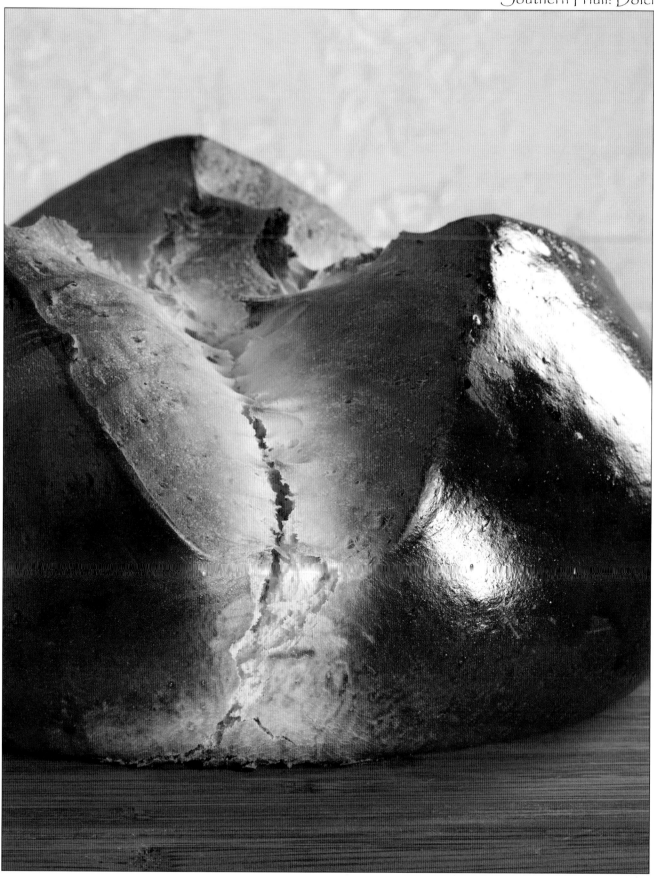

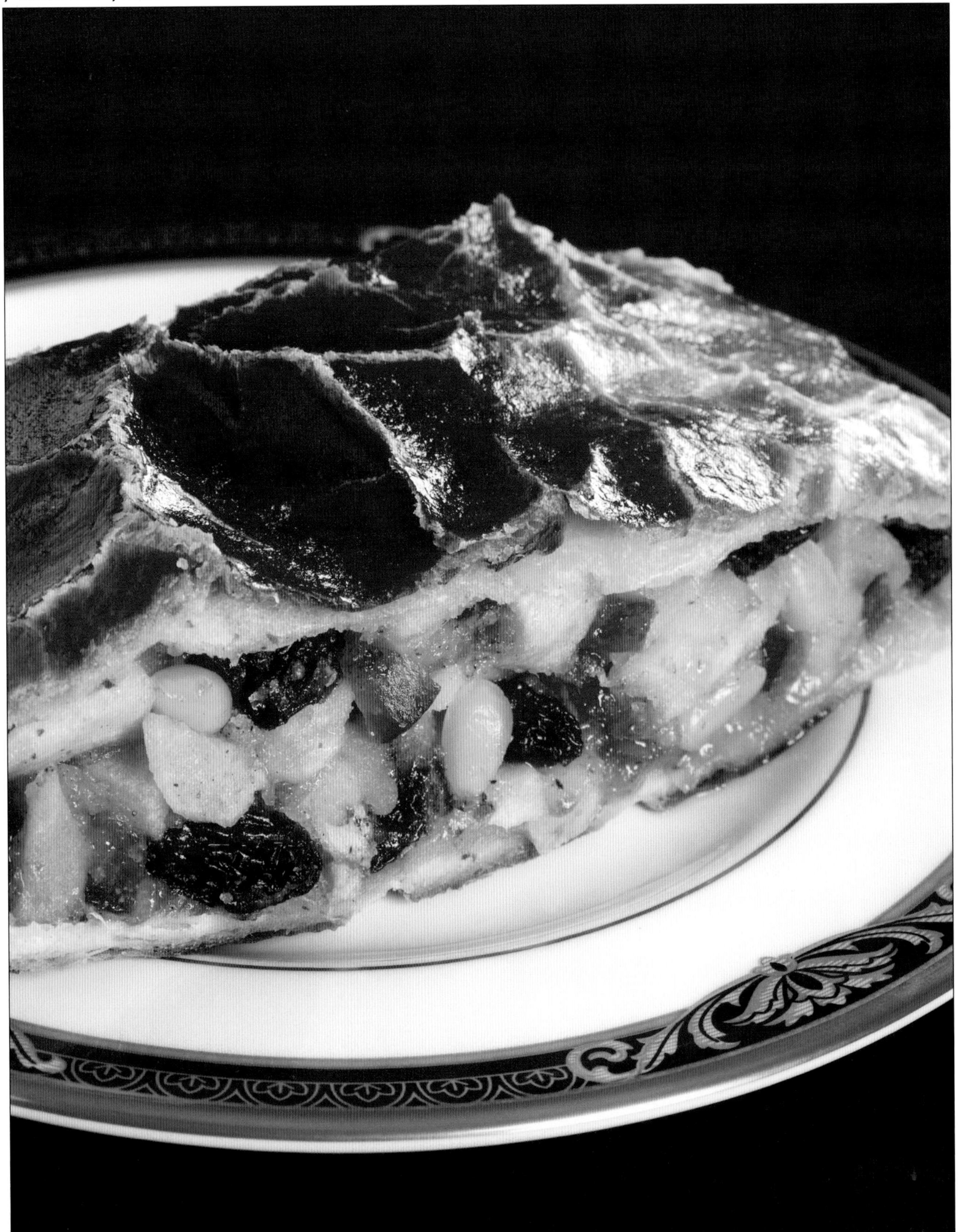

Strucolo de Pomi

Apple Strudel

Strudel—called "strucolo" in the Triestine dialect—is thought to have been inspired by the Turkish pastry baklava. Apples were added to the filling when variations on baklava were integrated into Austro-Hungarian cuisine after periods of Turkish invasion during the 16th century. Apples remain the most popular filling, although walnuts, cherries, apricots, plums, or ricotta cheese may be used as well. True Austrian strudel requires a paper-thin dough similar to phyllo; while you will find this type of dough in strudels throughout Friuli, puff pastry is a common substitute in many of Trieste's bakeries. This recipe comes from Pasticceria Penso.

FILLING:

3 medium apples (about 1 ¼ pounds), peeled, cored, and cut into ¼-inch pieces

½ cup finely crushed biscotti, amaretti, or savoiardi cookies

¼ cup raisins

¼ cup diced candied orange peel

¼ cup pine nuts

¼ cup sugar

1 tablespoon rum

1 tablespoon butter, melted

1 teaspoon freshly grated lemon peel

¼ teaspoon ground cinnamon

. . .

Puff Pastry Dough (see recipe on page 213)

1 egg, beaten to blend

FOR THE FILLING:

ẟ In a large bowl, combine the apples, crushed biscotti, raisins, candied orange peel, pine nuts, sugar, rum, melted butter, lemon peel, and cinnamon.

TO PREPARE:

ẟ Preheat oven to 400°F. On a lightly floured surface, roll the puff pastry dough to a 12- by 15-inch rectangle. Transfer the dough to a large sheet of parchment paper. Brush the surface of the dough with beaten egg. Spread the filling lengthwise along the center of the dough. Wrap the dough around the filling, tightly sealing all seams; carefully turn the strudel seam-side down. Transfer the strudel, along with the parchment paper, to a baking sheet. Brush the surface of the dough with beaten egg. Bake until golden brown, about 25–30 minutes.

Serves 8 to 10.

Torta Sacher

Chocolate Cake with Apricot Glaze and Ganache

While torta Sacher may be found throughout much of northeastern Italy, it is considered a local dessert due to Trieste's Austrian heritage. The cake was created in 1832 by Franz Sacher, cook and pastry chef for the Austrian prince Klemens von Metternich. In 1876, the chef's son Eduard founded Vienna's elegant Hotel Sacher and has ensured that the family recipe be kept a guarded secret. This version is based on Pasticceria Penso's recipe, which adds ground hazelnuts to the cake batter and Maraschino liqueur to the glaze.

CAKE:

1/3 cup hazelnuts, skinned and toasted (see instructions on page 342)

1/2 cup (1 stick) unsalted butter, softened

1 cup sugar

5 eggs, separated

1 teaspoon vanilla extract

3/4 cup cake or pastry flour, sifted

1/2 cup Dutch-process cocoa powder, sifted

Pinch salt

. . .

APRICOT GLAZE:

1/4 cup Maraschino liqueur

2/3 cup apricot jam

. . .

CHOCOLATE GANACHE:

4 ounces semisweet or bittersweet chocolate

1/2 cup heavy whipping cream

. . .

Chocolate sprinkles (optional)

FOR THE CAKE:

  Preheat oven to 325°F. Finely grind the toasted hazelnuts in a food processor.

  In a large bowl, beat the butter and sugar until light and fluffy. Beat in the egg yolks, one at a time, adding the vanilla extract with the last yolk; beat the mixture until thick and pale in color, about 5 minutes. Stir in the flour, cocoa powder, and ground hazelnuts. In a separate bowl, beat the egg whites with a pinch of salt until they form stiff peaks. Soften the batter by stirring in a little egg white; fold in the remaining egg whites.

  Pour the batter into a greased and floured 8-inch round cake pan. Bake until a wooden pick inserted near the center comes out clean, about 45 minutes. Cool 15 minutes before removing from the pan; cool completely before glazing.

FOR THE GLAZE:

  Slice the cake in half horizontally; shave a thin slice off the top layer to create a smooth surface. (Any air pockets may be filled in with the shaved-off pieces of cake.) Brush the Maraschino liqueur over the top and sides of both cake layers; repeat with the apricot jam. Stack the two cake layers on a wire rack.

FOR THE GANACHE:

  Melt the chocolate with the cream in a double boiler, stirring until smooth. Pour the ganache over the top and sides of the cake. Decorate the sides of the cake with sprinkles, if desired. Using a large spatula, transfer the cake to a serving plate; refrigerate until the ganache has set.

Serves 8 to 10.

Torta Dobos

Layer Cake with Chocolate Buttercream and Caramel

This cake was created by Hungarian pastry chef József Dobos for Budapest's National General Exhibition in 1885. The hazelnut paste in this recipe's buttercream frosting adds an Italian touch.

CAKE:

6 eggs, separated

2/3 cup sugar

1 teaspoon vanilla extract

1 teaspoon freshly grated
    lemon peel

1 cup cake or pastry flour,
    sifted

Pinch salt

· · ·

CARAMEL GLAZE:

1/2 cup sugar

2 tablespoons water

1 teaspoon lemon juice

· · ·

BUTTERCREAM FROSTING:

1/2 cup hazelnuts, skinned and
    toasted (see instructions on
    page 342)

1 1/2 cups (3 sticks) unsalted
    butter, softened

3 cups confectioners' sugar

1/2 cup unsweetened cocoa
    powder

FOR THE CAKE:

ᛠ Preheat oven to 350°F. Line three baking sheets with parchment paper. Trace two 8-inch circles onto each piece of paper.

ᛠ In a large bowl, beat the egg yolks, sugar, vanilla extract, and lemon peel to the "ribbon stage," about 5 minutes. (The batter will be pale in color and will leave a ribbon-like trail when drizzled over the surface of the batter.) Stir in the flour. In a separate bowl, beat the egg whites with a pinch of salt until they form stiff peaks. Soften the batter by stirring in a little egg white; fold in the remaining egg whites. Spread about 3/4 cup batter onto each of the six parchment paper templates. Bake until the edges are golden brown, about 10–12 minutes. Transfer the cakes, along with the parchment paper, to wire racks; cool completely before removing the paper. Choose the best-looking cake to reserve for the top layer.

FOR THE GLAZE:

ᛠ Combine the sugar, water, and lemon juice in a small saucepan; bring to a boil over high heat. Cook until golden amber in color, about 6–8 minutes. Pour the caramel immediately over the reserved cake layer. Spread using a buttered offset spatula, scraping away any caramel that has spilled over the edges. Wait a couple minutes, until the caramel has begun to solidify but is still warm to the touch. Using the blunt edge of a buttered knife, score the cake into twelve wedges. When the caramel has cooled to room temperature, cut the cake into twelve wedges using a sharp, buttered knife.

FOR THE FROSTING:

ᛠ Grind the toasted hazelnuts to a smooth paste in a food processor. In a large bowl, beat the hazelnut paste, butter, confectioners' sugar, and cocoa powder until soft and fluffy. Spread a thin layer of frosting over each of the remaining cakes, stacking to assemble the five layers. Spread additional frosting around the sides of the cake; use any extra to decorate as desired. Place the caramel-glazed wedges on top of the cake.

Serves 12.

Torta Rigojanci   *Chocolate Cake with Chocolate Cream Filling*

This sinful chocolate cake was named after the Hungarian gypsy violinist Jancsi Rigó, whose passionate affair with a beautiful American millionairess caused a worldwide scandal in the late 19th century. For picture-perfect slices, trim the cake edges before assembling.

CAKE:

6 eggs, separated

1 ¼ cups sugar

⅔ cup cake or pastry flour,
  sifted

½ cup Dutch-process cocoa
  powder, sifted

Pinch salt

. . .

CHOCOLATE GANACHE:

6 ounces semisweet or
  bittersweet chocolate

⅓ cup heavy whipping cream

. . .

CREAM FILLING:

8 ounces semisweet or
  bittersweet chocolate

3 cups heavy whipping cream,
  chilled

FOR THE CAKE:

&?; Preheat oven to 350°F. In a large bowl, beat the egg yolks and sugar to the "ribbon stage," about 5 minutes. (The batter will be pale in color and will leave a ribbon-like trail when drizzled over the surface of the batter.) Stir in the flour and cocoa powder.

&?; In a separate bowl, beat the egg whites with a pinch of salt until they form stiff peaks. Soften the batter by stirring in a little egg white; fold in the remaining egg whites. Pour the batter into a greased and floured 11- by 17-inch jelly-roll pan. Bake until a wooden pick inserted near the center comes out clean, about 20 minutes. Cool completely before removing from the pan. Slice the cake into two 8 ½- by 11-inch sheets.

FOR THE GANACHE:

&?; Melt the chocolate with the cream in a double boiler, stirring until smooth. Pour the ganache over one sheet of cake. Refrigerate until the ganache has set; slice into twelve squares.

FOR THE FILLING:

&?; Melt the chocolate in a double boiler, stirring until smooth; remove from heat. Pour the cream into a large bowl. (For best results, chill the bowl in advance.) Beat until the cream forms stiff peaks. Stir about 1 cup whipped cream into the melted chocolate. Pour the chocolate mixture into the bowl of whipped cream; whisk vigorously until the chocolate is thoroughly incorporated. Spread the chocolate cream over the remaining sheet of cake. Place the twelve glazed squares on top of the cream layer. Refrigerate until ready to serve.

Serves 12.

Cuguluf

Chocolate-Marbled Pound Cake

This Viennese cake is said to have been a favorite of Austrian emperor Franz Joseph. Called "kugelhupf" in German—and often referred to as "plumcake" throughout other parts of Italy—the cake is commonly eaten for breakfast or as a special treat with coffee or hot chocolate. While other recipes may include raisins, almonds, pine nuts, or candied fruit, this chocolate-marbled version is typical of bakeries in Gorizia.

3 1/2 cups cake or pastry flour, sifted

4 teaspoons baking powder

1 cup (2 sticks) unsalted butter, softened

2 1/2 cups sugar

5 eggs, separated

1 teaspoon vanilla extract

1/2 teaspoon freshly grated lemon peel

1 cup whole milk

Pinch salt

1/2 cup Dutch-process cocoa powder, sifted

. . .

Confectioners' sugar (optional)

„ Preheat oven to 350°F. In a medium bowl, combine the flour and baking powder. In a large bowl, beat the butter and sugar until light and fluffy. Beat in the egg yolks, one at a time, adding the vanilla extract and lemon peel with the last yolk; beat the mixture until thick and pale in color, about 5 minutes. Gradually beat in the milk; stir in the flour mixture.

„ In a separate bowl, beat the egg whites with a pinch of salt until they form stiff peaks. Fold the egg whites into the batter. Pour half the batter into a second bowl; stir in the cocoa powder.

„ Spoon half the plain batter into a greased and floured 12-cup fluted tube pan. Spoon in the chocolate batter, making a second layer; spoon the remaining plain batter on top. Bake until a wooden pick inserted near the center comes out clean, about 55–65 minutes. Cool 15 minutes before removing from the pan. Sprinkle with confectioners' sugar, if desired.

Serves 8 to 12.

Palacinche

Crêpes with Apricot Jam

Ubiquitous throughout central Europe, these crêpes are named after the Austrian palatschinke and the Hungarian palacsinta. While apricot jam remains the most popular filling, palacinche may also be served with chocolate cream, fresh fruit, cooked apples, ricotta cheese, or hazelnut, walnut, or chestnut cream. They may be folded into quarters, as shown here, or else rolled up jelly roll style.

2 cups all-purpose flour

4 teaspoons sugar

Pinch salt

4 eggs

2 1/2 cups whole milk

2 tablespoons unsalted butter,
   melted

1 teaspoon freshly grated
   lemon peel

. . .

2 cups apricot jam

Confectioners' sugar (optional)

◉ In a medium bowl, combine the flour, sugar, and salt. In a large bowl, whisk together the eggs, milk, melted butter, and lemon peel. Gradually whisk in the flour mixture.

◉ Preheat a 10- or 11-inch nonstick skillet over medium-low heat. Pour 1/2 cup batter into the skillet, swirling to allow the batter to coat the bottom of the skillet. Cook until the crêpe begins to turn light golden in color, about 1–2 minutes on each side. Repeat using the remaining batter. (Stack the crêpes between layers of parchment or waxed paper; they may be warmed in a low oven or microwave before assembling.)

◉ Spread each crêpe with about 3 tablespoons apricot jam; fold into quarters. Sprinkle with confectioners' sugar, if desired.

Makes 10 crêpes.

Fave dei Morti

Almond Cookies

Translated literally as "beans of the dead," fave dei morti are typically prepared during the months of October and November to celebrate All Saints' Day. While variations are found in regions throughout Italy, the cookies are especially popular in Trieste.

1 pound (about 4 cups)
    blanched slivered almonds
2 ½ cups sugar, divided, plus
    extra as needed
1 egg
1 tablespoon rum
1 tablespoon unsweetened
    cocoa powder
1 tablespoon Maraschino liqueur
1 teaspoon rose water
Pinch powdered red food color

    Finely grind the almonds in a food processor. Transfer to a large bowl, along with 2 ¼ cups sugar and the egg; mix until the dough forms a solid mass.

    Divide the dough equally among three medium bowls. Mix the rum and cocoa powder into the first batch of dough, the Maraschino liqueur into the second, and the rose water and a pinch of red food color into the third.

    Preheat oven to 300°F. Spread the remaining ¼ cup sugar on a plate. Roll half-teaspoonfuls of dough into small balls; roll in sugar to coat, adding extra sugar to the plate as needed. Place on baking sheets lined with parchment paper. Bake until the cookies are dry and crisp but not yet brown on the bottom, about 12 minutes.

Makes about 7 to 8 dozen of each flavor.

Toasted Hazelnuts—Instructions

Skinned and toasted hazelnuts are used in the following three recipes: presnitz (page 325), torta Sacher (page 330), and torta Dobos (page 333).

1 cup water

⅓ or ½ cup hazelnuts
 (see individual recipe
 instructions)

1 tablespoon baking soda

ଞ Preheat oven to 350°F. In a small saucepan, bring 1 cup water to a boil over high heat. Add the hazelnuts and baking soda; cook for 5 minutes. Remove the hazelnuts and place in a colander under cold running water; rub off and discard the skins. Transfer the skinned hazelnuts to a baking dish; toast until golden brown, about 15 minutes. Cool completely before using in recipes.

Pastries at Pasticceria Penso include torta Sacher, *as well as cakes flavored with mocha, cherries, and rum* (BELOW); *colorful Trieste-style* marzapane *in assorted flavors* (OPPOSITE).

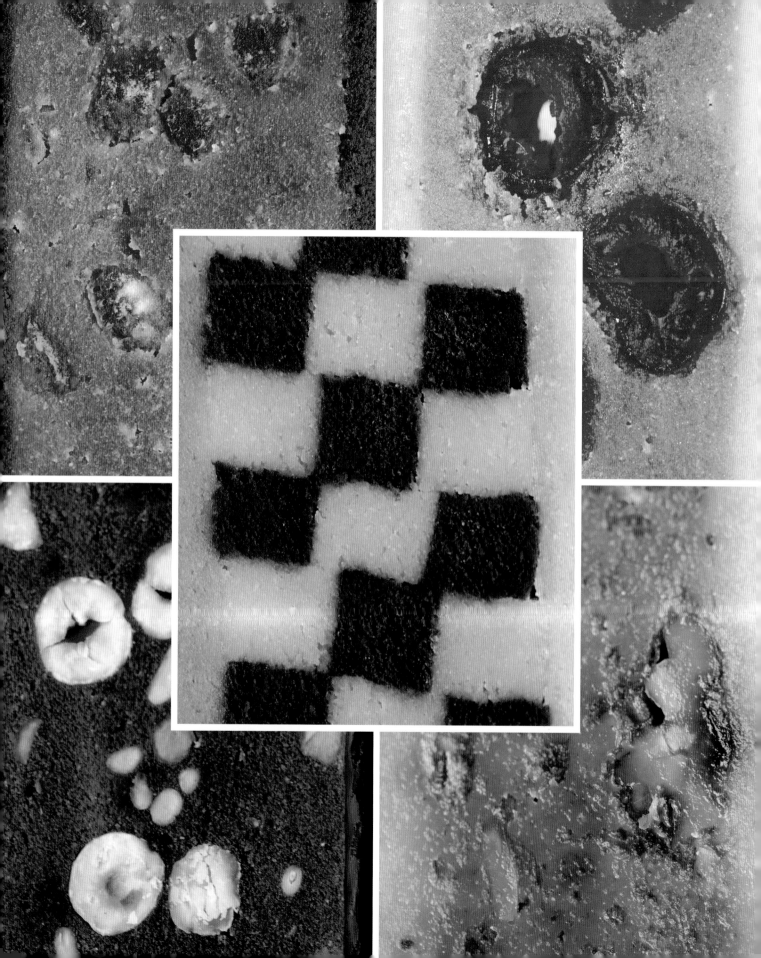

TRAVEL INFORMATION

This information is accurate at the time of publication and may be subject to change.

Restaurants

ANTICA TRATTORIA COOPERATIVA
Via Matteotti, 5
Tolmezzo
39/0433-44720

BUFFET DA PEPI
Via Cassa di Risparmio, 3
Trieste
39/040-366858

ENOTECA DI CORMÒNS
Piazza XXIV Maggio, 21
Cormòns
39/0481-630371

LOCANDA ALLA PACE
Via Roma, 38
Sauris di Sotto
39/0433-86010

OSTERIA AL VECCHIO STALLO
Via Viola, 7
Udine
39/0432-21296

RISTORANTE AI SETTE NANI
Frazione Prato, 30
Prato Carnico
39/0433-69013

RISTORANTE ALLE VECCHIE CARCERI
Via G. D'Artegna, 25
San Daniele del Friuli
39/0432-957403

RISTORANTE LA TECIA
Via San Nicolò, 10
Trieste
39/040-364322

RISTORANTE ROMA
Piazza XX Settembre, 14
Tolmezzo
39/0433-468031

RISTORANTE SALON
Via Peresson, 70
Piano d'Arta (Arta Terme)
39/0433-92003

TAVERNETTA ALL'ANDRONA
Calle Porta Piccola, 6
Grado
39/0431-80950

TRATTORIA AL CACCIATORE (LA SUBIDA)
Località Monte, 22
Cormòns
39/0481-60531

TRATTORIA ALLA LAGUNA (VEDOVA RADDI)
Piazza Garibaldi, 1
Marano Lagunare
39/0431-67019

Vacationers crowd the beach in Lignano Sabbiadoro (RIGHT); Chiesa di San Leonardo in Zuglio (OPPOSITE).

Festivals

ARIA DI FESTA
San Daniele: June
www.infosandaniele.com

BARCOLANA
Trieste: October
www.barcolana.it

CARNEVALE MUGGESANO
Muggia: February or March
www.carnevaldemuja.com

FESTA DEGLI ASPARAGI
Tavagnacco: May
www.protavagnacco.it

FESTA DEI FRUTTI DI BOSCO
Forni Avoltri: July
www.carnia.it

FESTA DELLA MELA
Tolmezzo: September
www.carnia.it

FESTA DELL'ASPARAGO DI BOSCO, DEL RADICCHIO
    DI MONTAGNA, E DEI FUNGHI DI PRIMAVERA
Arta Terme: May
www.carnia.it

FESTA DELLA ZUCCA
Venzone: October
www.prolocovenzone.it

FESTA DELLE ERBE DI PRIMAVERA
Forni di Sopra: June
www.fornidisopra.org

FESTA DEL PROSCIUTTO
Sauris: July
www.carnia.it

FESTA DEL SOLSTIZIO D'ESTATE
Ravascletto: June
www.turismoruralefvg.it

FESTA PROVINCIALE DELL'UVA
Cormons: September
www.cormons.info

FRIULI DOC
Udine: September
http://blog.friulidoc-vive.it

MITTELFEST
Cividale: July
www.mittelfest.org

MONDO DELLE MALGHE
Prato Carnico, Ovaro, Sauris: June–September
www.carnia.it

NOZZE CARSICHE
Monrupino: August (every 2 years)
www.carsoweb.com

SAGRA DEI CJALSÒNS
Pontebba: May
www.prodottitipici.com

SAGRA DEI OSEI
Sacile: August
www.prosacile.com

SAN SIMONE: SAPORE DI MONTASIO
Codroipo: October
www.comune.codroipo.ud.it

Producers

DISTILLERIA CASATO DEI CAPITANI
Via Cabia, 169
Cabia (Arta Terme)
39/0433-92240
www.cabia.net

FRIULTROTA
Via Aonedis, 10
San Daniele del Friuli
39/0432-956560
www.friultrota.it

ILLYCAFFÈ
Via Flavia, 110
Trieste
39/040-3890111
www.illy.com

MACELLERIA BIER
Via Roma, 1
Meduno (Pordenone)
39/0427-86189
www.pitina.com

MALGA POZÔF
Località Pozôf
Liariis (Ovaro)
39/368-3745660

MALGA PRAMOSIO
Frazione Cleulis
Paluzza
39/0433-775757

PASTICCERIA DUCALE
Piazza A. Picco, 18
Cividale del Friuli
39/0432-730707

The 20th-century Chiesa di Cristo Re in Timau (LEFT).

PASTICCERIA PENSO
Via A. Diaz, 11
Trieste
39/040-301530

PROSCIUTTIFICIO IL CAMARIN
Via San Luca, 24/26
San Daniele del Friuli
39/0432-942125
www.ilcamarin.it

PROSCIUTTIFICIO PROLONGO
Viale Trento e Trieste, 129
San Daniele del Friuli
39/0432-957161
www.prolongo.it

PROSCIUTTIFICIO WOLF SAURIS
Sauris di Sotto, 88
39/0433-86054
www.wolfsauris.it

Museums & Sights

BASILICA PATRIARCALE
Piazza Capitolo
Aquileia
39/0431-91067
www.comune.aquileia.ud.it

CASA CARSICA
Località Rupingrande, 31
Monrupino (Trieste)
39/040-327240
www.carsoweb.com

CASA DELLE FARFALLE
Via Canada, 1
Bordano
39/0432-988135
www.casaperlefarfalle.it

CASTELLO DI DUINO
Via Castello di Duino, 32
Duino Aurisina (Trieste)
39/040-208120
www.castellodiduino.it

CASTELLO DI GORIZIA
Borgo Castello, 36
Gorizia
39/0481-535146
www.comune.gorizia.it

CASTELLO DI MIRAMARE
Viale Miramare
Trieste
39/040-224143
www.castello-miramare.it

CASTELLO DI SAN GIUSTO
Piazza della Cattedrale, 3
Trieste
39/040-309362
www.retecivica.trieste.it

CASTELLO DI UDINE
Piazzale del Castello
Udine
39/0432-271591
www.udinecultura.it

CIVICO MUSEO ARCHEOLOGICO IULIUM
     CARNICUM
Via Giulio Cesare, 19
Zuglio
39/0433-92562
www.comune.zuglio.ud.it

GROTTA GIGANTE
Borgo Grotta Gigante 42/A
Sgonico (Trieste)
39/040-327312
www.grottagigante.it

Monte Santo di Lussari (telecabina)
Via Priesnig, 34
Camporosso (Tarvisio)
39/0428-653915
www.tarvisiano.org

Museo Archeologico Nazionale
Via Roma, 1
Aquileia
39/0431-91016
www.museoarcheo-aquileia.it

Museo Archeologico Nazionale
Piazza Duomo, 13
Cividale del Friuli
39/0432-700700
www.cividale.com

Museo Carnico delle Arti e Tradizioni
        Popolari "Michele Gortani"
Via della Vittoria, 2
Tolmezzo
39/0433-43233
www.carniamusei.org

Museo Diocesano e Gallerie del Tiepolo
Piazza Patriarcato, 1
Udine
39/0432-25003
www.musdioc-tiepolo.it

Risiera di San Sabba
Via Giovanni Palatucci, 5
Trieste
39/040-826202
www.risierasansabba.it

Tempietto Longobardo
Borgo Brossana
Cividale del Friuli
39/0432-700867
www.cividale.com

Terme di Arta
Via Nazionale, 1
Arta Terme
39/0433-929320
www.termediarta.it

Villa Manin
Piazza Manin, 10
Passariano (Codroipo)
39/0432-821211
www.villamanin-eventi.it

Agencies

Agenzia Turismo Friuli-Venezia Giulia
Piazza Manin, 10
Passariano (Codroipo)
39/0432-815111
www.turismofvg.it

Camera di Commercio di Udine
Via Morpurgo, 4
Udine
39/0432-273111
www.ud.camcom.it

Consorzio del Prosciutto di San Daniele
Via Umberto I, 26
San Daniele del Friuli
39/0432-957515
www.prosciuttosandaniele.it

Consorzio Tutela del Formaggio Montasio
Vicolo Resia 1/2
Codroipo
39/0432-905317
www.formaggiomontasio.net

FRIULI-VENEZIA GIULIA

AUSTRIA

ITALY

FORNI AVOLTRI

TIMAU

PAULARO

PRATO CARNICO

RAVASCLETTO

PONTEBBA

TARVISIO

CARNIA

TARVISIANO

SAURIS

OVARO

ARTA TERME

ZUGLIO

FORNI DI SOPRA

RAVEO

TOLMEZZO

VENZONE

ALTO FRIULI

BORDANO

GEMONA

SLOVENIA

CLAUZETTO

MANIAGO

SAN DANIELE

SPILIMBERGO

TAVAGNACCO

CIVIDALE

COLLI ORIENTALI

UDINE

VENETO

GRAVE DEL FRIULI

PORDENONE

CODROIPO

GORIZIA

COLLIO

CORMÒNS

SACILE

PALMANOVA

MARANO LAGUNARE

AQUILEIA

DUINO

CARSO

GRADO

OPICINA

★ TRIESTE

LIGNANO SABBIADORO

MUGGIA

ITALY

ADRIATIC SEA

CROATIA

BIBLIOGRAPHY

Artico, Melie. *Cucina della Carnia*. Italy: Chiandetti, 1998.

Benvenuto, Gianfranco Angelico, ed. *Cucina & Vini Friulani nel Mondo*. Italy: Camera di Commercio di Udine, 1992.

Buora, Maurizio. *Guida di Udine: Arte e Storia tra Vie e Piazze*. Italy: Edizioni LINT, 1986.

Busdon, Giorgio, and Germano Pontoni. *Sapori d'Acqua: Cucina di Terra e di Mare in Friuli-Venezia Giulia*. Italy: Editrice Leonardo, 2002.

Cigalotto, Paola, and Mariagrazia Santoro. *Vie del Gusto e Agriturismi in Carnia*. Italy: Forum Editrice, 2004.

Comin, Sonia, and Bepi Pucciarelli. *Il Mondo di Bepi Salon*. Italy: Camera di Commercio di Udine, 2005.

Contini, Mila. *Friuli e Trieste in Cucina*. Italy: Edizioni Gulliver, 1998.

Duomo di San Martino in Tolmezzo (ABOVE).

Cosetti, Gianni. *Vecchia e Nuova Cucina di Carnia*. Italy: Camera di Commercio di Udine, 2002.

Cremona, Luigi. *Un Amore Chiamato Friuli*. Italy: Camera di Commercio di Udine, n.d.

Del Fabro, Adriano. *Friuli in Cucina: La Cultura del Cibo, Le Ricette*. Italy: Edizioni La Libreria di Demetra, 1997.

————. *Le Ricette della Tradizione Friulana*. Italy: Edizioni La Libreria di Demetra, 1998.

De Vonderweid, Jolanda. *Ricette Triestine, Istriane e Dalmate*. Italy: Edizioni LINT, 2003.

Filiputti, Walter. *Friuli: Via dei Sapori*. Italy: Gribaudo, 2004.

Fonda, Cesare. *Cucina Triestina: Nuovissimo Prontuario per Professionisti ed Esperti*. Italy: Edizioni Italo Svevo, 1997.

Frausin, Maria. *Le Ricette Tradizionali di Trieste: i Sapori della Cultura Mitteleuropea.* Italy: Edizioni La Libreria di Demetra, 2000.

Mancini, Paola, and Adriano Del Fabro. *Feste, Sagre, Fiere, Mercati in Friuli-Venezia Giulia.* Italy: Edizioni La Libreria di Demetra, 1999.

Omero, Marta. *Le Ricette della Cucina Friulana dalla A alla Z.* Italy: Editrice Leonardo, n.d.

Plotkin, Fred. *Italy for the Gourmet Traveler.* New York: Little, Brown and Company, 1996.

———. *La Terra Fortunata: The Splendid Food and Wine of Friuli-Venezia Giulia.* New York: Broadway Books, 2001.

Pontoni, Germano. *La Zucca Si Sposa...* Italy: Editrice Leonardo, 2002.

Pradelli, Alessandro Molinari. *La Cucina del Friuli-Venezia Giulia.* Italy: Newton & Compton Editori, 1999.

Re, Giancarlo. *Dulcis in Fundo: Guida ai Dolci e alla Pasticceria in Friuli-Venezia Giulia.* Italy: Libra Edizioni, 2002.

———. *Montasio, per Primo e per Ultimo: dal Frico agli Antipasti, ai Dessert.* Italy: Libra Edizioni, 2003.

Rodgers, Rick. *Kaffeehaus: Exquisite Desserts from the Classic Cafés of Vienna, Budapest, and Prague.* New York: Clarkson Potter/Publishers, 2002.

Torossi, Ermanno. *Ristoranti, Osterie e Frasche del Friuli-Venezia Giulia.* Italy: Edizioni La Libreria di Demetra, 2000.

Vascotto, Anna. *Ricette Tradizionali dell'Istria e Quarnero.* Italy: Edizioni La Libreria di Demetra, 2000.

METRIC CONVERSION TABLES

Liquid Measures (volume)

U.S.	Metric
1/4 teaspoon	1.25 milliliters
1/2 teaspoon	2.5 milliliters
1 teaspoon	5 milliliters
1 tablespoon	15 milliliters
1 fluid ounce	30 milliliters
1/4 cup (2 ounces)	60 milliliters
1/3 cup	80 milliliters
1/2 cup	120 milliliters
1 cup	240 milliliters
1 pint (2 cups)	480 milliliters
1 quart (4 cups)	960 milliliters
1 gallon (4 quarts)	3.84 liters

Oven Temperatures

Farenheit	Celsius	Gas Mark
250°	120°	1/2
275°	140°	1
300°	150°	2
325°	160°	3
350°	180°	4
375°	190°	5
400°	200°	6
425°	220°	7
450°	230°	8
475°	240°	9
500°	260°	10

Dry Measures (weight)

U.S.	Metric
1 ounce	30 grams
2 ounces	60 grams
4 ounces	115 grams
8 ounces	225 grams
1 pound (16 ounces)	450 grams
2.2 pounds	1 kilogram

Length

U.S.	Metric
1/8 inch	3 millimeters
1/4 inch	6 millimeters
1/2 inch	12 millimeters
1 inch	2.5 centimeters
6 inches	15 centimeters
1 foot (12 inches)	30 centimeters

ଊ In these tables, the precise equivalents have been rounded for convenience.

Authentic Carnian cookware on display in Forni
Avoltri's ethnographic museum (OPPOSITE).

RECIPE INDEX

Chiesa dei Santi Pietro e Paolo in Tarvisio (ABOVE).

INDEX